THE CENTER OF A GREAT EMPIRE

Early Ohio locations featured in the text

THE CENTER OF A
GREAT EMPIRE

The Ohio Country in the Early American Republic

Edited by

Andrew R. L. Cayton and Stuart D. Hobbs

Ohio University Press   Athens

Ohio University Press, Athens, Ohio 45701
www.ohio.edu/oupress
© 2005 by Ohio University Press
Printed in the United States of America
All rights reserved
Ohio University Press books are printed on acid-free paper ⊚ ™

Cover illustration: "Pomeroy Coal Mines," from Henry Howe, *Historical Collections of Ohio,* 1848, page 352.

12 11 10 09 08 07 06 05   5 4 3 2 1

Library of Congress Cataloging-in-Publication Data

The center of a great empire : the Ohio country in the early American Republic / edited by Andrew R.L. Cayton and Stuart D. Hobbs.
   v. cm.
Includes bibliographical references and index.
   Contents: Introduction : the significance of Ohio in the early American Republic / Andrew R.L. Cayton — Reconsidering the ideological origins of Indian removal : the case of the Big Bottom "massacre" / Patrick Griffin — The changing political world of Thomas Worthington / Donald J. Ratcliffe — Ohio gospel : Methodism in the early Ohio valley / John Wigger — The evolution of racial politics in early Ohio / Ellen Eslinger — How colleges shaped a public culture of usefulness / Kenneth H. Wheeler — "My whole enjoyment & almost my existence depends upon my friends" : family and kinship in early Ohio / Tamara Gaskell Miller — The Ohio country in the political economy of nation building / Christopher Clark — Afterword : new directions in the history of Ohio in the early American Republic.
   ISBN 0-8214-1620-0 (cloth : alk. paper) — ISBN 0-8214-1648-0 (pbk. : alk. paper)
   1. Frontier and pioneer life—Ohio. 2. Ohio—History—1787–1865. 3. Ohio—Social conditions—19th century. 4. Ohio—Politics and government—1787–1865. 5. Ohio River Valley—History—18th century. 6. Ohio River Valley—History—19th century. I. Cayton, Andrew R. L. (Andrew Robert Lee), 1954– II. Hobbs, Stuart D. (Stuart Dale), 1961–
F495.C37 2005
   977.1'03—dc22

                                                    2004030590

CONTENTS

PREFACE

This book originated in the 1997–2003 restoration of Adena, the Chillicothe home of prominent early Ohioan Thomas Worthington. The restoration and the development of exhibits in a new museum and education center at the site was a major contribution of the Ohio Historical Society to Ohio's 2003 bicentennial celebration. Then OHS Chief Curator Amos Loveday suggested holding a conference that would focus on the life of Worthington as a way of exploring major themes in the history of Ohio and the Early American Republic. Members of the Adena team agreed that this was an excellent idea, and George Kane and Harry Searles at the Ohio Historical Society lent their support. Planning for the conference began in 2000 when Project Manager Stuart Hobbs sought the advice of Andrew Cayton in identifying participants.

Cancelled because of a lack of funding, the conference was reborn as a series of related sessions at the 2003 annual meeting of the Society for Historians of the Early American Republic (SHEAR) at the Ohio State University. The original drafts of these essays (with the exception of Patrick Griffin's paper, which was produced especially for this volume) were presented in a series of well-attended sessions. Nicole Etcheson, Craig Friend, John Larson, Peter Onuf, and Carrol Van West offered wide-ranging comments that helped the authors revise their essays for publication. Marion Winship also made important contributions to the shape of the final volume. In addition, we deeply appreciate the encouragement and flexibility of Jeff Pasley, chair, and the other members of SHEAR's program committee and of John Brooke, chair of local arrangements.

We thank David Sanders, director of Ohio University Press, and Gillian Berchowitz, senior editor, for supervising the transformation of our manuscript into a book. We are grateful for the map prepared by Mary Stephenson, formerly of the Ohio Historical Society Design Department, and the expert copyediting of Sharon Rose. Finally, we wish to say how much we enjoyed our collaboration as well as working with our contributors.

The essays that follow make only occasional references to Thomas Worthington. Nevertheless, they fulfill the original goal of illuminating the world in which he lived.

The Significance of Ohio
in the Early American Republic

ANDREW R. L. CAYTON

The late-eighteenth-century Congregational minister and land speculator Manasseh Cutler could scarcely restrain his enthusiasm when
he contemplated the future of trans-Appalachian North America.
The region between the Ohio River and Lake Erie was destined to
become "the garden of the world, the seat of wealth, and the *centre*
of a great Empire."[1] Educated Christian gentlemen would guide the
transformation of the "dreary abode of savage barbarity" into a place
where "the Gospel [would] be preached to the latest period of time;
the arts and sciences be planted; the seeds of virtue, happiness, and
glory be firmly rooted and grow up to full maturity."[2] Cutler happily
anticipated "beholding the whole territory of the United States settled by an enlightened people, and continued under one extended
government."[3]

Historians have found good reasons to scoff at Cutler's overheated
rhetoric. First, he had a financial interest in promoting settlement
north of the Ohio River. In the late 1780s Cutler was a director of
the Ohio Company of Associates and the Scioto Company, two speculative land schemes whose investors hoped to secure enough regular
income to live as gentlemen. Second, Cutler had no respect for the
American Indians and white settlers already living in the Ohio Valley. When he did not dismiss them as "lawless banditti," he simply ig-
nored them. One unique "advantage" of the land the Ohio Company purchased, according to Cutler, was its supposed virginity. "In

order to begin *right,* there will be no *wrong* habits to combat, and no inveterate systems to overturn—there is no rubbish to remove, before you can lay a foundation."[4] Third, Cutler was talking about a region in the interior of the continent far from his home in Massachusetts. Commerce and travel between the Atlantic Ocean and the Ohio Valley required an arduous trek through the Appalachian Mountains unless one went up the St. Lawrence River to lakes Ontario and Erie in British-controlled Canada or up the Mississippi River in Spanish Louisiana.

Fourth, the Ohio Country was a hotly contested borderland on the western fringes of the United States, itself a tenuous collection of states whose citizens were in the midst of debating the nature of authority in a republican empire few had imagined in 1775. Despite the creation of a system of colonial governance in the Northwest Ordinance of 1787, which allowed for the absorption of conquered territories as equal states, the United States exercised little real power in the Ohio Valley. American Indians as well as British and Spanish authorities were eager to stop the American advance. The struggle for dominion over the Ohio Valley that had commenced in the middle of the eighteenth century would continue long after Cutler had lost interest in trans-Appalachia.

None of this, however, should obscure the fact that Manasseh Cutler was prescient about the future of the Ohio Country. If anything, he underestimated it. The people who lived in what became the seventeenth state in the American Union in 1803 were not only at the center of a great empire, they were at the center of the most important historical developments in the revolutionary Atlantic World. Ohio embodied the major themes in the history of the Atlantic World from the middle of the eighteenth through the middle of the nineteenth century. It established patterns as well as represented them.

Ohio recapitulated the history of colonial encounter, conquest, and postcolonial development with breathtaking speed. When Cutler wrote, the region was a heavily forested world between Lake Erie and the Ohio River inhabited by a few thousand Indians and Americans locked in a bitter and brutal war for control of its future. Nowhere in North America was the struggle between Indians and Americans more prolonged than in the Ohio Valley. It was terrain contested in the 1780s and 1790s by people in villages along the Kentucky and Ohio rivers and people in villages along the Maumee and Wabash rivers. Raids and counter-raids were the norms of border warfare rooted in racial hostility and efforts at extermination that amounted to ethnic cleansing.[5]

In the 1780s the United States sought to exert its authority north of the Ohio River, first by outlining procedures for surveying land and organizing territories as well as negotiating several treaties with Indians, and then through military conquest. Miamis, Shawnees, and other Indians in the Wabash and Maumee valleys defeated military expeditions led by Josiah Harmar and Arthur St. Clair, however. It was not until 1794 that the Legion of the United States under the command of General Anthony Wayne subdued Indian resistance at the Battle of Fallen Timbers. The next year was a major turning point in the history of the region as well as the republic. The ratification of Jay's Treaty, by which the British finally evacuated forts south of the Great Lakes, the suppression of the Whiskey Rebellion in western Pennsylvania, and the signing of the Treaty of Greenville, by which Indians accepted white settlement north of the Ohio River, firmly established the authority of the United States. The Ohio Country would henceforth develop under its auspices and within the parameters of its constitutional requirements. By 1803 enough people had flooded the river valleys of southern Ohio that the region was able to achieve statehood. By the time Manasseh Cutler died in Hamilton, Massachusetts, in July 1823, Ohio was the fifth most populous state in the Union; of its 581,434 residents, some 370,000 were under the age of twenty-five.

Four decades later, on the eve of the Civil War, Ohio trailed only New York and Pennsylvania in population, with 2,339,502 people, of whom 36,673 were free people of color and 328,249 were born outside the United States. The Census of 1860 recorded only thirty Indians living within the borders of the state. Ranked third among American states in the value of its real estate and second in the cash value of its farms, Ohio was on the cutting edge of agricultural, commercial, and industrial development. Its largest city (Cincinnati) was one of the most ethnically diverse in the world. Its proliferating colleges inculcated ambition, discipline, and a taste for social reform. No other state was as strongly identified with the Underground Railroad or with resistance to the presence of African Americans. Ohio sent the most men per capita, including generals Ulysses S. Grant and William Tecumseh Sherman, into the Union army to suppress the Confederacy even as it nurtured the North's most prominent advocate of peace, Clement Vallandigham. More of its women joined the Women's Christian Temperance Union, which was founded in Cleveland in 1874, than did those of any other state. Within Ohio's borders, the American Federation of Labor (1886) and the United Mine Workers of America (1890) would be organized. Here John D. Rockefeller would develop Standard Oil. Ohio would be the home of the first professional baseball team, the Cincinnati Red Stockings (1869). It would attract tens of thousands of immigrants from all over Europe and North America. Ohio would set the standard in municipal reform and practical inventions. The citizens of the Wright Brothers' hometown of Dayton would hold more patents per capita in 1900 than those of any other city in the United States. An obvious measure of Ohio's position in the nation and the world was the fact that most American presidents between 1869 and 1923 were from the state.

These facts add up to something greater than the sum of its parts. They suggest the degree to which Ohio reflected larger developments in the Atlantic World. Indeed, the state's early history speaks to most of the major questions that have preoccupied the legion of historians who have revived the study of the early republic in the last several decades. As the essays in *The Center of a Great Empire* make clear, students of Ohio must deal with colonial conquest and resistance; massive migration; the formation of political parties; cultural rebellion and assimilation; tensions over the nature and structures of political authority; the proliferation of evangelical religious denominations, including Methodism and Mormonism; the reconfiguration of public space; the construction of identity in a dialectic between the demands of citizenship and the claims of family, community, and religion; critical arguments about the meanings of race; and the emergence of a provincial bourgeois culture rooted in domesticity and earnest piety.

Ohio, in short, was conquered, organized, and developed at a critical moment in the history of the world and of North America. To Ohio came people to work, farm, and own property that would provide them with previously unimagined standards of living. Five years after arriving in the Ohio Valley with his wife and eight children in 1803, Massachusetts native Thomas Carter owned a home and a prosperous grocery store in Cincinnati. He had twenty dollars for every one he had had in Reading. "If the people of New England would believe the truth" about Ohio, "they would flock to this country in the thousands."[6]

One who did come was Connecticut-born Harriet Beecher Stowe (1811–96). In her immensely popular novel *Uncle Tom's Cabin* (1852), enslaved Eliza looks at the Ohio River lying "like Jordan, between her and the Canaan of liberty on the other side."[7] The image of Ohio as a place that celebrated freedom and labor was a commonplace trope by the 1850s, a trope invoked by travelers (including Alexis de Tocqueville [1805–59]) and fugitive slaves alike.

People from all over North America and Europe constructed a government and a society in Ohio on principles derived from the global transformations of the eighteenth century. Here was a full-fledged experiment in republican government, in the power of the market, in democratic social organization, and in the necessity of organized competition in politics, religion, labor, and commerce. "All power," wrote Connecticut-born Chillicothe lawyer Michael Baldwin in 1802, ought to flow "from the people," for they were "fully competent to govern themselves" and were "the only proper judges of their own interests and their own concerns."[8] Methodist minister John Sale, who expected Ohio to be "as the Garden of God," was pleased "to live in a Country where there is so much of an Equallity & a Man is not thought to be great here because he possesses a little more of this Worlds rubbish than his Neighbour."[9]

Ohio was a world defined by the proliferation of villages as commercial crossroads sporting banks, stores, churches, and schools, all of them vying to acquire the keys to growth and prosperity—county seats, canals, roads, and colleges. It was hardly coincidental that when Lyman Beecher (1775–1863) set out to reform America and Isaac Meyer Wise (1819–1900) to reform Judaism, they came to Cincinnati. English critics Frances Trollope and Charles Dickens recoiled in horror from the materialism they found in Ohio because they thought it an exaggerated example of what was happening all over the Atlantic World in the nineteenth century. The Unitarian minister Moncure D. Conway, who met his wife and championed theater while living Cincinnati in the late 1850s and early 1860s, declared that in the Queen City of the West he "seemed for the first time to know something of all America" and that "every 'new thing' found headquarters there."[10]

While the essays in this book outline the major contours of these developments, their authors are most interested in helping us think about *how* and *why* these developments happened as they did, *where* they did. In other words, these historians are concerned less with

Ohio than with locating the experience of Ohio within larger transformations in the Revolutionary Atlantic World. Why was Ohio at the center of so much change? Why did Ohio attract so much interest from so many diverse people all over the world? Why did Ohio become such a startling success story in the eyes of most of its own citizens? Why was Ohio such a breeding ground for education, antislavery, political parties, and evangelical religion?

Constructing answers to these questions returns us to the concerns of a large coterie of Ohio men and women who came of age in the second quarter of the nineteenth century. Artisans and lawyers, clerks and ministers, teachers and farmers were stunned by the rapid development of the state and fascinated by how it had happened. The speed and thoroughness of the transformation of the Ohio Country were extraordinary even by the standards of the Age of Progress. Within a lifetime, forests had become fields and villages had been linked by railroads and telegraph wires. The rise of Ohio was a model of the possibilities of well-directed human power. Progress, while inevitable in the long run, was anything but inevitable in the short run. It was created and nurtured by the character and actions of thousands of individuals. Celebrating Ohio as the very model of a liberal society, many citizens (not just educated Yankee professionals in Cincinnati) were beginning by the 1830s to think self-consciously about what the state's history said about human history.

What made Ohio work so well for so many in such a short period of time? Kentucky-born Dr. Daniel Drake of Cincinnati informed members of the Union Literary Society in Oxford in 1834 that Ohio was an experiment in the viability of a new kind of society. The "restraints employed by an old social organization, do not exist—the government of fashion is democratic—and a thousand corporations,—literary, charitable, political, religious, are combined into an oligarchy, for the purpose of bringing up one set of artificial and traditional standards, the feelings, opinions, and actions of the rising generation; and thus the mind of each individual is allowed, in a great degree, to form on its own constitutional principles." Of all the advantages of Ohio, the most "salutary" were the cultivation of "a love of nature . . . a feeling of romance and enthusiasm—a keen sensibility to whatever is touching or magnanimous in the human character—a taste, in short, for all which the natural and moral world can present, to stir the imagination, and warm and elevate the feelings."[11]

Offering a romantic, democratic revision of Cutler's vision, Drake exhorted the students: "You will contribute to raise up a mighty people, a new world of man, in the depths of the new world of history" by "prescribing the direction, and laying down the rule of action."[12] In the center of the American empire, according to Cincinnati poet and journalist William Davis Gallagher (1808–94), was "an Experiment in Humanity, higher in its character and sublimer in its results" than in any other place. The agents of the founding of "the freest forms of social development and the highest order of civilization" were "the schoolmaster and the missionary." A new day was dawning, when people would awaken "to a just sense of their real dignity and importance in the social scale, by proclaiming to them that they are neither slaves nor nonentities, but true men and women."[13] The Buckeye tree, exclaimed Drake, does "not bow its head and wave its arms at a haughty distance, but it might be said to have held out the *right hand of fellowship.*"[14]

Like most nineteenth-century Romantics, these Ohioans assumed that progress was intrinsically valuable and that the triumph of their values was inevitable.[15] Yet they also believed in the contingency of their history, ascribing their victory to superior character both revealed and refined in an intense struggle to transform the Ohio Country. American Indians and rough-hewn frontierspeople mattered mightily in these narratives because their subordination confirmed the righteousness of the victors. Nineteenth-century Ohio was revolutionary to the extent that it eclipsed alternative as well as older worlds. The pioneers were remarkable for overcoming all sorts of difficulties with unparalleled labor, discipline, piety, and commitment to a cause larger than themselves. "The lights of science and art have removed the long reign of darkness, and the simple aborigines of the forest have been supplanted by civilization and the cultivation of the white man," wrote Marietta doctor and historian Samuel Prescott Hildreth (1783–1863) in an echo of Manasseh Cutler. As for Indians, "although we may deplore their misfortunes and pity their calamities in their removal from the land of their fathers, yet who shall say that the hand of God hath not directed it?"[16]

By the 1830s Ohio's historians had singled out individual Indians to admire as great men who had tested the virtue of the state's settlers. True glory rested in vanquishing a worthy opponent. Particularly prominent in this narrative was the Shawnee Tecumseh, who had tried to build a pan-Indian movement and was killed at the Battle of the Thames in 1813. Benjamin Drake, brother of Daniel and a Cincinnati lawyer and journalist, offered Tecumseh as an ideal American. Opposed to polygamy, simple in manner, temperate, industrious, manly, "uniformly self-possessed," a "poet of the heart," he was above all "a patriot." It was "his love of country [that] made him a statesman and a warrior," not "mere prejudice or self-interest." The defeat of so impressive a man testified to the righteousness as well as the inevitability of American conquest. As "Hannibal was to the Romans, Tecumseh became to the people of the United States." "[B]ut for the power of the United States," he "would, perhaps, have been the founder of an empire which would have rivaled that of Mexico or Peru."[17]

The authors of the following essays are not Buckeye patriots, and their accounts are neither celebratory nor romantic. Still, they are pursuing issues that have fascinated people interested in Ohio for two centuries. Addressing familiar questions, they offer new answers and open up new paths of inquiry through investigations of general subjects such as race, education, politics, religion, commerce, colonialism, family, and communication. The essays emphasize contingency rather than inevitability and contention rather than progress. Downplaying the frontier character of Ohio, they stress the extent to which developments in the state were tied to developments in the Atlantic World. They focus on general developments in Ohio as a whole rather than on individual case studies. They are intended to question conventional wisdom and to identify areas for further research and reflection. And they are founded on the hope that future scholars will think of the history of the state as significant without as well as within its borders.

Manasseh Cutler would have been flabbergasted if he could have visited Ohio in the middle of the nineteenth century. If the state was not exactly what he had imagined it would be, its development still constituted an amazing phenomenon. At a terrible cost to American Indians and disappointed settlers, more of whom were migrating out of than into the state by the 1850s, the Ohio Country had been transformed with astonishing speed and thoroughness into a recognizable variation on Cutler's relentlessly upbeat sales pitch. "Ohio is as good a place as I want to live in," a Madison County schoolteacher wrote in his diary in summer 1853. "Perhaps it is not the garden of the world, yet I think it comes the next thing to it."[18]

Notes

1. Manasseh Cutler, *An Explanation of the Map which Delineates that Part of the Federal Lands* . . . (Salem: Dabney and Cushing, 1787), 14.

2. Manasseh Cutler, "Sermon Preached at Campus Martius, Marietta, . . . August 24 1788," in *Life, Journals, and Correspondence of Rev. Manasseh Cutler,* ed. William Parker Cutler and Julia Perkins Cutler, 2 vols. (Athens: Ohio University Press, 1987 [1888]), 2:445.

3. Cutler, *Explanation of the Map,* 21.

4. Ibid., 20.

5. Daniel K. Richter, *Facing East from Indian Country: A Native History of Early America* (Cambridge: Harvard University Press, 2001), 189–236.

6. Quoted in Steven J. Ross, *Workers on the Edge: Work, Leisure, and Politics in Industrializing Cincinnati, 1788–1890* (New York: Columbia University Press, 1985), 5.

7. Harriet Beecher Stowe, *Uncle Tom's Cabin* (New York: New American Library, 1966 [1851–52]), 64.

8. Michael Baldwin to the Electors of Ross County, *Chillicothe Scioto Gazette,* August 26, 1802.

9. John Sale to Edward Dromgoole, February 20, 1809, in *The Methodists,* vol. 4 of *Religion on the American Frontier, 1783–1840,* ed. William Warren Sweet (Chicago: University of Chicago Press, 1964), 160.

10. Moncure D. Conway, *Autobiography,* 2 vols. (London: Cassell and Co., 1904), 1:230.

11. Daniel Drake, *Discourse on the History, Character, and Prospects of the West: Delivered to the Union Literary Society of Miami University, Oxford, Ohio* (Cincinnati, 1834), in *The First West: Writing from the American Frontier, 1776–1860,* ed. Edward Watts and David Rachels (New York: Oxford University Press, 2002), 356, 358.

12. Ibid., 366.

13. William Davis Gallagher, "Address to the Historical and Philosophical Society of Ohio" (1850), in Gallagher, *Facts and Conditions of Progress in the North-West* (Cincinnati: H. W. Derby, 1850), 26, 27, 9, 47.

14. Quoted in W. H. Venable, *Beginnings of Literary Culture in the Ohio Valley* (Cincinnati: R. Clarke and Co., 1891), 319.

15. David Levin, *History as Romantic Art: Bancroft, Prescott, Motley, and Parkman* (Stanford: Stanford University Press, 1959).

16. Samuel Prescott Hildreth, *Biographical and Historical Memoirs of the Early Pioneer Settlers of Ohio* (Cincinnati: H. W. Derby, 1852), 482–83.

17. Benjamin Drake, *Life of Tecumseh* (Cincinnati: E. Morgan and Co., 1841), 226, 230, 229, 235.

18. John M. Roberts, Diary, July 31, 1853, in *Buckeye Schoolmaster: A Chronicle of Midwestern Rural Life, 1853–1865,* ed. J. Merton England (Bowling Green, OH: Bowling Green State University Popular Press, 1996), 49.

ONE

Reconsidering the Ideological Origins of Indian Removal

The Case of the Big Bottom "Massacre"

PATRICK GRIFFIN

If we believe what we read, it would seem that Indian-white relations were poisoned during nearly every period of early American history. Historians working on the seventeenth century argue that the crucial break occurred in 1676. Warfare against the small eastern tribes of New England, as some contend, or against the dispersed tribes of the Chesapeake, as others would have it, doomed the constitution of any sort of middle ground between the groups.[1] Eighteenth-century historians tell us that the relationship between natives and newcomers irrevocably soured in the 1750s and early 1760s. Pontiac's War or the slaughter of innocent Indians by the Paxton Boys in 1763 usually fills the climactic role.[2] Or was it the American Revolution? The massacre of ninety Indians at Gnadenhutten in 1783 by western Pennsylvanians, perhaps? White settlers in such instances, we have learned, twisted the liberating logic of the Revolution to justify killing Indians and grabbing land.[3] And specialists of the early republic point to their period as the turning point. The year 1815 usually marks the falling out. Decades of warfare—forty, fifty, or sixty years, depending on starting or ending points—turned backcountries defined by fluid relations between Indians and whites into frontiers of hardened lines and identities.[4] Admittedly, some scholars do not point to specific moments; rather, they argue that the cultural chasm between Europeans and European American settlers and Indians loomed too large for any sort of cultural accommodation.[5] But most pick the period they focus on as the "seminal" moment.

Each of these episodes has a bottom-up and a top-down component. Most historians agree that common settlers on the frontier harbored anti-Indian attitudes. Bearing the brunt of Indian hostility, these men and women came to view Indians as essentially suspect. More complex are the views of elites. While most settlers developed racist attitudes, officials usually living far to the east of the frontier articulated ideologies of human difference that amounted to, as one scholar puts it, "de facto" racism.[6] Elites ranging from John Winthrop to Thomas Jefferson did not view Indians as inherently or essentially inferior but argued that cultural circumstances created native "savagery." While this vision admitted the possibility of Indian redemption—that is, if they abandoned backward practices and embraced more civilized ways—in practice this ideology consigned Native Americans to the margins of society. In any event, Indians at each crucial juncture that historians study found themselves trapped between the wrath of a racist rabble in their midst and the ethnocentric views of powerful elites living far away.[7]

What is striking about these dates, the wars that gave them meaning, and the ideologies that somehow emerged is that the processes that led to the intercultural Rubicons appear strikingly similar. Here is how many of the stories go: poorer whites seeking competency leave core settlements and encroach on Indian land on frontiers far from established authority. They lash out as Indians contest the movement and then try to get eastern officials involved. Officials prove reluctant, fearing that jumping into a struggle will only exacerbate problems. Whites on the margins styling themselves vigilantes kill with racist intent, pressuring officials to respond with force by threatening the government with violence or disorder. Elites act, and Indians lose. And in so doing, there is no going back to the way things were before. At this point in the story historians imply that we are now on the road to the Trail of Tears, as elites begin the ideological work of marginalizing Indians. In many of these studies, events that occur in one region and place taint a broader white society as irredeemably racist. Each episode, therefore, either creates or canonizes one of the significant facets of an essential "American character," or, as one scholar recently put it, an American "identity" defined by race.[8]

But—and this is a simple question—if the irrepressible racist genie emerges from the bottle in, say, 1676 in New England, how is he forced back in, only to reemerge, as others would tell us, in 1763, or 1783, or 1815? In other words, individually each of the studies that broach the subject can offer persuasive explanations for the ideological origins of Indian removal. Collectively, however, the logic of a golden age declining into an irreversibly racist society at a given moment seems less than persuasive.

In this essay I would like to argue that most treatments of the development of anti-Indian attitudes miss one crucial point. They fail to take into account the role of the state, or if they do they miss its significance. During the colonial period, Indians and whites living in close proximity in the backcountry or frontier lived in a state of intercultural flux, moving between moments of conflict and cooperation. Even brutal violence, the kind witnessed during King Philip's War or Bacon's Rebellion, did not lead all whites to consign Indians to perpetual racial inferiority. Did the Puritans and adventurers who killed with glee and impunity harbor racist sentiments? Of course they did. But in years after, the descendants of these selfsame whites could jettison such beliefs, and in the meantime new "middle grounds" would be created in different settings. And the frontier drama would unfold once more.

That is, until the American Revolution. During the 1790s in particular, the federal government took over the role of ordinary men and women in clearing the way for white settlement. Officials of the new nation did not do so willingly. But they acted once they understood the significance of two developments in the West. First, it became clear that after nearly forty years of unremitting warfare on the frontier—and the Ohio Valley in particular—common settlers would not stand for the old pattern of conflict-accommodation-conflict to resume once more. Second and more significantly, elites in frontier settlements had little choice but to jettison their "civilizing mission" to the Indians and subscribe to violence and racist assumptions to challenge Indians. These men were not living in Boston, Williamsburg, or Philadelphia, far to the east of frontier struggles. They lived amid violence and hostility. And they would use their influence in these and other centers to leverage the federal government to protect them and open the way for white settlement. Hence the active role the state would play in ensuring whites and Indians would not live together grew from the rather novel nature of frontier society in the later stages of the Revolution and the years thereafter, as well as from the convergence of interests between two groups of whites, usually at odds with one another. With the wealthier and the poorer sorts thrown together, regional threats to far-off government authority caused alarm in far-off capitals. Once this happened, Indian removal became the de facto policy of the new nation, only to be formally enshrined with the Indian Removal Act of 1830.

I will examine this dynamic by discussing the changing pattern of Indian-white relations in the Ohio Country in the years after the Revolution—its similarity to, but more tellingly its difference from, earlier frontier episodes. The crucial breakdown of relations and the concomitant shift in state response occurred in the Ohio Country in 1791 in the wake of the so-called Big Bottom massacre. What happened here was neither unique nor exceptional in the annals of early American history. Indeed, its typicality makes it an ideal episode to examine. But the effects of this massacre were far-reaching, not for what happened between whites and Indians, but for the new understandings brokered between different groups of whites and the resulting response of government officials. The event itself did not amount to a watershed. Rather it reveals how the broader context of Indian-white relations was shifting in the years after the Revolution. Only with the birth of a nation could conflict and racial subordination become the rules rather than the exceptions.

Ohio's history—and troubles—began in 1785 with agreements and disputes over land. In that year Congress passed a land ordinance establishing the region north and west of the Ohio River as federal land. As officials of the federal government tried to get out from under the crushing debt of the Revolutionary War, they laid out the Northwest Territory as a virtual "land bank" for repaying debt while allowing orderly white settlement. States that had historic claims—real and imagined—to the region also received grants as they relinquished these claims to the federal government. In the same year, the federal government also made the first attempts to free these lands from Indians. At Fort MacIntosh officials met with Delaware, Wyandot, Chippewa, and Ottawa representatives to treat for peace and secure land in Ohio for white settlement. The following year emissaries from the Shawnees did likewise at Fort Finney. The treaties, in short, allowed the government to make good—on paper, at least—on the land ordinance.

The more famous Northwest Ordinance of 1787 inscribed the relationship between land and Indian treaties into law. "The utmost good faith," the ordinance read, "shall always be observed towards the Indians, their lands and property shall never be taken from them without their consent." The act went on to declare, "In their property, rights and liberty, they shall never be invaded or disturbed." The ordinance's goal was to settle the region while maintaining "peace and friendship" with the Indians, that is, "unless in just and lawful wars authorized by Congress."[9]

Under the ordinance, private joint-stock companies and individuals could redeem their now-worthless continental certificates for land in the region. The Ohio Company was organized in Boston in 1786 along these lines. The company's associates agreed to "raise a fund in continental certificates for purchasing LANDS in the western territory belonging to the United States." A share cost one thousand dollars in certificates or ten dollars in gold or silver, and no shareholder could buy more than five shares. As the 1787 ordinance was under debate, a group of wealthy New Englanders bought a million and a half acres between the Muskingum River and the Scioto Valley. Led by veterans of the war, officers all, they hoped to establish a new, orderly settlement with its headquarters at the confluence of the Muskingum and the Ohio. On April 7, 1788, forty-eight settlers landed at the spot, followed by nearly 150 more over the course of the year. As the first settlers spent the following summer constructing not only their homes but also the works of a civilian fort called Campus Martius, company officials scouted out promising plots for future settlement.[10]

These were heady times. And these members of the company hoped to establish a settlement where the principles of the Revolution—their reading of them, in any event—would flourish. Rufus Putnam, one of the organizers of the company and soon to be a brigadier general in the army, took control of the settlement and called its first grand jury. One of the first measures passed in the territory for bringing order to the territory spoke volumes. Territorial governor Arthur St. Clair issued a proclamation banning "the use of intoxicating liquor in the Northwest Territory." Until peace could be achieved with the Indians, authorities were authorized to seize "all spirituous liquors in the hands of private citizens."[11]

Officers of the company wanted only the best and brightest to settle Ohio. To ensure this, they would give free land to members of the company who owned at least one share. The thinking went that "in order to begin *right,* there will be no *wrong* habits to combat, and no inveterate systems to overturn—there is no rubbish to remove, before you can lay a foundation." Good people would bring good government. "Many of our associates," a settler gushed in 1788, "are distinguished for wealth, education and virtue; and others, for the most part, are reputable, industrious, well informed planters, farmers, tradesmen and mechanics." In the wake of the Revolution, these New Englanders suggested, the habits of industry for the lower orders would compliment the abilities of the well-heeled and virtuous to knit together a more perfect society than the one they were leaving.[12]

Like their Puritan forefathers, the new patriarchs of Ohio realized that disorderly Indians could destroy order and imperil their republican errand into the Ohio wilderness. Unlike their Puritan ancestors, however, the New Englanders at Marietta tried their damnedest to get along with Indians in the region. Trouble may come, one prominent settler warned during a Fourth of July speech in 1788, but if it did, "it is our duty as well as our interest to conduct towards them, with humanity and kindness." As settlers were in the process of "reducing a country from a state of nature to a state of cultivation," they had to "endeavor to cultivate a good understanding, with the natives, without much familiarity." In other words, the speaker warned that "going native" would not produce the orderly society these new Englanders envisioned, but neither would alienating the Indians. To make good on these sentiments, the settlers offered toasts after the speech to the United States, George Washington, and "Captain Pipe, Chief of the Delawars, and an happy Treaty."[13]

Accomplishing this mission required dutiful vigilance. In particular, it meant ensuring that the wrong sort of person stayed off their grant. Officials were shocked to find that despite warnings, "several vagabonds had presumed to improve the lands . . . which have been appropriated . . . for the redemption of depreciation certificates." Officials throughout the western world feared "deluded combinations of men . . . who forgetful of all obligations human and divine, seem intent only on rapine and anarchy."[14] In Ohio, federal authorities feared that the "country will soon be inhabited by a banditti whose actions are a disgrace to human nature." As soon as Congress had passed the first land act and officials had posted proclamations warning them off the land, they were "moving to the unsettled country, by forties and fifties." By April 1785, three hundred families had settled by the Hocking River and an equal number on the Muskingum, and more than fifteen hundred had squatted in the Miami and Scioto river valleys. "From Wheeling to that place," as one official put it, "there is scarcely one Bottom on the river but has one or more families living thereon." The West in general but the Ohio Country in particular "is in almost a state of nature."[15]

Settlers agreed that they had to keep out the Virginians who were settling south of the Ohio River. New Englanders styled themselves a more enlightened set than those who lived across the Ohio River. Recent studies of the common "western world" Virginians and New Englanders inhabited aside, in the minds of the men and women who settled Marietta, the Ohio River divided two distinct worlds. The North in their eyes stood for enlightened principles, civilized society, and orderly rule. The South did not. And officials north of the river feared that the fertility of land there "very much attracts the attention of these fellows who wish to live under no government." While some Kentuckians and transplanted Virginians made murmurs of declaring themselves "not only independent of the State of Virginia, but of the United States altogether," the "New England settlers are very industrious" and were creating a settlement both "strong and very secure." At Marietta, as opposed to the rest of the western world, "Gay Circles of Ladies, Balls, etc." were held. "These were the changes," a proprietor of the company noted, "which this three years ago Wilderness has undergone."[16]

Here the federal government also established its western beachhead. Named after the military commander of the territory, Lt. Col. Josiah Harmar, Fort Harmar had arisen just across the Muskingum from Campus Martius and Marietta. Small numbers of troops fanned out from this fort to garrison smaller posts along the Ohio and its many tributaries. Order was the order of the day. Authorities had less rarified reasons than did the associates of the Ohio Company for securing order in the region. They wanted to avoid the sordid land grabs and the subsequent squabbling that had defined the early Kentucky experience.[17] Good management and a small but vigorous federal presence in the region could also forestall a dreaded and expensive Indian war. It was too late to salvage Kentucky, but it was not too late to save the Northwest.

Federal authorities in the region, therefore, had a stake in the company's success. Josiah Harmar was a proprietor of the Ohio Company. Rufus Putnam, a commanding figure in early Marietta, served in the army, earning promotion to brigadier general while he was serving as chief judge of Ohio. Blurring military and civilian roles did not seem to bother any of the principals. Indeed, Secretary of War Henry Knox owned stock in the Ohio Company. Nor was there talk of conflicting interests. Binding one's personal interests to the state's prerogatives was both solid policy and—to men like Alexander Hamilton, also an investor—sound business.

Unsurprisingly, army officials preached the same message of order that company directors did. Harmar faced the sticky challenge of conciliating Indians while paving the way for orderly white settlement. Much as the British had conceived Indian policy in 1763 in the wake of Pontiac's War, men like Harmar realized that maintaining peace with neighboring Indians would keep costs down and keep the frontiers quiet.[18] Harmar and his subordinates were eager to inform the government that in 1785 the Delawares and Wyandots in the region seemed "friendly" and that the Shawnees "make great professions of peace" even as he admitted to others that "the Indians down the river, viz. the Shawnees, Miamis, Cherokees, and Kickapoos have killed and scalped several adventurers, settlers on their land." Men like Harmar and St. Clair understandably did all in their power to "brighten the chain" of friendship with Indians, going so far as to hold regular discussions with disaffected groups. Therefore Harmar could without a hint of irony inform Henry Knox that "I am endeavoring all in my power to conciliate the minds of the Indians" and at the same time (to make sure that the region served its larger purpose of helping the government stave off bankruptcy) could order his troops to "cover the Continental surveyors" who worked the region.[19]

The gravest threat to this plan came from the poorer sort, who were streaming into the West. These masterless men, Harmar feared, could undo the soundest policy. Not only did they settle on land without permission but they also harbored an intense hatred of Indians. Before the Revolution, poorer men and women had settled where they liked. Now this arrangement had changed. "These men upon the frontiers," Harmar argued, "have hitherto been accustomed to seat themselves on the best of lands, making a tomahawk right or Improvement, as they term it, supposing that to be sufficient Title." Harmar believed them "in general to be averse to federal measures, and that they would wish to throw every obstacle in the way to impede surveying of the western Territory."[20]

Federal troops, therefore, took a vigorous approach to warning off squatters. As early as 1785, troops moved throughout the region north and west of the river, destroying cabins and ordering people to leave behind the corn they had planted. In one such instance, an Ensign Denny gave a family two weeks to quit its claim because one child lay sick with a snakebite. After the child recovered, the family was instructed to leave the region and tear down its own cabin. Such magnanimity proved exceptional. On one mission Denny reported that he had torn down twenty-three cabins.[21] In general, if squatters asked for time to take in their crops before leaving, they received no "Lenity." Any standing cabin that troops came across was to be "burned and destroyed." Troops would not only "dispossess" such individuals but also "severely chastise them for their insolence, and defiance of the Supreme Authority."[22]

Squatters, as they had historically been wont to do, resisted this new Ohio vision. In this instance they argued that such evictions flew in the face of the Revolution's principles. In the Ohio Country, settlers claimed to be "true and faithful subjects of the common wealth of America, and are as we have always have been ready to venture our Lives in the common defense of the same." That is, "presuming hitherto we were in our present circumstances and state safe under the protection of Government." Yet "to our great surprise we have received advice that an armed party are on their way with orders from Government to dispossess us and to burn and destroy our dwellings."[23] Some cooperated, some pleaded for mercy, others resisted. John Armstrong, an officer charged with warning squatters off land west and north of the Ohio River, ran into one settler who was "determined to hold his possession" and who informed Armstrong "that if I destroyed his House he would build six more in the course of a week." He then "cast many reflections on the Honourable the Congress the Commissioner and the commanding Officer," warning Armstrong he was not acting alone and that if threatened he would fire on troops "as Enemies to my country.[24]

Harmar and his men were playing a dangerous game. Common settlers and squatters from Bacon's "giddy multitude" to the Paxton Boys and their ilk created unmitigated headaches for officials and Indians. Governments in the past that had tried to deal with Indians in a straightforward fashion and that had privileged Indians over settlers had reaped whirlwinds. These governments had also hoped to foster good relations with Indians, but they could not control the type of people that Mariettans called "Virginians" from destroying this vision. The governor of Virginia, for example, learned of "incursions having been made by parties from this State, upon the tribes of Indians in amity with the United States." Beverley Randolph found this movement to be "highly dishonorable to our national Character," but because it occurred far from Richmond there was little he could do. Similarly, Harmar had learned of "several lawless villains in the neighborhood of Wheeling, [who] have threatened to way lay and murder . . . friendly Indians." Such people would, Harmar bellowed, "suffer the brunt of *federal Law*."[25]

At the same time, officials in Ohio invited Indians to settle in the region that they had warned white settlers to steer clear of. Indeed, peaceful Indians in some instances could "be assured of the friendship and protection of the United States." And whereas squatters saw their fields burned to the ground, such Indians would receive corn. To add insult to injury, federal officials like Josiah Harmar believed that the tension between illicit settlers and Indians could create more order in the region. "The circumstance of a few adventurers (settlers on the Indian lands) down the river, having been kill'd and scalp'd, has had a good effect," Harmar argued. "It has halted them in their rapid emigration." Harmar also contended that white Indian killers should be "executed in the presence of the Indians."[26]

Creating a world without such "adventurers" would prove crucial to both the government's and the company's plans for Ohio. The enlightened principles which animated Marietta's founding, the associates hoped and believed, would naturally lead to better relations with Indians. And elites in the territory pinned their hopes on this approach. Hostility to Indians did not derive from a "natural" animosity between two races. On the contrary, wise rule, enlightened principles, the right sort of settler, and vigilance, company leaders argued, would deliver them from the sorts of troubles with Indians that nearly every settlement in British North America had experienced. In fact, they boasted that their plan was already reaping dividends less than a year after initial settlement. The Indians' "depredations since the last year, have been trifling," a settler argued, "and their murders few in number." Indeed Indians seemed to cause more problems for the unruly men and women across the river. "They have murdered some individuals in the Kentucky settlement," he continued, "and have stolen horses from the Virginians. But in most instances of the kind, they have professedly avenged some injury, which they before had sustained."[27] Rufus Putnam, one of the principal organizers of the Ohio Company, believed that the slaughter of Virginians, while tragic, was understandable. Virginians stole horses from Indians from time to time. Indeed, "a Gang of Robbers" was working over the Indians in western Virginia settlements. North of the river all appeared different. "The kind and friendly treatment of the Indians by the first settlers," argued a Mariettan, "has conduced greatly" to relations "without blood-shed" and to settlement "without opposition."[28]

Because most settlers of Marietta came from the east, they did not have, according to Rufus Putnam, "those prejudices against the natives which commonly arise from long wars with them," and could therefore enjoy "the prospect of peace and tranquilety to the frontiers." People with these principles would prove an "advantage" to Ohio. "The western country," he argued, "should in their maners, morrals, relegion, and policy take the eastern States for their modle." He asked—rhetorically—"Is the Genus, education, etc., of any people So favorable to republican government as theirs; and Should they not then . . . take the lead, and give a tone to the New States forming in the western quarter?"[29]

The settlers expected and hoped to achieve nothing short of creating a "new" New England in the Ohio wilderness. And as late as 1790 it seemed to be working. During the summer of that year Delawares and Ottawas came in and out of Marietta, trading deerskins and meat for corn.[30] One migrant to Marietta, Minerva Nye, wrote to her friends back home, "I suppose by this time you have heard that we are all killed by the Indians." But such a belief could not have been further off the mark. Nye gushed that "we find the Country much more Delightsome than we had any idea of: we have formed some acquaintance that are all very agreeable," adding that "yesterday we had the honor of drinking tea with Genl. Harmar." Instead of "being serenaded with howlings of wild beasts," a settler boasted, "and horrid yells of savages, which ye were warned to expect, on the delightful banks of Muskingum ye are favored with the blandishments of polished social intercourse." This errand seemed to be succeeding. "Are we, indeed, in a wilderness? The contemplation of the scene before me, would almost lead me to distrust my sense."[31]

They should have paid more attention to their "senses." The world around Marietta swirled with Indian-white hostility. In 1785 at Pittsburgh, a Delaware killed one inhabitant and wounded three more. In western Virginia, settlers feared they were "daily surrounded" by hostile Indians. In general they argued that men could not "go out to work but Expects our Women and children will be Destroyed." In May 1790 a settler in Ohio County complained that "the present Behavior of the Indians to us is very alarming." In one month's time, he explained, "they have killed two persons, taken five prisoners burnt ten houses stole a number of horses and killed Cattle." Indians had also waylaid nine boats heading down the Ohio River.[32] In Kentucky, Indians and settlers made good on the region's reputation as a "dark and bloody ground." Farther west in the Northwest Territory, where the reach of the federal government was attenuated, whites slaughtered Indians with gusto and Indians paid these settlers back in kind. Even just a few miles from the Muskingum seven or eight people had been killed by Indians just a few years before the settlement of Marietta. The following year a Mrs. Moore and her eldest daughter were taken by Cherokees to a Shawnee settlement. There they were "scalped their ears cut off and their arms and then ham stringed and threw into the fire and Burnt to death." Most settlers understood the nature of the world they were entering. One group moving west, for example, implored the president for protection because of "the numerous accounts in the public papers" of atrocities.[33]

Such atrocities were to be expected. Settlers throughout the Ohio Valley from Kentucky to western Pennsylvania were, after all, encroaching on lands that Native Americans regarded as their own. Officials had two treaties in hand which said otherwise. But the 1785 Treaty of Fort McIntosh and the one signed at Fort Finney with some Shawnees the following year were worth hardly more than the paper they were written on. The treaties ceded much of the Ohio Valley to American settlement, but even the signatories conceded that most Native Americans viewed them as worthless and fraudulent. The same could be said of the 1789 Treaty of Fort Harmar, which amounted to a desperate attempt to try to keep the fictions of the older treaties alive. Violence, therefore, would and did occur. But if bloodshed could be kept to acceptable levels, combative Indians could be diplomatically and militarily isolated. The key, as the architects of this policy noted, was to rein in only those groups of Indians that seemed to contest settlement or that refused to come to the negotiating table.

From time to time local officials took up the cudgel against such Indians, but not with an eye to conquest. To be sure, Kentuckians organized expeditions to slaughter natives. But north of the river officials treaded more carefully. In 1790, because of what Henry Knox called "incursions of small parties of Indians on the western frontier," the government had authorized the dispatch of spies at government expense. But when in Knox's estimation the trouble had passed, the authorization for spies was "to be considered as having ceased and terminated." Sending out spies, "that expensive species of militia," was considered a "temporary measure." Knox argued that the government would undertake only "reasonable measures" to protect frontier settlements.[34] In that year Harmar also led a small force largely composed of militia against some Indians from western Ohio who had been attacking Kentucky settlements. Although this attempt failed—indeed, it infuriated Indians living in Ohio—it did not amount to an attempt to conquer Indian land or even to rationalize the fraudulent and now forgotten treaties with Indians signed in the wake of the Revolution. Rather, the Harmar campaign was an attempt to "chastise" wayward Indians; to bring them back into line.[35]

In this western world of seething hostility, the question the New Englanders faced was could they keep a larger world at bay, or, in other words, could the ideology of Indian-white relations they constructed keep pace with reality. The answer, of course, was no. And they would learn of the fate of their errand in 1791 at a place called Big Bottom. In the years after the initial founding of Marietta, company associates sponsored only smaller settlements nearby. In this way Indians in the region—and many of these were peaceable Christian Delawares—would not be alarmed. In autumn 1790, the company permitted thirty-six men to settle on donation lands on the river bottom on the east bank of the Muskingum about thirty miles upriver from Marietta.[36] The men came from Massachusetts, Rhode Island, Connecticut, and New Hampshire. At this time, the company sponsored similar settlements at a number of points on the streams feeding into the river, including Belpre, Waterford, and Wolf Creek. Each settler received one hundred acres of land, which he was expected to improve within a few years.[37]

The settlement at Big Bottom was a rather modest affair. The young men erected a blockhouse of large beech logs. Not far from the blockhouse two settlers, Francis and Isaac Choate, built a cabin and began clearing the woods. Up from the bottom, two Virginians named Asa and Eleazar Bulard had already settled in a cabin. Although the region around them seethed with violence, the settlers at Big Bottom demonstrated little vigilance and even less sense. Within a few weeks of their arrival the weather had turned bitterly cold, and the river froze over a few days before Christmas. Because clay also froze in these conditions, they did not chink between the logs. They rarely posted sentries. They did not even leave their dogs outside the blockhouse to sound an alarm. Nor did they construct palisades around the blockhouse, despite the fact that on the opposite bank of the river ran an old Indian path from Sandusky to the mouth of the Muskingum. Perhaps they thought they were immune to the bloodshed engulfing other frontier settlements. We will never know.[38]

On the afternoon of January 2, a raiding party of Delawares and Wyandots from the Upper Sandusky area traveling on the old path encountered the settlement on the opposite bank of the river. The Big Bottom settlement, apparently, had not been their objective. But, poorly planned, it proved a target of opportunity. After dusk, the twenty-five young men broke into two parties and crossed the frozen river on foot. The smaller party entered the Choate cabin in a friendly manner and sat down for dinner before seizing the men and restraining them with leather thongs. The Choates submitted without resistance. Meanwhile the larger party headed to the blockhouse undetected. One raider smashed open the door while others ran in. They had found the occupants at supper. From outside, other Indians aimed their guns between the un-chinked logs and shot a few men by the fire. The wife of Isaac Meeks, one of the Virginians, resisted. She attacked one of her assailants with an axe, which she plunged into his shoulder. She was quickly killed, as were the others in the blockhouse. One young man tried to escape by a window but was shot as he clambered on the roof. The only survivor was Philip Stacy, who hid under some bedding in the corner of a room. When the raiders discovered him after the killings, they spared his life and took him, along with the two Choates, as a captive. All told, twelve persons perished in the attack.[39]

The raid seemed to precipitate more attacks throughout the Ohio Valley. In Ohio County, Virginia, a group of Indians took two boys, "one of which they have killed, the other has got in, tho' he is scalped and badly Tomahawk'd." By March 1791 officials up and down the Ohio Valley from Pennsylvania to western Virginia and Kentucky reported fresh outrages. The county lieutenant of Ohio County, Virginia, sent reports back east detailing the "continual depredations of the Savages upon our frontier during the later part of Winter." The enemy forces appeared widespread, so much so that even the governor of Pennsylvania had taken notice.[40] Even Josiah Harmar sensed something different in the air. He reported to one of his officers just a few days after Big Bottom that "a body of savages to the amount of 200 besieged a small station" using flaming arrows for twenty-five hours. As one frontier settler put it, while attacks seemed to be multiplying throughout the Ohio Valley, "we can Expect nothing but an Indian War."[41]

Such attacks had occurred before Big Bottom. But only after the massacre did settlers in Ohio interpret isolated incidents up and down the frontier as part of larger design. Putnam blamed the failed Harmar expedition against the Shawnees. But he insisted, everything he and others had said notwithstanding, that the attack did not come as a total surprise. "I have Sometime ben of the opinion that the Spring would open with a general attack on the frontier," he suggested. Government was to blame, and only government could solve the problem. "I consider the event," he wrote, "as a foreruner to other attacks of a more serious nature and which may involve us in complet ruin unless prevented by Government imediately taking measures for our protection."[42] After Big Bottom, the reasoning went, the "horror committed by the savages . . . multiplied upon all points of the Ohio." "There is not a single doubt," white Ohioans now believed, "that all the Indians are agreed to make war and destroy all the settlements formed on the right bank of La Belle Riviere."[43] On this point they were right, and they were wrong. The Indian confederation in their midst was indeed making war on white settlements throughout the region. But Ohio Company settlers could not admit that they represented part of the problem. By their logic any attack on Ohio Company land had to be part of a general war against Americans in the West. Their minds could not grasp the possibility that Indian raids could have been caused by the New Englanders in Ohio.

The massacre revealed the flawed foundations of Ohio. "Our prospects," Rufus Putnam lamented, "are much changed. Instead of peace and friendship with our Indian neighbors a hored Savage war Stairs us in the face." Officials scrambled to prepare adequate defenses for what they feared awaited the Ohio colony. They appealed to the federal troops in the region for help. They sent out spies of their own. They refitted hastily built palisades. They removed women and children from exposed outposts. After the event, elites in Marietta wasted little time in petitioning the government for protection. Putnam issued a terse and harried letter to Secretary of War Henry Knox, pleading for help. "The unhappy fate of the persons who fell victim to savage barbarity" necessitated the government "as soon as possible" to "take effectual measures to prevent a repetition of Indian depredations by making a powerful inroad into their country, and establishing strong posts there."[44] They had become Kentuckians.

They had ready allies. John Brown, a member of Congress from the Kentucky district, informed his friends that "a few days ago a party of Indians made an attack on a fort on the Muskinghan, took it and murdered the greater part of the Inhabitants." The attack, he believed, was already spawning other raids closer to home. "Since that time," he reported, "an attempt has been made by a party of one hundred-fifty Indians to take a Station on the Miami." He warned that "on most of our frontier Stations there is every reason to apprehend severe attacks." Harry Innes, a transplanted Virginian from a wealthy family living in Danville, Kentucky, warned Secretary Knox of "the consequences if government is not more active and more decisive in the business." Innes informed Knox that people "who had settled here and bore with fortitude all the cruelties of a savage Warr then hoped that the attention of general Government would be turned towards quieting the hostile tribes of Indians."[45]

Kentuckians and westerners in general had aired such grievances before. Even before Big Bottom they had complained of the failure of eastern governments to protect western settlements. Because, as one settler put it, "the Seat of that Government is far distant," it was difficult for the state to offer "relief." But after the events of the early 1790s, the tone of westerners became more shrill and alarming. "Nature," one prominent Kentuckian wrote, "has done everything for us; Government everything against us." Although Indians raided to "murder [their] wives and children," the central administration also trampled their rights. Kentucky elites argued, "We are too distant from the grand seat of information; and are too much hackneyed in the old fashioned principles of 1776, to receive much light from the . . . new fashioned systems and schemes of policy, which are the offspring and ornament of the present administration." They warned officials living out East to "take care they do not drive us" to secession.[46]

In the wake of the Big Bottom attack and the newest wave of unrest in the West, the territorial governor planned another expedition to "chastise" wayward Indians. Writing from Fort Washington, Arthur St. Clair wrote that the county lieutenants of western America were now "authorized by the President of the United States to embody at the Expense of the United States as many Militia, by voluntary enlistment or otherwise as the Law directs." U.S. troops also arrived at frontier posts to relieve the militia.[47] St. Clair, of course, led a hastily raised force against Native Americans in the Ohio Country, making a last ditch effort to keep the old policy of chastisement alive. The army sent west was not up to the task. Its troops were "picked up and recruited from the off-scourings of large Towns and Cities." Corrupted "by Idleness, Debaucheries and every species of Vice, it was impossible they could have been made competent to the arduous duties of Indian Warfare." The government, moreover, had mismanaged the affair from the start. The army was "badly cloathed, badly paid, and badly fed," and supplied with "very bad powder." They did not stand a chance, and a confederation of Indians routed them, killing six hundred.[48]

Squatters, who had suffered the brunt of Indian raids, clamored for revenge. When the number of attacks seemed to be escalating, the lower sort began taking things into their own hands. A number of such men, for example, killed five Indians on Beaver Creek in Allegheny County, Pennsylvania. "Parties of volunteer militia" from the counties of western Pennsylvania—including the Washington County militia which had been responsible for the massacre at Gnadenhutten—"fell in with a party of friendly Indians at the block house on Beaver Creek." The Indians called out to them in English, and a number of them were "Moravian Indians." Nonetheless, the patrol butchered the Indians "known to several" on the raid.[49] The governor, Thomas Mifflin, offered a reward for the capture of the men who had perpetrated what he called an "atrocious act." But officials living in the region disagreed, interpreting such murders as justice. As exposed settlers had been wont to do since the days of the earliest American frontier, they wanted to vent their fury on "the Tawny Enemies who frequently Infest the Good people."[50]

After Big Bottom, officials at Marietta discovered a newfound appreciation for such sentiments. An army officer serving in Ohio concluded that far from condemning an atrocity at Beaver Creek that "appears very much like deliberate murder," the "majority of people on the Ohio" approved of it.[51] Indeed, squatters, especially those who had suffered at the hands of Indians, now proved useful. And at this juncture Ohio officials changed their tune. Now they could no longer "be silent," as they put it, while others were being killed. The officers of the company now conceded, "It is with pain we have heard the cruel insinuations of those who have been disaffected to the Settlement of this Country." They continued that "it is not possible that those men who have pursued into these woods that path to an humble competence . . . should be doomed the Victims of a Jealous policy." That policy, which had been sponsored and supported by men like Harmar and Putnam, was now revealed for what it was. It seemed unjust to use "the mangled bodies of their friends exposed as a Spectacle to prevent emigration."[52]

It is at this moment, as interests converged, broaching lines of class and region, that we can say that a "western vision" emerged. In their 1793 "Address to the Inhabitants of the United States West of the Allegany and Appalachian Mountains," members of the Democratic Society of Kentucky charged that the federal government exhibited "a neglect bordering on contempt" for western protection. Although they had hoped that the new government under the Constitution would have the "requisite energy" to safeguard the frontier," they found instead that only "our brethren, on the Eastern Waters, possess every advantage." They, in effect, decried the effects of what they referred to as "a Local policy."[53] In the early 1790s westerners began a concerted campaign to lobby the federal government to recognize the "degraded and deserted situation of this Country, both as to its commerce and protection." They resolved that "the inhabitants of the Western Country have a right to demand, that their frontiers be protected by the general government."[54] Protection, western elites claimed, "has not been extended to us," while the "strong nerved government, extends its arm of protection" to all others. Patriotism, they warned, "like all other things, has its bounds," and "attachments to governments cease to be natural, when they cease to be mutual."[55] To make good on these principles, westerners began clamoring for committees of correspondence to be created to "give and receive communications on these subjects" with other frontier regions.[56]

After the St. Clair debacle, pressure on the government mounted considerably. Settlers rushed a letter to the governor of Pennsylvania, Thomas Mifflin, asking for any help from state or federal authorities he could muster. They feared "the present defence-less state of their frontiers, now exposed to the cruel ravages of a powerful and savage foe." They considered themselves "unprotected as well as destitute of arms and ammunition for defending them-selves." But as John Brown informed his constituents in early 1792, a new plan for dealing with the Indian threat was being "calculated upon a much larger scale." Brown claimed that the War Department estimated that it would need upwards of a million dollars to destroy the Indians in Ohio. "The augmentation of the Military establish-ment is alarming to many," Brown wrote, "but notwithstanding I be-lieve the plan will be agreed to by a Majority of Congress."[57]

The federal government had to respond. It had little choice. The rank-and-file of the West had often clamored against govern-ment. That was nothing new. But elites losing confidence in the gov-ernment and subscribing to the racist views of the rabble around them was another matter. Here lay the real possibility of losing the West. At this moment the government was faced with the choice of either allying with whites by engaging in an expensive war of con-quest or acting as an honest broker for Indian concerns. The choice did not prove difficult. Writing from Philadelphia in March 1791, one of Harmar's lieutenants wrote that "the great people here have at length determined to carry on a another campaign against the savages upon a more extensive plan than the last."[58]

The federal government's response is well documented and does not need to be recounted in detail here. After Big Bottom the government wanted to end permanently what it regarded as a prob-lem. In 1792 President George Washington called Anthony Wayne, a veteran of the Revolution, out of retirement. For nearly two years he trained a force of five thousand regulars for the rigors of frontier warfare. And in 1794 his force defeated a confederation of Native Americans on the Maumee River at a place called Fallen Timbers.

The 1795 Treaty of Greenville both canonized what had al-ready happened in the West and presaged what was to come to pass. Westerners conceded that Wayne's victory in military terms was not devastating for Indians. But its implications were great. "The loss on both sides was trifling," a prominent Kentuckian explained, "but as it is the first stand the arms of the U. States have ever made against the Indians, I think it will produce good consequences."[59] After Big Bottom, whites and Indians could not live together in Ohio. And although this arrangement might have indeed proven ephemeral in other places and times, now there was no turning back. To ensure fiscal solvency, order, and national unity, the government would have to act as a force for expansion and establish formal and informal guidelines to keep the races apart. No longer would squatters act as a vanguard for unregulated or unmediated white settlement. The government would from this point forward be in this business. There would be no meaningful "middle ground" again.

Consider the forces arrayed against Native Americans at this time to get a sense of what they confronted. The lower orders saw Indians as impediments, immediate threats, and as members of a "perfidious" race to be eradicated. Elites north and south of the river now saw them in a similar light. And the federal government had put itself in the position of achieving this frightening vision. The array of these forces ensured that Indian-white relations were doomed from this point forward. Thomas Jefferson wrote to an acquaintance in Kentucky on the eve of Wayne's offensive that "it is very interesting to the United States to see how this last effort for living in peace with the Indians will succeed. If it does not, there will be a great revolution of opinion here as to the manner in which they are to be dealt with." Jefferson prophesied that "if war is to follow, the event of this campaign will probably fix the kind of instrument to be used," adding that "this summer is of immense importance to the future condition of mankind all over the earth: and not a little so to ours."[60]

Jefferson, of course, was right, but in ways he could scarcely have imagined. The Ohio River Valley and the events occurring there in the late 1780s and early 1790s represented an American Rubicon over which no return passage was possible. And the presidency of Jefferson would speak volumes to the transformed reality of Indian-white relations he would confront as well as the ways he would navigate those rocky shoals. He would, of course, resort to the language of "civilization" and "progress" to explain the marginalization of Native American culture within a broader white society, most notoriously in his infamous *Notes on the State of Virginia*. But he would take to heart the lessons learned in Ohio in the 1790s. During his presidency that hardened line between the races would begin inching westward. And he was one of the first to envision an eastern America—from the Atlantic to the Mississippi—free of Indians.[61]

The Treaty of Greenville line amounted to the early republic's "Proclamation Line" dividing two distinct worlds. But unlike the

British line, which used the Appalachian Mountains as its marker, the new line would know no such geographic bounds. Beyond the line lived Indians whose lives, liberty, and property had been compromised. They now confronted squatters and elites, Ohioans and Kentuckians, the army, and state and federal governments, thrown together by the events and decisions of the early 1790s. This line, unlike the British line, would move to find its proper geographic bounds. At first the Mississippi River served that purpose; eventually the Pacific Ocean did.

Notes

1. See Edmund S. Morgan's analysis of Bacon's Rebellion in *American Slavery, American Freedom: The Ordeal of Colonial Virginia* (New York: Norton, 1975) and Jill Lepore's take on King Philip's War in *The Name of War: King Philip's War and the Origins of American Identity* (New York: Knopf, 1998).

2. Gregory Evans Dowd, *War under Heaven: Pontiac, the Indian Nations, and the British Empire* (Baltimore: Johns Hopkins University Press, 2003); Daniel Richter, *Facing East from Indian Country: A Native History of Early America* (Cambridge: Harvard University Press, 2001).

3. Eric Hinderaker, *Elusive Empires: Constructing Colonialism in the Ohio Valley, 1673–1800* (New York: Cambridge University Press, 1997). Alternatively, the Revolution witnessed a shift apparent especially in Kentucky from a frontier society based on hunting and commonality with Indians to one premised on settlement and agriculture, which precluded white-Indian cooperation. On this see Stephen Aron, *How the West Was Lost: The Transformation of Kentucky from Daniel Boone to Henry Clay* (Baltimore: Johns Hopkins University Press, 1996).

4. Richard White, *The Middle Ground: Indians, Empires, and Republics in the Great Lakes Region, 1650–1815* (New York: Cambridge University Press, 1991); D. C. Skaggs and L. L. Nelson, eds., *The Sixty Years' War for the Great Lakes, 1754–1815* (East Lansing: Michigan State University Press, 2001); Gregory Nobles, *American Frontiers: Cultural Encounters and Continental Conquest* (New York: Hill and Wang, 1997). On the shift from backcountry to frontier, see Hinderaker and Peter Mancall, *At the Edge of Empire: The Backcountry in British North America* (Baltimore: Johns Hopkins University Press, 2003).

5. See, for example, James Merrell, *Into the American Woods: Negotiators on the Pennsylvania Frontier* (New York: Norton, 1999).

6. George Fredrickson, *Racism: A Short History* (Princeton: Princeton University Press, 2002).

7. Anthony F. C. Wallace, *Jefferson and the Indians: The Tragic Fate of the First Americans* (Cambridge: Belknap Press of Harvard University Press, 1999).

8. See Lepore, *The Name of War.* In a similar vein, we also have studies that discuss how European Americans discovered or invented their "whiteness" as this process unfolded. The wages of whiteness, it would seem, were doled out even on the frontier. See Jane Merritt, *At the Crossroads: Indians and Empires on a Mid-Atlantic Frontier, 1700–1763* (Chapel Hill: University of North Carolina Press, 2003).

9. Wallace, *Jefferson and the Indians,* 163.

10. Ohio Company, *Articles of an Association by the Name of the Ohio Company* (Worcester, MA: Isaiah Thomas, 1786), 2–3; S. P. Hildreth, *Biographical and Historical Memoirs of the Early Pioneer Settlers of Ohio* (Cincinnati: H. W. Derby, 1852), 104, 250.

11. Hildreth, *Pioneer Settlers of Ohio,* 104; Court and Legal Papers, Backus-Woodbridge Papers, Box 5, File 1, 1422–1428, MSS-128, Ohio Historical Society, Columbus (hereafter OHS).

12. Manasseh Cutler, *An Explanation of the Map which Delineates that Part of the Federal Lands . . .* (Salem: Dabney and Cushing, 1787), 20; James Mitchell Varnum, *An Oration Delivered at Marietta, July 4, 1788* (Newport, RI: Peter Edes, 1788), 5.

13. On New Englanders and Indians in the seventeenth century, see James Axtell, *Natives and Newcomers: The Cultural Origins of North America* (New York: Oxford University Press, 2001), 145–73; Varnum, *Oration Delivered at Marietta,* 5, 10, 8.

14. Harmar to John Dickinson, May 1, 1785, Josiah Harmar Papers, Letterbook A, 54, Clements Library, University of Michigan, Ann Arbor (hereafter Harmar Papers); Proclamation of Governor of Virginia, August 20, 1794, Pittsburgh and Northwest Virginia Papers, Series NN, vol. 5, 66, Draper Manuscripts (microfilm copies of originals that are held at the University of Wisconsin, Madison).

15. John Armstrong to Harmar, April 13, 1785, Harmar Papers, vol. 2, 56; William Irvine to Harmar, May 31, 1785, Harmar Papers, vol. 2, 77.

16. Harmar to Knox, May 14, 1787, Harmar Papers, Letterbook B, 80; Harmar to Knox, December 15, 1788, and February 10, 1789, Harmar Papers, Letterbook E, 10–11, 45; Harmar to John Doughty, April 28, 1789, Harmar Papers, Letterbook E, 80. Kim Gruenwald, *River of Enterprise: The Commercial Origins of Regional Identity in the Ohio Valley, 1790–1850* (Bloomington: Indiana University Press, 2002).

17. On the Kentucky mess, see Hinderaker, *Elusive Empires,* and Aron, *How the West Was Lost.*

18. Reginald Horsman, "American Indian Policy in the Old Northwest, 1783–1812," *William and Mary Quarterly,* 3rd Ser., 18 (1961): 35–53. For differing views on the significance of the Proclamation Line, see Hinderaker, *Elusive Empires;* Patrick Griffin, "Empires, Subjects, and Pontiac," *Reviews in American History,* 31 (2003): 363–71; and Dowd's *War under Heaven.*

19. Harmar to Knox, June 1, 1785, Harmar Papers, Letterbook A, 65–66; Harmar to General Mifflin, June 25, 1785, Harmar Papers, Letter-

book A, 75; Harmar to Knox, September 4, 1786, Harmar Papers, Letterbook A, 145; Harmar to Knox, October 22, 1785, Harmar Papers, Letterbook A, 98–99.

20. Harmar to Knox, August 4, 1786, Harmar Papers, Letterbook A, 145.

21. Harmar to Richard Henry Lee, May 1, 1785, Harmar Papers, Letterbook A, 55–56; Ensign E. Denny to Harmar, August 23, 1785, Harmar Papers, vol. 2, 110.

22. Harmar to Knox, October 22, 1785, Harmar Papers, Letterbook A, 98–99; Orders delivered to Captain John Doughty, Fort McIntosh, October 3, 1785, Harmar Papers, Letterbook A, 96–97; Harmar to John Carpenter, April 26, 1789, Harmar Papers, Letterbook E, 76.

23. "Resolution of Settlers West of the Ohio River," April 5, 1785, Harmar Papers, vol. 2, 51.

24. John Armstrong to Harmar, April 12, 1785, Harmar Papers, vol. 2, 55.

25. Beverley Randolph to County Lieutenant of Nelson, March 10, 1790, Harry Innes Papers, Container 1, General Correspondence, 1790, 29, Library of Congress (hereafter Innes Papers); Harmar to Knox, August 4, 1786, Harmar Papers, Letterbook A, 145 (emphasis Harmar's).

26. Resolution of Congress, August 24, 1786, Harmar Papers, vol. 4, 9; Harmar to Knox, August 1, 1785, Harmar Papers, Letterbook A, 90; Harmar to Knox, July 7, 1787, Harmar Papers, Letterbook B, 115.

27. Varnum, *Oration Delivered at Marietta,* 13.

28. Rufus Putnam to George Washington, July 24, 1790, in *The Memoirs of Rufus Putnam,* ed. Rowena Buell (Boston: Houghton Mifflin, 1903), 232–33; Solomon Drowne, *An Oration, Delivered at Marietta, April 7, 1789* (Worcester, MA: Isaiah Thomas, 1789), 8.

29. Putnam to Fisher Ames, 1790, *Memoirs of Rufus Putnam,* 244–45, 246.

30. S. P. Hildreth, *Pioneer History: Being an Account of the First Examinations of the Ohio Valley* (Cincinnati: H. W. Derby, 1848), 428.

31. Minerva Nye to Mrs. Stone, September 19, 1788, Tupper Family Papers, Box 2, Folder 1, 4–5, Marietta, Ohio Collection, OHS; Solomon Drowne, *Oration,* 9.

32. Josiah Harmar to Michael Huffnashe, May 14, 1785, Harmar Papers, Letterbook A, 60; Petition of People of Grave Creek, May 18, 1790, Shepherd Papers, Series SS, vol. 2, 173, Draper Manuscripts; Shepherd to General Knox, May 10, 1790, Shepherd Papers, Series SS, vol. 2, 171–72, Draper Manuscripts.

33. Obediah Robins to Harmar, August 28, 1785, Harmar Papers, vol. 2, 113; Obediah Robins to Capt. Ferguson, September 29, 1786, Harmar Papers, vol. 4, 43; "Appeal to the President of the United States," May 19, 1790, Scioto Land Company records, Correspondence File, 1790, Historical Society of Pennsylvania, Philadelphia.

34. Knox to Shepherd, July 17, 1790, Shepherd Papers, Series SS, vol. 2, 181–83, Draper Manuscripts.

35. On chastisement, see Andrew R. L. Cayton, *The Frontier Republic: Ideology and Politics in the Ohio Country, 1780–1825* (Kent, OH: Kent State University Press, 1986), 36, 38.

36. A. B. Hulbert, ed., *The Records of the Original Proceedings of the Ohio Company*, 2 vols. (Marietta: Marietta Historical Commission, 1917), 2:57, 59.

37. Hildreth, *Pioneer Settlers of Ohio*, 104.

38. Hildreth, *Pioneer History*, 429–30.

39. Ibid., 431–33.

40. David Shepperd to Col. Beard, May 5, 1792, Samuel Brady and Lewis Wetzel Papers, Series E, vol. 1, 99, Draper Manuscripts; Benjamin Biggs to Beverley Randolph, March 1791, Pittsburgh and Northwest Virginia Papers, Series NN, 23–24, Draper Manuscripts.

41. Harmar to Hamtramck, January 15, 1791, Harmar Papers, Letterbook I, 6–7; Shepherd to unknown recipient, January 25, 1791, Shepherd Papers, Series SS, vol. 3, 1, Draper Manuscripts.

42. Putnam to unknown recipient, January 6, 1791, *Memoirs of Rufus Putnam*, 248.

43. Capt. De Luziere to Gov. St. Clair, February 20, 1791, in *The St. Clair Papers*, ed. William Henry Smith, 2 vols. (Cincinnati: R. Clarke, 1882), 2:199.

44. Putnam to unknown recipient, January 6, 1791, *Memoirs of Rufus Putnam*, 247; Hulbert, *Records of the Ohio Company*, 2:67–71; Putnam to Knox, January 27, 1791, *Memoirs of Rufus Putnam*, 249.

45. John Brown to Harry Innes, February 1, 1791, Innes Papers, General Correspondence, 1791, 57; Harry Innes to General Knox, July 7, 1790, Innes Papers, General Correspondence, 1790, 40–41.

46. Shepherd to unknown recipient, 1789, Shepherd Papers, Series SS, vol. 2, 157–58, Draper Manuscripts; John Breckenridge to Samuel Hopkins, September 15, 1794, Breckinridge Family Papers, vol. 2, Library of Congress.

47. St. Clair to John Brown, June 25, 1791, Innes Papers, General Correspondence, 1791, 75; Richard Butler to Shepherd, June 11, 1791, Shepherd Papers, Series SS, vol. 3, 43, Draper Manuscripts.

48. "Winthrop Sargent's Diary of St. Clair Expedition, October 10, 1791," Winthrop Sargent Papers, Reel 1, 10, Massachusetts Historical Society, Boston. For the best treatment of Native American motivations and responses to Harmar and St. Clair, see Richard White's *Middle Ground*.

49. Isaac Craig to General Knox, March 6, 1791, in Smith, *St. Clair Papers*, 2, 201.

50. Benjamin Biggs to Beverley Randolph, March 1791, Pittsburgh and Northwest Virginia Papers, Series NN, 23–24, Draper Manuscripts; Henry Bidinger to Shepherd, October 27, 1791, Shepherd Papers, Series SS, vol. 3, 59, Draper Manuscripts.

51. Major Isaac Craig to General Knox, March 6, 1791, in Smith, *St. Clair Papers,* 2, 202.

52. Hulbert, *Records of the Ohio Company,* 2:72–73.

53. "Address to the Inhabitants of the United States West of the Allegany and Appalachian Mountains, December 13, 1793," Innes Papers, Miscellany, 84. In *The Other Founders: Anti-Federalism and the Dissenting Tradition in America, 1788–1828* (University of North Carolina Press, 1999), Saul Cornell argues that westerners tended to see their rights only within "local" contexts. Westerners would seem to have disagreed.

54. Citizens of Kentucky, *On Saturday the 24th Instant a Numerous Meeting of Respectable Citizens . . . in Lexington* (Lexington: Bradford, 1794).

55. "Remonstrance of Citizens West of the Allegany Mountains to the President and Congress of the United States of America," n.d., Innes Papers, Miscellany, 106.

56. Citizens of Kentucky, *Saturday the 24th.*

57. *Pennsylvania Gazette,* January 4, 1792; Brown to Harry Innes, January 20, 1792, Innes Papers, General Correspondence, 1792, 89.

58. Lt. Denny to Harmar, March 9, 1791, in Smith, *St. Clair Papers,* 2, 200.

59. John Breckenridge to Samuel Hopkins, September 15, 1794, Breckenridge Family Papers, vol. 2.

60. Jefferson to Harry Innes, May 23, 1793, Innes Papers, General Correspondence, 1793, 115.

61. Thomas Jefferson, *Notes on the State of Virginia,* ed. David Waldstreicher (New York: Palgrave, 2002), 121–25. On Jefferson's presidency and his policy toward Indians, see Wallace, *Jefferson and the Indians.*

TWO

The Changing Political World
of Thomas Worthington

DONALD J. RATCLIFFE

Thomas Worthington was not quite what he seems. Moving from western Virginia to the Ohio Country in 1798, Worthington (1773–1827) won renown as the "father of Ohio statehood" and became the state's best-known politician, both nationally and at home, until after the War of 1812. Most historians have regarded him as a scion of the Virginia gentry who easily established himself as a leading notable in the western territories. They see him almost inevitably becoming a Jeffersonian Republican and necessarily leading a statehood movement in Ohio that gave local autonomy and political command of the new state to its leading men. Worthington's object has been defined as a stable and open society guided by local "men of proven talents," as befitted a political culture that accepted naturally the social and political propriety of deference to the rich and the well-born. In other words, he endeavored to provide the enlightened leadership needed to maintain a liberal and decentralized but hierarchical society. As a person with such views, his day would seem to have passed by the 1820s, when a boisterous frontier democracy apparently made political power dependent on the popular will.[1]

This view of Worthington fits closely with the tradition of seeing the older political ways of the eighteenth century as continuing into the nineteenth century. Most historians currently see the early republic as still maintaining the elitist, deferential, and aristocratic

36

ways of colonial America, with local political structures based on the principles of communal solidarity and subordination to social superiors. The object of the republican system was to secure enlightened leaders who would pursue the general welfare, and that meant limiting popular power in significant ways. These habits of mind, historians insist, persisted through the Jeffersonian era, and the prevalence of antiparty attitudes ensured that the conflict between Federalists and Jeffersonian Republicans would not become an all-absorbing, all-penetrating mass party contest like those of later periods. Not until the 1820s and 1830s, with the election of Andrew Jackson and the rise of the Second Party System, did American politics enter the brave new political world of egalitarian rhetoric, popular participation, democratic values, and mass partisanship.[2]

Unfortunately, Worthington's political career does not quite fit that view. He was something rather different, someone less easy to generalize about confidently; there is a fascinating contrast between his presumed ideological outlook and his political behavior. Undoubtedly he and his allies grew up in that older political world that respected elitism and deference, and their ambition in the Ohio country was to place power in the hands of those who deserved it. In practice, however, they deliberately encouraged mass participation in politics and worked to distribute power as broadly as possible. Far from preserving upper-class privilege, Worthington helped to extend the right to vote and hold office to (in effect) all adult white males in Ohio, he helped to remove limitations on the power of the people's representatives, and between 1807 and 1812 he struggled to reduce the power of the judiciary to defend property rights and so in practice endeavored to establish unchallenged legislative supremacy.[3]

Similarly, at various stages in his life Worthington expressed great doubts about the virtues of political parties, in a manner typical of a pre-party age. In the late 1790s, far from being an original Jeffersonian Republican, he disavowed the growing partisanship of the day, instead lavishing praise on John Adams and pandering to Federalist authorities as late as 1800. Yet between 1802 and 1804 he helped to introduce partisan considerations into Ohio elections, causing candidates to be judged essentially by their national party labels and giving office only to those who were on the right team. He used party devices to keep power in the hands of his political friends, and then in 1810, when some Jeffersonian Republicans refused to clip the judges' wings, he participated in the creation of the Tammany Society, a tight inner group designed to confine effective power to those who supported the full application of Democratic Republican principle. Arguably, Worthington was involved in efforts to extend the power of the people and their representatives that were far more radical than anything Andrew Jackson's supporters attempted, and for a time he endeavored to impose a degree of party discipline far more thoroughgoing than anything later conceived by Martin Van Buren.

Thus if Worthington's influence declined after 1818, it was not because the world became more democratic. He had shared in the disillusionment with extreme partisanship after 1812 and so, as governor of Ohio between 1814 and 1818, had helped to destroy one key basis of his earlier political preeminence. More important, he became too closely associated with special economic interests, notably his own. Damned by his connections with banks before and during the Panic of 1818–19, after 1821 this revered Republican statesman lacked influence with the new generation of internal improvers because he favored handing essential public works over to private companies, potentially to his own considerable advantage. To the would-be canal builders he became a "holy saint of speculators" who typified a Tammany influence that had always "opposed any thing liberal or generous." He was therefore suspected as a potential betrayer of the people's legitimate demand to benefit from positive and constructive policies undertaken at their behest by popularly elected governments.[4]

These apparent paradoxes within Worthington's political career are best explained by the changing political world in which he found himself. Worthington's great achievement—early statehood for Ohio—amounted to a political revolution that brought self-government to the main area of settlement in the Old Northwest before it had acquired the population specified by the Northwest Ordinance as the minimum for statehood. But, more significantly, Ohio's statehood also established (though only for adult white males) one of the most democratic constitutional systems in the United States, a system that would satisfy Jacksonian Democrats right down to 1850. That democratic transformation was what forced on Worthington the changes that often compelled him to behave in ways that contradicted his apparent cultural assumptions.

Were Worthington and Ohio unusual, or were they part of a process of political transformation that was taking place all over the republic? After all, some historians have argued that the process of democratization had begun in the United States even before Worthington's birth in 1773. Already in the late colonial period, especially in the middle colonies, they claim, socially dominant elites could not command automatically deferential voters, while the Revolution itself legitimized popular sovereignty and increased popular political awareness.[5] As a consequence, the party conflicts of the years between 1794 and 1816 were marked by populistic appeals, high levels of voter participation, and popular rejection of social superiors who favored the unpopular side. The range of those actively participating in politics broadened, especially with the growing importance of partisan newspapers, and traditional leaders drawn from the professions and the landed gentry had to cooperate with men of a more artisanal background.[6] Did politics indeed become more democratic (in this admittedly limited way) across the nation, or did the process of transformation depend upon social, economic, and cultural characteristics that varied from one part of the country to another? Did the Ohio Country undergo experiences that prompted the development of a brand of politics that was peculiar to itself?

When Worthington arrived in the Ohio Country in 1798, he entered a recognizable political world. The Northwest Territory was entering on the second stage of government laid down in the Northwest Ordinance, which gave it a political system akin to those of eighteenth-century Britain and most British American colonies. The new territorial legislature represented only substantial landowners, since the ordinance required at least five hundred acres for membership in the appointed legislative council and two hundred acres for the house, which was elected. The suffrage rules excluded about half of the adult male population because only owners of fifty-acre freeholds (or the equivalent in town lots) qualified to vote. The restriction of polling stations to the county seats at a time when the future Ohio, for example, was divided into only five or six counties reduced participation even further. Some voters had to ride through eighty miles of thick forest to vote, so it is not surprising that, at most, only 22 percent of adult white males actually cast votes in territorial elections. At the polls, the elector had to approach a table occupied by the sheriff and the clerks, announce his preference publicly, and have his name and vote inscribed in the pollbook. This *viva voce* election opened voters to the scrutiny and pressure of employers, landlords, creditors, and men of influence in a way that was perfectly familiar to aspiring Virginians like Worthington who were making their fortunes settling the Scioto Valley.[7]

The political influence of the landed gentry was, however, restricted by the territorial governor, Arthur St. Clair, who owed his appointment entirely to the federal government and, as a committed Federalist, was devoted to ensuring that the territory became thoroughly integrated into the Union. This periwigged old Scot enjoyed many prerogatives and controlled a patronage system that gave jobs to about one in ten of adult males in the territory, not counting his command of the militia. Since opponents could never win control of the executive power and its patronage through the territory's internal political processes, the politically ambitious were easily tempted to join "King Arthur's Court." So Worthington's obsequious course in seeking office and preferment from this Federalist governor shows him playing the old-fashioned game in time-honored fashion, at least down to 1800.

More ominously, the governor could summon, prorogue, and dissolve the newly installed assembly at will, determine its apportionment, nominate the upper house, and exercise an absolute veto on all legislation. As he was paid by the federal government, St. Clair enjoyed a degree of financial independence that enabled him, unlike the king of England or most British colonial governors, to actually exercise his veto. At the close of the first Territorial Assembly in December 1799, the governor vetoed a significant number of reform measures passed by the legislature and in so doing alienated Worthington and his Chillicothe friends. Not only had the governor nullified measures they favored but he had, in effect, proclaimed that he alone could determine the limits of the assembly's power.

Thereafter Worthington and his friends opposed the "tyranny" of King Arthur, but they could not actually change the executive and so could form only what was traditionally called a "Country" opposition. Then St. Clair, in Walpolean fashion, bought off some opposition leaders by offering them jobs, appealed to the self-interest of different power centers in the territory, and thereby ensured that the next assembly would be more amenable to his wishes. In December 1801 this assembly accepted St. Clair's plans for dividing the future Ohio into two territories and so postponing statehood, a division that would incidentally do irreparable harm to Chillicothe's ambitions. Yet even now Worthington and the Chillicothe gentry continued to think in terms of the established *ancien régime:* they worked for St. Clair's removal rather than the end of the territorial yoke and looked for relief after March 1801 to the new dispenser of patronage in Washington, President Jefferson.

But circumstances rapidly pushed Worthington and his Chillicothe friends on to the more revolutionary object of early statehood for Ohio. On the one hand, Jefferson refused to cooperate by dismissing Federalist officeholders in the territory; on the other, a vociferous popular demand was already building up for statehood to be secured more quickly than the Chillicothe gentry wanted. Worthington and his allies organized a massive petition campaign to demonstrate to the new powers in Washington the degree of discontent with the proposed division of the territory and so deliberately appealed to the small farmers, squatters, and urban workers who were formally excluded from the territory's electoral process. The public responded favorably but advanced a demand for immediate statehood that the Country opposition could not deny. Sent as an emissary to Washington, Worthington persuaded Congress in April 1802 both to "enable" early statehood and—fearful of the support St. Clair could still command—to extend the right to vote for the constitutional convention to "all actual residents." As a result, in the critical elections of October 1802 for the constitutional convention, the proportion of adult white males who voted would more than double compared with earlier territorial elections, producing a smashing victory for the statehood forces.[8]

In this new electoral situation politicians had to change the way in which they approached the electorate. In Worthington's Ross County, the nearest thing in Ohio to a Virginia transplant, Chillicothe was "glutted with hand-bills and long tavern harangues," candidates were questioned in the press, and only those who gave satisfactory answers got elected. In eastern Ohio, established leaders who were keenly attached to the *ancien régime* accommodated to the new reality; even the committed Federalist Bezaleel Wells issued handbills announcing his conversion to the statehood cause and favoring a democratic constitution. As Jonathan Mills Thornton has written of Jacksonian Alabama, when candidates have to explain their views to the voters, deference is dead and elections belong to the electorate.[9]

The campaign for the convention revealed a popular demand for near-universal adult white male suffrage and the removal of all restraints on the popular will. The Republican Society in Cincinnati, which espoused the principles of the Jacobin club of Paris, publicly argued for an equal distribution of power in the new state and the extension of the right of suffrage "to every free male inhabitant." Similarly, three obscure farmers from an isolated rural township in the Scioto Valley issued a handbill demanding a constitution "that will annually leave it in the power of the electors to continue in office or discontinue them that fill the various departments of government"; they wanted to "set the natural rights of . . . the most abject beggar upon an equal footing with those citizens of the greatest wealth and equipage." Widely reprinted in the press, such radical arguments were critical in forcing many candidates for the constitutional convention to commit themselves in advance to formulating a democratic instrument of government.[10]

In the convention, a few leading Republicans of Virginian origin looked for constitutional limitations on the popular will, but for the most part the wealthy "men of talents & information" from Virginia, as well as from Maryland and Pennsylvania, were "among the most zealous to secure inviolably the equal rights of the people." The new constitution opened up officeholding to all resident taxpayers, provided for equitable apportionment, and introduced the secret ballot to secure the independence of the voter. Worthington himself had been privately told by "Some of the People" of his own county that the public demanded "frequent elections and a general suffrage to elect, making all officers responsible to the people." In the convention, he voted consistently for the broadest possible distribution of power and for extending the franchise beyond the nominal taxpayer qualification. By granting the vote also to everyone who was compelled to labor on Ohio's roads, he helped to enfranchise virtually every resident adult white male.[11]

However democratic the new state's constitution, in reality its operation might well have turned out to be, as St. Clair had predicted, "democratic in its form and oligarchic in its execution." Right on cue, Worthington and his Republican allies used their control of the new state government to favor their friends and even tried to entrench their power by making local government dependent on appointment by the state legislature. However, a voter rebellion in 1803 challenged their control, and the resulting legislative assembly of 1803–4 shifted the election of key local officers from the legislature to the local electorate. This reversal swiftly taught Worthington and his fellows that the new electorate they had created would not tolerate a close monopoly of office or central direction of local affairs by any aristocracy.[12]

Some historians claim that Worthington's league of gentlemen subsequently, in 1809, created the Tammany Society as a means of restoring their control of patronage and power.[13] Certainly the more doctrinaire Republican Democrats used it to gain control of the legislature and then, in January 1810, dismissed state officeholders of whom they did not approve. But then, in the fall elections of 1810 and 1811, a populistic campaign bearing some resemblance to the anti-Masonic crusade of twenty years later demonstrated once more that the voters would not accept dictation by any set of self-constituted leaders. The assembly of 1811–12 overthrew the new dispensation and destroyed the influence of St. Tammany in state affairs. Clearly Ohio was not a political society that could be commanded by social authority, that accepted deference as proper, or that would tolerate the erection of elitist political structures. Everything about the new state—its social structure, its political and governmental systems, its values, its political traditions—prevented the Chillicothe gentry from erecting the sort of world that has been identified as their ideal. Why? What was it that obstructed the creation of a gentry-led Ohio?

Undoubtedly, social conditions in the frontier Northwest militated against the maintenance or erection of any kind of regime based on aristocratic influence and voter deference. Such a political structure could persist in nineteenth-century America in long-settled rural areas that were culturally homogeneous and demographically stable, as Maryland's Eastern Shore, but traditional ways could not be established or survive in more heterogeneous areas that were facing the sort of dynamic changes and population growth that the nascent Ohio was undergoing. Even in Virginia in the mid-eighteenth century, wealthy men had failed to achieve in the newly settling Southside the predominance they enjoyed in the older parts of the Tidewater and Northern Neck, even though the structure of governmental institutions throughout the state facilitated elite rule.[14] In frontier Ohio, much early settlement occurred in isolated forest clearings, where individual pioneers established their homesteads and only slowly built a sense of community with their neighbors. In such circumstances, any acquiescence in the rule of the rich and the well-born derived not from a cultural acceptance of the social and political propriety of deference to established leaders but from externally enforced legal obligation or economic dependence.

But the legal and economic foundations of upper-class influence were shaky in the Old Northwest. On the frontiers of northern New England and New York, landed magnates could maintain their command because they possessed (or acquired) land grants that had been awarded by British imperial authorities long before either proper survey or even the beginnings of white settlement; these claims had then been confirmed by state legislatures following the Revolution and were supported by the forces of law and order. In frontier Maine, for example, large landed claims were protected against popular resistance by the Massachusetts authorities. In the Old Southwest, the parent states inflicted an inequitable and careless maldistribution of land on Kentucky and Tennessee, a maldistribution which they then insisted that the new states give legal protection to as the price of independence.[15] In the Ohio Country there were a few large arbitrary land grants—the Miami Purchase, the Connecticut Land Company's Western Reserve, and the Ohio Company Purchase—that had been awarded by the Congress in the 1780s and enforced thereafter by the federal government. However, Ohio landowners in these areas could not impose demands for large payments on those who settled or squatted on their lands, as happened in Maine. The Ohio proprietors' bargaining position was weak because of the slow rate of settlement before 1795, the scarcity of cash, their own indebtedness, and the willingness of frontiersmen and squatters to move on. Unlike the situation in Maine, in the Ohio Country much good land was available close at hand, and the opening of public sales persuaded most large proprietors and land speculators to sell more quickly and cheaply than they wished. In particular, they could sell only on terms comparable with those offered by the federal government, terms which became especially competitive after the passage of the Harrison Land Act of 1800.[16]

The result was an unloading of land that helped to ensure a considerable broadening of landownership and a consequent shift in social and political influence. In 1802 some magnates still possessed the title to immense landed properties, but many of them were nonresidents who lived in the seaboard states. As such they held little direct power in territorial affairs except through the influence of the federal government and its appointees. After statehood their influence could operate only through agents within Ohio, and most of the largest owners of Ohio lands found themselves excluded from office and power. Landowners who had supported statehood retained their political influence, but they too suffered from federal competition. In particular, as the price of early statehood, they had accepted that lands sold by the federal government would be exempt from state taxation for five years after sale, which put all established owners and would-be sellers at a disadvantage.

Moreover, all large landowners suffered from the tax policy of the new state. The state's main source of revenue was the land tax, which increased by 25 percent annually in the early years of statehood and weighed heavily on those holding large tracts of land off the market in the hope of future capital gains. From the start land was taxed according to its quality as potential farmland rather than its state of improvement or its present commercial value, and the dissident assembly of 1803–4 penalized nonresident landowners by requiring that taxes be paid separately in each township in which lands were held and by confiscating 60 percent of the land if taxes were not paid. Resident landowners with smaller properties liked the system because it compelled nonresidents to bear much of the cost of government at the local as well as the state level, and they refused to elect anyone they suspected of sympathizing with nonresident owners. The burden fell heavily on all land speculators who did not enjoy the five-year exemption, and many of them had to cash in some of their holdings in order to pay their tax bills.[17]

As a result, by 1810 landowning in Ohio was, in Lee Soltow's words, "widespread and substantial" as the size of landholdings shrank in the older settled counties of the state. Some men continued to own several huge properties, but such men were not separated from the rest of the landowning class since there was no clear class demarcation in the distribution of landed wealth. In 1810 at least half the male population over the age of twenty-six owned land outright and paid taxes on it in their own names. Of those landholders, 82 percent held only one property and were almost certainly working farmers, while at least 98 percent of them owned more than forty acres. The median landholding was 150 acres, which, as Soltow says, was a "bountiful or munificent" allotment by any standard, and certainly compared with the 20 improved acres that was the median in Massachusetts in 1771.[18]

These "middle-class" farmers were not necessarily grateful to those from whom they had bought or borrowed. Notoriously, John Cleves Symmes had possessed a mighty domain in southwestern Ohio but had handled it so irresponsibly that he was deeply unpopular with the settlers of his huge Miami Purchase. As early as 1796 he was denounced by a public meeting in Columbia as "the greatest land-jobber on the face of the earth." By 1800 he was involved in ruinous lawsuits brought by settlers who had bought from him land that Congress said he never owned. More responsible and respected speculators, such as Bezaleel Wells in eastern Ohio, found that they could promote settlement only by making generous concessions that encouraged the participation of smaller property owners and the creation of alternative sources of political power. In other words the great proprietors quickly discovered that partial sale of their speculative holdings prompted the emergence of a class of independent men who were not always inclined to follow their lead. Even Worthington and the so-called Chillicothe Junto discovered in the early years of statehood that they could not control their own county in the face of popular discontent at the county seat and in the outlying parts of the countryside.[19]

Similarly, deference could not survive in situations of cultural competition. Some communities had moved west as established communities, *en bloc,* re-creating older ways in the backwoods, and loyalty to traditional leadership could survive among settlers who possessed a heightened sense of communal solidarity or of ethnocultural self-awareness. Thus in consolidated and relatively homogeneous settlements such as Waterford or Gallipolis or Dayton, community feeling accepted recognized leaders as magistrates and spokesmen for the community. Such closed communities, however, lasted only as long as frontier isolation protected them. Those like Marietta that were always accessible to the passing world attracted a more diverse population fairly quickly and so took on the variegated and conflictual character typical of the river towns that were the main early centers of population.[20]

Even communities noted for their cultural solidarity were shaken by the great religious revival that swept across southern Ohio about the time of the famous Cane Ridge meeting in Kentucky in 1801. The revival broke up many religiously united communities, transforming Presbyterians into New Lights and Halcyons, and spread doctrines that weakened hierarchical structures and promoted the abolition of clerical monopolies. Significantly, most of the denominations associated with settled, homogeneous communities—the Presbyterian, Congregationalist, and Episcopalian churches—gravitated toward the Federalist *ancien régime,* while Methodism and Baptism, both rapidly expanding, fostered evangelical attitudes that favored a more open and egalitarian political system.[21]

Methodism in particular contributed hugely to the popular arousal and liberal impulses that Republicanism exploited in the buildup of its electoral support. Worthington himself and his popular brother-in-law Doctor Edward Tiffin—who became Ohio's first governor—had both been converted to Methodism in Virginia in 1790–91, and Tiffin had become (and remained) an active preacher. However, Worthington himself had no formal connection with the church, and Bishop Francis Asbury felt for a time in 1809 that Tiffin's involvement in the practicalities of "land and politics" interfered with "the work of God . . . in his soul." Indeed, in 1811 Tiffin was temporarily suspended from his ministerial functions because of his political activities, as some Methodists began to show some signs of disenchantment with the Democratic Republican predominance. In Ohio such ever-dissolving religious diversity did not directly challenge an existing church establishment, as it had in Virginia, but it did help to reduce the cozy internal harmony of communities that might otherwise have sustained deference to established leaders.[22]

These growing obstacles to the creation of aristocratic structures and deferential behavior largely reflect the free and open conditions of the northwestern frontier as understood by Frederick Jackson Turner and his disciples.[23] Yet in Upper Canada after 1791 similar frontier conditions did not lead to a revolt against a similar constitutional setup. The failure of Canadians to protest against the Constitutional Act of 1791—which, like the Northwest Ordinance, was designed to ensure imperial control by limiting local participation—had obvious roots: many of the early Canadian settlers were Loyalist refugees who rejected republican ways and valued social hierarchy, traditional authority, and deferential behavior as the true basis of liberty. Similarly, the older French settlers, like their counterparts south of the border, were happy with paternalistic institutions that reduced the burden of taxation. Such attitudes were reinforced locally by imperial authorities who had no doubts about the virtues of the regime and were determined to defend it against the revolutionary and democratic tendencies that they saw triumphing in the United States. After 1800 the challenge to this imperially imposed establishment came from the rapidly growing number of American immigrant settlers, who were commonly identified as favoring greater local self-rule and an extension of popular power. By 1806 these radicals were gaining some voice in the provincial assembly, and only the effectiveness of British and Loyalist resistance to the U.S. invasions of 1812–13 prevented an internal political crisis and curbed American influences. No observer doubted that the demand for greater democracy in Upper Canada came not from frontiersmen as such but from a particular immigrant group that was defined by its common political experience and shared political culture.[24]

In fact political culture south of the border had for a long time been remarkably sympathetic to broad participation in politics. Whatever the theoretical limitations placed on the franchise in the eighteenth century, in practice the right to vote had been widespread in most American colonies, and at times—certainly in Maryland, Delaware, and New Jersey—over half the adult white male population turned out to vote.[25] Popular participation served the American cause well during the struggle with Britain, and the Revolution enshrined the doctrine of popular sovereignty as the only legitimate basis for government. By the 1780s many state governments had fallen under the control of broad electoral majorities; candidates increasingly came from nonelite sources, made their views known to voters, and deliberately kept in touch with opinion in their constituencies. The U.S. Constitution may have been intended to shift power back to an enlightened elite nationally, but in practice it did little to reduce popular power within the states or provide the "filtration of talent" that James Madison advocated. Moreover, the final say on the Constitution was given to popularly elected conventions, and Federalists were forced to use popular arguments in order to justify its ratification. In effect the rightfulness of widespread participation in politics was becoming more broadly accepted, and over the years that followed states in the East and West removed the barriers to adult white male suffrage and officeholding.[26]

The brave souls who crossed the mountains to settle in the Northwest Territory after 1788 found there a political anachronism deliberately created in 1787 to keep the West under national control and to establish stable, law-abiding societies in frontier areas. The suffrage provisions of the Northwest Ordinance were more restrictive than those in any of the original thirteen states; not one of the thirteen gave its governor the prerogatives and patronage that St. Clair enjoyed. Long before Worthington arrived in the territory, pioneer politicians were damning the territorial regime as a return to British colonialism and complaining that they were denied the political rights they had enjoyed in the East as citizens of the new republic and ratifiers of the Constitution. Repeatedly they drew the colonial parallel and called for a new American Revolution to destroy the tyranny of the "British Nabob" set to rule over them; they saw statehood as simply securing for Ohio what independence had secured for the eastern states.[27]

Even the Federalists, so commonly dismissed as reactionary supporters of the *ancien régime,* appreciated the justice of some criticisms, although they insisted on the need to maintain national control of an unreliable colony. From the start the Federalist-dominated territorial legislature operated more democratically in practice than the ordinance required: it published its proceedings, recorded its votes, accepted that constituents could "instruct" their representatives, broadened the opportunity to vote, and adopted the secret ballot in territorial elections. The assembly extended the opportunity to vote by increasing the number of polling places and first proposed the extension of the franchise along the lines ultimately adopted in the Republicans' Ohio Enabling Act. St. Clair had formally approved these measures and was the first to propose the secret ballot, adopted by the territorial assembly in January 1802.[28] In the 1802 campaign many Federalists shifted to favor statehood and supported many democratic reforms in the constitutional convention. In contrast with Upper Canada, the main beneficiaries of the colonial regime in the Northwest Territory, including the imperial authorities—in this case the federal government—were not absolutely committed to maintaining it in every conservative detail.

In accepting the new state's democratic constitution, the Ohio Federalists were accepting that popular participation was becoming an essential feature of the republic. Like the Republicans, they were adjusting to a fundamental shift in western culture after 1760—a shift that, slowly but increasingly, placed more value on individual wills and the capacity of ordinary people than on the elite's perception of the general good. This challenge to hierarchical assumptions and exclusivist structures affected political developments in Britain under George III, where popular discontents were voiced, both among the governing classes and more roughly by the politically excluded. This surging tide broke through the traditional restraints in France after 1789 and roused a popular radicalism in Britain that was restrained only by government repression and the patriotic appeals of wartime. In the United States the restraints were less well entrenched, the popular demand more confident, and the resistance less effective. As one Massachusetts Federalist acknowledged in 1801, "The spirit of our country is doubtless more democratic than the form of our government," and so constitutional barriers could not prevent popular power from penetrating, in some degree, every part of the government. Even in the Northwest Territory, the imposition of a colonial regime to restrain popular licentiousness could not be maintained in the face of popular opposition, as the Ohio revolution demonstrated.[29]

Yet in some places the process was effectively resisted during the republic's early decades. The pressure for a more democratic polity succeeded only where the ideological drive met favorable social and political conditions. For example, the same democratic aspirations that triumphed in Ohio in 1802 were expressed earlier in Kentucky, but the gains of 1792 were cut back in 1799; the landed elite in Kentucky opposed democratic concessions, unlike in Ohio, where the Republican elite needed radical support in order to overthrow the territorial regime. In general, the southern states were slower to broaden suffrage, distribute power, and make representation more equitable because slaveholders wished to retain institutional protections for slavery against the majority of nonslaveholders in their midst. They had the power to do so partly because the combination of large landed estates and slave labor allowed them to build up far larger agricultural operations than could any northern farmer and so they could retain a social hegemony impossible in many parts of the rural North. As Gordon Wood has argued, it was the combination of corrosive political principles and relatively free land that explained the growth of democracy.[30]

From that point of view, territories of the United States containing a large portion of federal land had the advantage that the process of sale was likely to distribute the land more equitably despite the operations of speculators. On the other hand, these territories faced the disadvantage that Congress insisted on providing centrally controlled colonial government for these newly settling areas, and such restraint inherently contradicted the aspirations of settlers who shared the democratic values of their fellows in the older states. Right through the nineteenth century—right down to New Mexico and Arizona in the early twentieth century—territories would have to undergo a process of decolonization and democratization similar to that undergone by Ohio in 1802.[31] Thus the coming of statehood in Ohio was really less revolutionary than it felt: in reality, it amounted to little more than the removal of the artificial constraint of territorial status that had prevented political participation of the kind increasingly common in many eastern states by the 1790s.

But something more was needed to drive on the sudden democratic transformation in Ohio in 1802. What encouraged voters to turn against their social superiors at this time was the agitation of public issues of massive significance. "Issue-oriented campaigns," as Joan Wells Coward observed of parts of Kentucky in the 1790s, "undercut deference."[32] Of course there had been a tradition of contested elections in the East as well as in the Northwest Territory, but usually such contests allowed the electorate simply to choose which members of the elite should represent them and often operated merely as measures of respective social influence. Otherwise, backcountry areas normally showed little interest in politics, instead deferring to local leadership and rousing themselves only occasionally when local leaders appeared to be neglecting the interests of their local community. In such instances the arousal could often take the form of communal coercion and armed resistance to outside interference, as in the Whiskey Rebellion or the insurgency in Maine in 1807–8, but it was commonly followed by a retreat into political nonengagement. What transformed popular disquiet in Ohio into something more lasting was the process of politicization that resulted from the gradual spread of national party divisions in the 1790s.

The contest between Federalists and Republicans bit far more deeply than many historians assume. The issues raised by Hamilton's domestic measures and, above all, by the French Revolution's descent into extremism provoked fundamental questions about the future of the American republic, divided the political classes, polarized public opinion, and aroused popular passions; though deeply personal in its origins, the argument slowly began to generate a two-party conflict based on mass formations of voters. Even in the Northwest Territory the national party division generated partisan commitments and provoked interest in federal elections that its inhabitants had no say in. As early as 1794 partisan hostility to President Washington's policies was being expressed publicly in Cincinnati, and committed Republicans began damning the territorial government as part of the Federalist tyranny. By 1800 leading politicians recognized the existence of partisan proclivities among the electorate of the future state, and this recognition affected the various schemes for dividing the territory and postponing statehood. The demand for emancipation from colonial status gained real emotional bite from its intertwining with the new national partisanship, and Worthington and his friends had no choice but to ally with these Jeffersonian Republicans in order to mount a credible opposition to St. Clair.[33]

Of course this strategy also gave the statehood leaders the advantage of being able to tie themselves into a national competition and forge links with the new ruling majority in Washington. The experience of battling the Federalist territorial regime and working with local Republicans inevitably reinforced their partisan identity and gave them confidence in working with the lower orders. Whereas the Federalist elite had thought of pioneer farmers as ill-disciplined, lawless, uncivilized, disorderly, and potentially disloyal, Ohio's Republican gentlemen felt they could trust them. The large Virginian landholders of south-central Ohio could identify with those who cleared the forest and broke the land because they themselves—including Worthington—had often established a moral right to their lands by their own labor of surveying, and some of the largest landowners—notably Nathaniel Massie and Duncan McArthur—had risked their necks before 1795 surveying land not yet ceded by the native tribes. More to the point, the Virginia gentry could trust the poorer elements excluded from voting under the territorial regime, the squatters and backcountry farmers, because they were generally recognized to be inclined toward the Republicans. Thus partisanship encouraged even the most traditionally minded Virginia gentlemen to appeal downward and agitate the lower orders, particularly in areas where their opponents were strong. The political division within the elite made those out of power only too willing to offer political influence to other classes if that was the price of ensuring the defeat of their rivals. The erosive effect of this political competition has been underestimated even by

those most persuaded of the democratization of American life before 1815.[34]

The best example of the dissolving effect of party competition in
Ohio may be found in Washington County, the original Ohio Company foundation of 1788, which was dominated by tightly knit New
England communities that had been overwhelmingly Federalist in
territorial elections. However, in 1802 the few prominent Jeffersonians began to agitate for statehood and Republican issues and appealed to "every dirty scoundrel that could be met with on the
street." The Federalists responded in kind, with the result that, as
one prominent local Federalist complained, "From being one of the
most harmonious communities, we have been forced on to a most
tremendous, boisterous sea of revolutionary politics." The Federalists kept control of the country in 1802, but the uprising of the un-
washed meant that in 1803 the Republicans won two-thirds of its
votes, and the former Revolutionary War officers who had founded
Marietta and had "always considered themselves a kind of noblesse"
with a prescriptive right to office and power soon found themselves
excluded from federal, state, and local office.[35]

In the town of Cincinnati, too, the Federalists were predominant
overall and occupied positions of great influence, which they used
to the prejudice of Republican activists. However, the Republican
minority organized the Republican Corresponding Society on the
lines of the democratic societies founded earlier in eastern cities to
support the radical principles of the French Revolution. Led by a
handful of professional gentlemen and artisans, this society mobilized a strong minority vote in Cincinnati and coordinated its nominations with colleagues in similar township societies throughout
Hamilton County. In 1802 they produced a Republican and statehood ticket that carried eight of the county's ten seats in the constitutional convention. So, too, in late-eighteenth-century England,
had the influence of landed magnates in borough elections been reduced in some places when townsmen formed independent clubs
capable of organizing political opposition.[36]

Though party organization would in time make it possible for
political elites to manipulate blocs of committed voters, in Ohio's
critical early years formal party institutions provided the means for
further democratizing the political process. In Hamilton County the
township corresponding societies continued to elect the county's Republican delegate convention, which produced tickets that continued

to win majority support in Hamilton County until the panic over St. Tammany in 1810. In eastern Ohio the nomination of candidates at the local level was taken over by popularly elected delegate conventions. In such instances leading Republicans at the county seat called on party members to choose delegates, usually at the April township elections. These delegates then met in a county convention and selected candidates, whom those taking part in the process were bound to support. As in the Jacksonian era, such popularly elected delegate conventions were a significant symbol of democratic control. Some critics, however, insisted that delegate conventions were a device to enable the few to dictate county politics. In general, though, the nominating meetings were well attended and were usually accepted as honest representations of local Republican opinion. Proponents of the "delegate system" justified it specifically on the grounds that it prevented the domination of the electoral process by the rich and the well-born; undoubtedly many who opposed convention nominations were prominent landowners or professional men who had held elected office and objected when the principle of rotation in office was applied to themselves.[37]

Formal nominating procedures at the local level were effective because of the power of national party attachments to provide linkages between people in all sorts of social situations. The simple categorization of politics into Republican and Federalist, black and white, good and evil made politics more understandable to the less politicized members of society, roused their enthusiasm, and gave them the means of identifying their own team in the political game. Nominating conventions retained popular confidence in the face of powerful local opposition because they appealed to the partisan preferences and loyalties of voters. Partisanship also had the effect of tying the aggrieved members of society, such as the more marginal squatters, into the political and institutional process. The tradition of civil disobedience that had been seen during the Whiskey Rebellion recently and for decades in other frontier areas gave way to a greater willingness to secure redress through the political process, especially when Jeffersonian victories brought some measure of relief and redress. Of course many Republican leaders, such as Worthington and his fellows, were themselves of sufficiently high status to be unlikely to show too much sympathy with the socially aggrieved and economically deprived, but disillusionment with the Republicans then provided opportunities for the opposition party to co-opt their support within the political system.

Moreover, partisanship had important cohering effects in other ways. Partisan ties provided connections between pioneers and the people back home; indeed, the sense of partisanship had often been stimulated by news of party battles back home in the East. The use of a common political language also enabled newcomers who had already taken their stand on the national question to identify the colors of Ohio politicians and understand what was happening in state politics. Because the most salient political division in early Ohio derived from national politics and formed a bond of union with party fellows in other states, the peculiar needs of the new northwestern states did not divide them from the rest of the nation. Only after 1815, with the decline of the first national parties and the growing demand for federal internal improvements, would the special needs of the "Western interest" begin to foster a separate regional political identity.

After Ohio's emancipation in 1802, the political development of the rest of the Old Northwest continued to be obstructed by a constitutional instrument no one really believed in. The ordinance remained in place under the Jeffersonians, but Ohio's example ensured that Indiana and Illinois did not have to go down the same road of near revolution. Neither territory had to press for statehood before its population size justified it, and no great rousing of the populace was necessary. Admittedly, William Henry Harrison governed the Indiana Territory after 1800 in the same autocratic, patronage-wielding style as St. Clair, but once the territory's political system was democratized in 1809 and 1810 Harrison never tried to obstruct the territorial assembly's will as St. Clair had. But then Harrison was a Jeffersonian Republican, and there were very few Federalists west of Cincinnati, so that he and his masters in Washington had little to fear politically from statehood. Lacking the bite of partisan competition after 1815, both Indiana and Illinois adopted constitutions that were, if anything, more conservative than Ohio's because the politics of the governing class were more acceptable to the underlings.[38] The peculiar circumstances of 1802 had passed away, and the transition to statehood proved easier farther west because the partisan issues of the age of revolutions had come off the boil as the focus shifted to the problems of internal development.

In most of the West and South, states and communities tended to prefer the Jeffersonian Republicans, and in such circumstances traditional leaders tended to preserve their command. But wherever the party contest produced local competition, well-heeled leaders were impelled to work with a broader range of people. Such competition was unusual in most of the South, though there were brief exceptions, notably in the critical contest of 1798–1800. Though a slave state, Maryland developed a vigorous party contest in the 1800s, and several patterns of community leadership developed: established oligarchs retained their hold in traditional, slaveholding communities; alternative power bases developed in the more heterogeneous (and politically divided) rural areas; while in Baltimore a cosmopolitan elite retained power by accommodation with other elements of Jeffersonian support. Through much of New England and the Middle Atlantic states, a vigorous party competition after 1807 provoked an arousing of the electorate that forced politicians to embrace the electorate in populistic campaigns and to democratize their nomination processes. In New York, according to a Massachusetts Federalist in 1802, the "line of division" between the political parties "was more obscurely marked" than in other states because the voters "were more under the domination of personal influence," but even there landed magnates of Federalist persuasion were overthrown in 1801 by a Republican campaign appealing to the electorate as "Friends of the People."[39]

The enthusiastic Democratic Republican Benjamin Latrobe—who happened also to be the architect of Worthington's Adena—claimed in 1806 that in recent years "actual and practical democracy and political equality" had spread "over the whole union."[40] The claim was exaggerated but pardonable because Latrobe was making the common equation between democracy, meaning popular participation in politics, and "the democracy," a term describing Mr. Jefferson's party. Of course the equation was naïve: the Republican leadership in many localities was not greatly different from that of the Federalists, and often only the accidents of personal allegiance or frustrated ambition or special interest explain why a man of substance and education and Federalist connections—like Worthington—joined the Republican opposition. The regime of the Jeffersonian Republicans would not prove less interested in pursuing the private ambitions of well-placed men than its predecessor had been.

Yet in Ohio the verdict was justified. There the Jeffersonian triumph had brought statehood, self-government, and a democratic political structure for white adult males. Beyond that, Jeffersonian politicians had come to power as part of a voting coalition, and that required them to negotiate with other elements in the community and to keep constituents happy. Ironically, it would be their own internal arguments as much as the testing opposition of the Federalists that, over the next decade, would invigorate political argument and force the Jeffersonians to develop and extend the democratic methods and values they had developed during the statehood campaign.

Notes

1. Alfred B. Sears, *Thomas Worthington: Father of Ohio Statehood* (Columbus: Ohio State University Press, 1958); Andrew R. L. Cayton, *The Frontier Republic: Ideology and Politics in the Ohio Country* (Kent, OH: Kent State University Press, 1986).

2. Ronald P. Formisano, "Deferential-Participant Politics: The Early Republic's Political Culture, 1789–1840," *The American Political Science Review* 68 (1974): 473–87; cssays by Formisano and William G. Shade in *The Evolution of American Electoral Systems,* ed. Paul Kleppner et al. (Westport, CT: Greenwood Press, 1981).

3. This essay draws heavily on Donald J. Ratcliffe, *Party Spirit in a Frontier Republic: Democratic Politics in Ohio, 1793–1821* (Columbus: Ohio State University Press, 1998). For the assumption that Worthington and the Chillicothe gentry opposed the wide distribution of political power, see Cayton, *Frontier Republic,* 81–109, and his "Land, Power, and Reputation: The Cultural Dimension of Politics in the Ohio Country," *William and Mary Quarterly* 47 (1990): 275.

4. Benjamin Tappan to Ethan Allen Brown, December 4, 1819, and Alfred Kelley to Brown, January 16, 1822, Ethan Allen Brown Papers, OHS; Donald J. Ratcliffe, *The Politics of Long Division: The Birth of the Second Party System in Ohio, 1818–1828* (Columbus: Ohio State University Press, 2000), 66, 67.

5. Gary B. Nash, *The Urban Crucible: Social Change, Political Consciousness, and the Origins of the American Revolution* (Cambridge: Harvard University Press, 1979); Benjamin H. Newcomb, *Political Partisanship in the American Middle Colonies, 1700–1776* (Baton Rouge: Louisiana State University Press, 1995); Jackson T. Main, "Government by the People: The American Revolution and the Democratization of the Legislatures," *William and Mary Quarterly* 23 (1966): 391–407; Edward Countryman, *A People in Motion: The American*

Revolution and Political Society in New York, 1760–1790 (Baltimore: Johns Hopkins University Press, 1981).

6. David Hackett Fischer, *The Revolution of American Conservatism: The Federalist Party in the Era of Jeffersonian Democracy* (New York: Harper and Row, 1965); Jeffrey L. Pasley, *"The Tyranny of Printers": Newspaper Politics in the Early American Republic* (Charlottesville: University Press of Virginia, 2001).

7. Donald J. Ratcliffe, "Voter Turnout in Early Ohio," *Journal of the Early Republic* 7 (1987): 223–52, especially 231–33; Charles S. Sydnor, *Gentlemen Freeholders: Political Practices in Washington's Virginia* (Chapel Hill: University of North Carolina Press, 1952).

8. Worthington to [William B. Giles?], March 20, 1802, Thomas Worthington Papers, Ross County Historical Society, Chillicothe; Ratcliffe, "Voter Turnout," 231–33.

9. John Cleves Symmes to Worthington, June 24, 1802, and James Pritchard to Worthington, October 23, 1802, Thomas Worthington Papers, OHS; Jonathan Mills Thornton, *Politics and Power in a Slave Society: Alabama, 1800–1860* (Baton Rouge: Louisiana State University Press, 1978), 72.

10. *Cincinnati Western Spy*, July 24, August 21, October 2, 1802; *Chillicothe Scioto Gazette*, June 5, July 17, 1802. For the complication as to whether blacks should vote, see Radcliffe, *Party Spirit*, 69–71.

11. Samuel Huntington to Turhand Kirtland, December 3, 1802, in Mary Lou Conlin, *Simon Perkins of the Western Reserve* (Cleveland: Western Reserve Historical Society, 1968), 54; "Some of the People" to Worthington, Pickaway, and Green townships, October 11, 1802, Worthington Papers, Ross County Historical Society; *Journal of the Convention of the Territory of the United States North-west of the Ohio River* (Chillicothe, 1802), reprinted in Daniel J. Ryan, ed., "From Charter to Constitution," *Ohio Archaeological and Historical Society Publications* 5 (1897): 103, 104, 113–14, 122.

12. *The St. Clair Papers: The Life and Public Services of Arthur St. Clair*, ed. William Henry Smith, 2 vols. (Cincinnati: Robert Clarke, 1882), 2:482; Ratcliffe, *Party Spirit*, 77–80.

13. Andrew R. L. Cayton and Peter S. Onuf, *The Midwest and the Nation: Rethinking the History of an American Region* (Bloomington: Indiana University Press, 1990), 68–69.

14. Whitman H. Ridgway, *Community Leadership in Maryland, 1790–1840* (Chapel Hill: University of North Carolina Press, 1979); Richard R. Beeman, *The Evolution of the Southern Backcountry: A Case Study of Lunenburg County, Virginia, 1746–1832* (Philadelphia: University of Pennsylvania Press, 1984).

15. Alan Taylor, *Liberty Men and Great Proprietors: The Revolutionary Settlement on the Maine Frontier, 1769–1820* (Chapel Hill: University of North Carolina Press, 1990); Thomas P. Abernethy, *From Frontier to Plantation in Tennessee* (Chapel Hill: University of North Carolina Press, 1932); Stephen Aron, *How the West Was Lost: The Transformation of Kentucky from Daniel Boone to Henry Clay* (Baltimore: Johns Hopkins University Press, 1996).

16. Randolph C. Downes, *Frontier Ohio, 1788–1803* (Columbus: Ohio State Archaeological and Historical Society, 1935), 60–68, 73–76, 83–87; Timothy J. Shannon, "This Unpleasant Business: The Transformation of Land Speculation in the Ohio Country, 1787–1820," in *The Pursuit of Public Power: Political Culture in Ohio, 1787–1861*, ed. Jeffrey P. Brown and Andrew R. L. Cayton (Kent, OH: Kent State University Press, 1994), 15–30.

17. Ratcliffe, *Party Spirit*, 111–13.

18. Lee Soltow, "Inequality amidst Abundance: Land Ownership in Early Nineteenth Century Ohio," *Ohio History* 88 (1979): 133–51; Bettye Hobbs Pruitt, "Self-Sufficiency and the Agricultural Economy of Eighteenth-Century Massachusetts," *William and Mary Quarterly* 41 (1984): 338. Soltow himself puts a slightly different gloss on his statistics, which are drawn from the tax assessments for 1810. For my doubts as to whether they accurately reflect the ownership of land, see Ratcliffe, *Party Spirit*, 46, 102, 103–4, 271nn9–10.

19. Downes, *Frontier Ohio*, 86, 181–82, 190–92; Ratcliffe, *Party Spirit*, 107–13.

20. Andrew R. L. Cayton, "The Contours of Power in a Frontier Town: Marietta, Ohio, 1788–1803," *Journal of the Early Republic* 6 (1986): 103–26; Emil Pocock, "Evangelical Frontier: Dayton, Ohio, 1796–1830," PhD diss., Indiana University, 1984.

21. Ratcliffe, *Party Spirit*, 89–94; Andrew R. L. Cayton, "'Language Gives Way to Feelings': Rhetoric, Republicanism, and Religion in Jeffersonian Ohio," in *Pursuit of Public Power*, ed. Brown and Cayton, 31–48.

22. *The Journal and Letters of Francis Asbury*, ed. Elmer T. Clark, J. Manning Potts, and Jacob S. Payton, 3 vols. (Nashville: Abingdon Press, 1958), 2:614, 649, 3:509; Ratcliffe, *Party Spirit*, 165–66.

23. Frederick J. Turner, *The Frontier in American History* (New York: Henry Holt, 1920); John D. Barnhart, *Valley of Democracy: The Frontier versus the Plantation in the Ohio Valley, 1775–1818* (Bloomington: Indiana University Press, 1953).

24. Fred Landon, *Western Canada and the American Frontier* (1941; Toronto: McClelland and Stewart, 1967), 1–58; Jane Errington, *The Lion, the Eagle, and Upper Canada: A Developing Colonial Ideology* (Kingston and Montreal: McGill-Queen's University Press, 1987), 1–86; David Mills, *The Idea of Loyalty in Upper Canada, 1784–1850* (Kingston and Montreal: McGill-Queen's University Press, 1988), 3–33.

25. Richard P. McCormick, *The History of Voting in New Jersey, 1664–1911* (New Brunswick: Rutgers University Press, 1953); Gary B. Nash, "The Transformation of Urban Politics, 1700–1765," *Journal of American History* 60 (1973): 630–31; Robert J. Dinkin, *Voting in Provincial America: A Study of Elections in the Thirteen Colonies, 1689–1776* (Westport, CT: Greenwood Press, 1977), 144–80; Bruce Bendler, "Two Colonial Elections in Kent County, Delaware," *Delaware History* 24 (1991): 211–16.

26. Jack N. Rackove, "The Structure of Politics at the Accession of George Washington," in *Beyond Confederation: Origins of the Constitution and*

American National Identity, ed. Richard Beeman, Stephen Botein, and Edward C. Carter II (Chapel Hill: University of North Carolina Press, 1987), 261–94; Jackson T. Main, *Political Parties before the Constitution* (Chapel Hill: University of North Carolina Press, 1973); Gordon S. Wood, *The Creation of the American Republic, 1776–1787* (Chapel Hill: University of North Carolina Press, 1967), 519–63; Robert Rutland, *The Ordeal of the Constitution: The Antifederalists and the Ratification Struggle of 1787–1788* (Norman: University of Oklahoma Press, 1966); Chilton Williamson, *American Suffrage from Property to Democracy, 1760–1860* (Princeton: Princeton University Press, 1960).

27. Donald J. Ratcliffe, "The Experience of Revolution and the Beginnings of Party Politics in Ohio, 1776–1816," *Ohio History* 85 (1976): 187–92.

28. Ratcliffe, *Party Spirit,* 47–49.

29. George Cabot, quoted in Williamson, *American Suffrage,* 174; Robert H. Berkhofer, "The Northwest Ordinance and the Principle of Territorial Evolution," in *The American Territorial System,* ed. John Porter Bloom (Athens: Ohio University Press, 1973), 45–55.

30. Joan Wells Coward, *Kentucky in the New Republic: The Process of Constitution Making* (Lexington: University Press of Kentucky, 1979); Gordon S. Wood, *The Radicalism of the American Revolution* (New York: Knopf, 1992), 310–11.

31. Howard R. Lamar, *Dakota Territory, 1861–1889: A Study of Frontier Politics* (New Haven: Yale University Press, 1956), 1–27, and *The Far Southwest, 1846–1913: A Territorial History* (New Haven: Yale University Press, 1966), 16–18, 178–201, 478–504; Kenneth N. Owens, "Pattern and Structure in Western Territorial Politics," in *American Territorial System,* ed. Bloom, 161–79.

32. Coward, *Kentucky in the New Republic,* 165.

33. Ratcliffe, *Party Spirit,* 19–21, 26–31, 33, 38–39, 58–67.

34. In *Radicalism of the American Revolution,* Gordon Wood underestimates the significance of party competition in undermining deference because he accepts the view that parties did not exist at this period (298–305).

35. Ephraim Cutler to Manasseh Cutler, Marietta, August 31, 1802, Ephraim Cutler Papers, Dawes Memorial Library, Marietta College; Jared Mansfield to William Lyon Jr., February 20, 1804, Jared Mansfield Papers, Ohio Historical Society.

36. Ratcliffe, *Party Spirit,* 55–57, 60–62. For England, see John Brewer, *Party Ideology and Popular Politics at the Accession of George III* (Cambridge, UK: Cambridge University Press, 1976), and Frank O'Gorman, *Voters, Patrons, and Parties: The Unreformed Electorate of Hanoverian Britain* (Oxford: Oxford University Press, 1989).

37. Ratcliffe, *Party Spirit,* 125–35, 164; Noble E. Cunningham, *The Jeffersonians in Power, 1801–1809* (Chapel Hill: University of North Carolina Press, 1963), 196–200.

38. Barnhart, *Valley of Democracy,* 161–215; Peter S. Onuf, *Statehood and Union: A History of the Northwest Ordinance* (Bloomington: Indiana University

Press, 1987), 86–87; Andrew R. L. Cayton, *Frontier Indiana* (Bloomington: Indiana University Press, 1998), 228–61.

39. Theodore Sedgwick, quoted in Alan Taylor, *William Cooper's Town: Power and Persuasion on the Frontier of the Early American Republic* (New York: Knopf, 1995), 233, 256–91; Ridgway, *Community Leadership in Maryland.*

40. Latrobe, quoted in Williamson, *American Suffrage,* 209.

THREE

Ohio Gospel

Methodism in Early Ohio

JOHN WIGGER

In 1806 young John Campbell Deem moved with his family from Campbell County, Kentucky, to Butler County, Ohio, to escape the "*Curse of Slavery*" and an uncertain land title. Deem later remembered Butler County as an "almost unbroken forrest" with so many wolves that shortly after their arrival the family's two large dogs had had enough. They returned to Kentucky on their own, swimming the Miami and Ohio rivers along the way. Prior to the family's arrival on their new land, Deem's father built a rough log cabin measuring sixteen by twenty feet. It was still not complete when the family moved in, lacking windows, a chimney, and a floor. Yet within days of their arrival, as Deem stood in the doorway watching the rain, a man rode up and asked "if there was a Methodist family living there." Deem's parents had joined the Methodists in about 1800 in Kentucky, and he later remembered that his mother's "heart was Swelled with Emotion" at the sight of a Methodist preacher at their new home. The preacher stayed for supper and then led the family in singing and prayer, as was customary. Thereafter, the Deems regularly hosted preaching at their home, and John Campbell eventually became a circuit rider himself.[1]

Methodism entered the Ohio Country in earnest in the 1790s, prospering there in a way that was remarkable even by the standards of early Methodist growth. Methodist expansion in Ohio quickly outstripped growth in nearly every other state or region, making the future state a model of Methodist success. Methodism was the largest and most dynamic popular religious movement in America between the Revolution and the Civil War. By 1850 one-third of all religious adherents in the United States were Methodists. Hence understanding the church's development in one of its key strongholds is important for understanding the development of American popular religion as a whole in the pivotal early republic. By 1870 Ohio Methodists owned 2,115 church buildings; their next closest competitor, the Presbyterians, could claim only 625 churches in the state. By 1890 Ohio Methodists numbered 272,000, more than all Ohio Baptists, Congregationalists, Lutherans, Presbyterians, and Episcopalians combined.[2]

Methodism's appeal to the people of Ohio was the result of familiar and unfamiliar forces, as Deem's experience illustrates. As in other regions, Methodists mobilized a dedicated core of local and itinerant preachers to reach out to the region's frontiers before most other religious groups could establish a presence. The church also fostered community through class and society meetings, circuit preaching, and camp meetings. It offered communal discipline and an economic and social safety net, often in the absence of any comparable social institution, at least in the early years of rapid white settlement. As was the case with Methodism almost everywhere, women joined in greater numbers than men. The church also appealed to potential converts through its boisterous worship and keen supernaturalism, aspects which led one 1789 migrant to the region to describe Methodism as a "boiling hot religion." What was unique to Ohio was the absence of conflict over slavery and the relative lack of organized opposition from other religious and political groups. As a result of all these factors, the largest churches of colonial America—the Congregationalists, Episcopalians (descendants of the Church of England), and Presbyterians—could not keep pace with the Methodists.

The Methodist system was organized around class meetings, societies, and circuits. By the time Methodists hit Ohio, the standard was a four-week circuit (one which took four weeks to complete) about four hundred miles in circumference, with preaching appointments nearly every day of the week. The itinerant preachers who rode these circuits were mostly young unmarried men with little formal education. Most had farmed or worked at a trade before turning to preaching, and they received little pay for their preaching efforts. Instead they were motivated by a white-hot conviction that it was their duty to save sinners from hell. Circuit riders who married and settled down to farm or pursue a trade usually became local preachers, offering their services for free in their spare time. For many of these local preachers the zeal of their circuit-riding days remained little diminished. It is impossible to understand this kind of Methodist without an appreciation for the depth of their religious beliefs.[3]

This was the kind of religion that Philip and Elizabeth Gatch brought with them to Ohio. Born in 1751 near Baltimore to nominally Anglican parents, Philip experienced Methodist conversion in 1772 and soon after began circuit preaching. In 1778 he married Elizabeth Smith of Powhatan County, Virginia, and shortly thereafter settled down to take up farming. Two years later Gatch liberated the nine slaves whom his wife had brought into the marriage. Still he "could not feel reconciled to die and leave my posterity in a land of slavery." So in 1798 Gatch sold the one thousand acres he owned in Virginia and purchased land on the Little Miami River. Gatch became active in the local community and eventually gained an appointment as a justice of the peace for Clermont County, Ohio. At the same time he continued to preach as an unpaid local preacher, joining Francis McCormick and other local preachers who had settled in the area. The same year the Gatches moved to Ohio, John Kobler became the first full-time itinerant preacher appointed to the territory, followed in 1799 by Lewis Hunt and Henry Smith. When no itinerant preacher was sent to ride the Miami Circuit in 1800, Gatch and four or five local preachers took it upon themselves to keep the circuit meetings going. The Gatches and other local families took the lead in hosting quarterly meetings (in many ways the predecessors to camp meetings), with Elizabeth arranging to board fifty to one hundred visitors in their home, the women sleeping in the house and the men in the barn.[4]

The early preachers proved their zeal in part by the hardships they endured. Smith recalled that one family he lodged with on the Miami Circuit had taken their horse into their cabin the previous winter to save it from the weather. This rendered the cabin "not as pleasant as it might have been." On this occasion Smith claimed to be undaunted by the horse's presence, but in 1800 his fortitude was put to a more "severe trial." After preaching a funeral sermon on the Scioto Circuit, Smith agreed to stay the night with the grieving widow, but "when bed-time came I was conducted to the room from which the corpse had been taken a few hours before, to sleep on the bedstead, perhaps the very bed, on which the young man had died, without the house having been scrubbed and properly aired." If this was not enough, fleas and barking dogs kept him awake all night, but Smith stuck it out. "If I was but poorly qualified for a missionary in every other respect, I was not in *one thing;* for I had long since conquered my foolish prejudice about eating, drinking, and lodging," Smith wrote. "I could submit to any kind of inconvenience when I had an opportunity of doing good."[5]

John Kobler experienced similar challenges during his first year preaching in Ohio in 1798. As he made his way from Kentucky into Ohio that summer, he was immediately impressed with the beauty of the land. "This country is the most beautiful for situation—the most fertile of any I ever saw," he recorded in his journal in August. "If the remains of paradisi[a]cal glory is yet to be found with any part of the creation, shurely it is here," he wrote a few months later. The settlers in Ohio were another matter, however. "The people are generally of low circumstances, & many of them the poorest of the poor," Kobler observed. At one house on the Great Miami River, he ended up sleeping "in a bed to[o] filthy for a Swine to lodge in." To make matters worse, an "army" of fleas attacked him that night in such numbers that they threated to "eat [him] up at one Meal." Nevertheless, Kobler continued to ride and preach relentlessly wherever he could gather an audience. By April 1799 his new Ohio circuit contained ninety-nine members.[6]

The content and style of Methodist preaching also worked to draw audiences in. Preaching extemporaneously in a colloquial style that most settlers could easily grasp, Methodist preachers urged their hearers to take the initiative in accepting God's grace and pursuing their own salvation. Methodist sermons wove scripture texts together with anecdotes and illustrations from everyday life. At their most effective, these preachers established an easy connection with their audiences while at the same time challenging them to rethink the fundamental meaning of their lives. Philip Gatch noted that when John Kobler preached, "his aims were more at the heart than the head." Henry Smith in turn described Gatch as "a close home preacher" who "called things by their proper names, and spared neither sin nor the sinner." "Our hearts were sometimes made to burn within us while we talked of Jesus and his love," Smith recalled. "Sound Wesleyanism," according to the early Ohio preacher James

Quinn, was best represented by "a truly-evangelical sermon—no philosophical chaff or metaphysical froth."[7]

As the Gatches' story indicates, the expansion of early Ohio Methodism was as much a product of decentralized lay initiative as it was of centralized clerical planning. This is a common theme in Methodist growth across the early republic, but other factors were unique to Ohio. Since slavery was largely absent north of the Ohio River, Methodists there did not have to contend with the kind of pro- and antislavery debates that had torn at the fabric of the movement in the South. After an unsuccessful attempt by Francis Asbury and others to expel slaveholders from the church in 1784, white Methodists remained deeply divided on the issue. Largely because of controversies over slavery, white membership fell across the South during the 1790s, including in Virginia and Kentucky. Ohio became a refuge for Methodists from these states seeking to escape the "curse of slavery." Such was not the case south of the Ohio River. Kentucky Methodism benefited from a sustained revival beginning about 1799 but still lost ground to the Baptists and never equaled Ohio Methodism in its pervasive influence.[8]

Like the Gatches, Methodist migrants to Ohio frequently identified the absence of slavery as one of their motivations for settling in the state. The strength of this conviction can be seen in a collection of letters written by a number of these migrants to Edward Dromgoole between 1802 and 1812. Dromgoole emigrated to America from Ireland about 1770 and began circuit preaching in 1773, mostly in Virginia and North Carolina. In 1786 he left the itinerancy to become a successful planter, merchant, and slaveholder in Brunswick County, Virginia. By 1798 he owned more than eight hundred acres and six slaves, and in 1803 the buildings on his property were valued at $2,050.[9] A few years after moving to Ohio Gatch wrote to Dromgoole urging him to leave the "land of slavery," where Gatch himself had been "unwilling to lay [his] Bones."[10]

In 1807 several of Dromgoole's former Methodist neighbors who had recently moved to Ohio also wrote urging him to come to Ohio and offering to help with the details of the move. While they extolled the abundance of good land and the economic promise of Ohio (Peter Pelham reported that his "wife had fatten'd much on the Journey" to Ohio), the absence of slavery was a persistent theme in their letters. For Frederick Bonner, one of the best things about

Ohio was that "once planted here our children are saved from the bane full practice of trading on there fellow creatures." "When the Legislature of Va. has determined against liberty & our preachers & people will be purchasing slaves without a prospect of liberating them[,] what can we think will be the condition of the church in the state where slavery is encouraged & liberty suppress't in a few Years[?]" asked Bonner. Peter Pelham also wrote to tell Dromgoole how "glad" he was that "we ever came to this fruitful Land, and place of *Liberty*." "I would not be situated to spend my Days where I came from for half the State of old Virginia," he concluded. Bennett Maxey, a former circuit rider, also wrote urging Dromgoole to escape "that land of oppression" for "a fare more excellent place," as did the Ohio District's presiding elder, John Sale. Perhaps moved by these appeals, Dromgoole sent his son Edward Jr. to scout out Ohio in the summer of 1807. With Pelham's help, the younger Dromgoole purchased more than four hundred acres near his former Virginia Methodist neighbors. But in the end Edward Dromgoole himself never left Virginia.[11]

Clearly, one of the primary attractions of Ohio for many southern Methodists was the absence of slavery. But it seems equally clear that they wished to avoid living in the presence of African Americans altogether. None of those who wrote to Dromgoole suggested that Ohio ought to become a refuge for free blacks. What Ohio Methodists failed to realize and probably would have resisted acknowledging was that the absence of conflict over slavery came at a price. African Americans had contributed significantly to the vitality of southern Methodism even as they were relegated to the periphery of the official church. Their presence would be felt only indirectly in Ohio, where Methodism quickly became more racially monolithic and respectably middle class than had been the case across much of the South.[12]

Ohio Methodists were also more politically active than was the case just about anywhere else in early-nineteenth-century America. In other regions before 1800, a politically powerful elite was already in place before the Methodists showed up. But this was by and large not the case in Ohio.[13] Hence Methodists were able to establish themselves in the political community without facing organized opposition. Whereas Methodists in Delaware were predominantly Federalists, in Ohio they were mostly Jeffersonian Republicans, the party that quickly came to dominate the region's early political life. Dan

Young, a former New England circuit rider and later a member of the Ohio legislature, noted that because Methodists were not seen as social outsiders in early southern Ohio, "I soon found that there was no such systematic opposition to Methodism here as we had to contend with in New England." The Methodist preacher Alfred Brunson likewise observed that as Methodist numbers grew in northern Ohio and northwestern Pennsylvania, local politicians "favored us, though they might be skeptical as to religion" since Methodist "votes counted as fast at an election as any others." In nearby Meadville, Pennsylvania, according to Brunson, the result was that leading politicians "attending upon our ministry drew out others, so that the old courthouse was usually filled with hundreds of attentive hearers."[14]

Though Methodist voting patterns in early Ohio have never been studied in detail, it seems apparent that the Methodist-Republican alignment helped to propel a number of Methodist candidates into office.[15] In no other state before Ohio did Methodists hold so many prominent political offices. Philip Gatch won election to Ohio's constitutional convention of 1802 and served as an associate judge in Clermont County for more than twenty years. Though he came from a Quaker background, Thomas Worthington, who served as a U.S. senator from Ohio and then as governor of the state (1814–18), was a longtime friend of Bishop Francis Asbury's and often attended Methodist meetings. Thomas Scott, a member of the 1802 constitutional convention and of the Ohio legislature and an Ohio supreme court judge from 1809 to 1815, was a Methodist elder and former itinerant preacher. Scott itinerated from 1789 to 1795, converting, among many others, the longtime preacher Henry Smith. Another former itinerant preacher, James Quinn, briefly served as an associate judge for Fairfield County before returning to circuit preaching in Ohio in 1808. While most Methodists hesitated to draw direct connections between religion and the election process, it is significant that in Ohio they were not automatically at a political disadvantage because of their religious affiliation. For Methodists, the boundary between religion and politics was more permeable in Ohio than just about anywhere else.[16]

One of the more interesting of the early Ohio politicians, from a Methodist perspective, was Edward Tiffin. Born in England in 1766, Tiffin moved with his family to Berkeley County, Virginia (now West Virginia), in 1784. Soon after their arrival Tiffin began studying medicine. He was converted to Methodism in about 1790, joining the church under Thomas Scott, whose legal career Tiffin later helped to launch. Tiffin almost immediately began preaching and in 1792 was ordained a deacon by Bishop Francis Asbury. In 1789 Tiffin married Mary Worthington, sister of Thomas Worthington. When Mary inherited sixteen slaves, she and Edward emancipated them as a demonstration of their Methodist faith. The Tiffins moved to Ohio in 1798, the same year as Philip and Elizabeth Gatch. Tiffin quickly rose through the ranks of Republican politics and was instrumental in ousting Federalist territorial governor Arthur St. Clair and in pushing Ohio toward statehood. As a result, he was elected Ohio's first governor in January 1803 and later served as a U.S. senator from the state.[17]

Tiffin continued to preach as a local preacher throughout his career, but it was his wife Mary who seemed closer to mainstream Ohio Methodism. She regularly welcomed Methodist preachers into her home, regardless of their sometimes shabby appearance, and was particularly close to Bishop Asbury. In 1805 the twenty-nine-year-old itinerant Jacob Young was struck with typhoid fever while riding the Marietta Circuit. Arriving at the Tiffins' in a feverish condition, Young thought that the governor "treated me rather rudely," Tiffin having apparently judged Young "an ignorant young man" and "not worthy" of his attention. But when Mary Tiffin arrived, "I found her to be a mother in Israel. If I had been her own son, she could not have paid me more attention," Young wrote. Henry Smith, who preached at the Tiffins' in 1799, described Mary Tiffin as "one of the most conscientious and heavenly minded women I ever saw. She was a mother in Israel indeed." At the same time, according to Smith, Edward Tiffin "refused to take any part in religious exercises in Chil[l]icothe out of his own family: he had his reasons for it." Smith does not explain what these reasons were, but it seems clear that Tiffin held himself at some distance from ordinary Methodists. After visiting Tiffin in September 1809, a year after Mary's death, Asbury complained that Tiffin seemed to want to talk of nothing but land policies and politics. Edward Tiffin may have been a faithful Methodist, but he was not immune to the kind of social ambition that came to characterize much of Ohio Methodism in the early nineteenth century. Tiffin was a genuine believer, but his brand of Methodism looked away from a radical past toward a respectable future.[18]

Perhaps no Ohio Methodist was more politically successful than John McLean. McLean's Presbyterian father, Fergus McClain, left

Ireland in 1775 and settled for a time in New Jersey, where he married Sophia Blackford. After John's birth in 1785 the family moved to West Virginia, then to Kentucky, and finally to Warren County, Ohio, about 1797. In 1804 John McLean, who had little formal education, entered an apprenticeship to the clerk of the court of common pleas of Hamilton County. He married in 1807 and began publishing a Jeffersonian newspaper, the *Western Star,* that same year. In 1811 he experienced conversion under the preaching of John Collins and joined the Methodist church, an affiliation he maintained to the end of his life. In 1812 McLean won election as a U.S. congressional representative, a position he held until his appointment to the Ohio supreme court in 1816. Next McLean briefly served as commissioner of the Public Land Office, a federal appointment in Washington, before becoming postmaster general of the United States in 1823. Andrew Jackson appointed McLean to the U.S. Supreme Court, a position he held from 1829 to 1861. But McLean's political ambitions did not stop there. From 1832 to 1860 McLean actively sought a presidential nomination in every election cycle, usually as a Whig at first and later as a Republican. No other Methodist of this period occupied such a prominent position on the national political stage. McLean's Methodism became a component of his view of a well-ordered society, which also rested on adherence to the law and dedication to public service. Though he held antislavery views, which are reflected in many of his judicial decisions (most notably *Dred Scott*), he was less of an abolitionist than his wife, and his positions rarely satisfied those who looked for a radical solution to the problem of slavery. Moderation and respectability characterized the way that McLean projected his faith into public life, but it was a respectability built on humble beginnings and evangelical sensibilities. As it had for Tiffin, Ohio offered McLean the chance to draw together his religious convictions and political ambitions.[19]

Political success, or at least its possibility, exerted a significant pull on early Ohio Methodism. But the influence was not only one way. Across the nation Methodism exerted a pull of its own on the political world of the nineteenth century, as Richard Carwardine has so powerfully demonstrated. This was no less the case in Ohio. Methodists succeeded politically only after projecting much of their respect for the opinions of common people onto the political landscape. Unlike their colonial predecessors, antebellum politicians knew that they had to connect with common people, something that the plain, pietistic language of Methodism allowed men like Tiffin, Worthington, and McLean to do with relative ease. For Tiffin and Worthington in particular, writes Andrew Cayton, "the familial, heart-felt, revelatory language of evangelical Protestantism" formed the "foundation of their public success."[20]

No one had a better feel for the development of Methodism in the West, or perhaps of the West in general, than Francis Asbury. Asbury was born in 1745 in Great Barr, a village about four miles outside Birmingham, England. His father, Joseph, was a farm laborer and gardener who likely worked for one or two local wealthy families and may have been employed by the brewery to which the family's cottage was attached. At his father's insistence, Francis began attending a nearby school and could read the Bible by age six or seven. But his schoolmaster was severe and often beat him, so that at about age thirteen he left school, briefly working as a servant in the home of a wealthy family before becoming a metalworker's apprentice. As an apprentice in Birmingham's rapidly shifting metalworking industry and the son of a gardener, Asbury understood the kinds of hopes and fears that tempted people to move to frontier Ohio, a land of both risk and opportunity.[21]

Following his mother's urging, Asbury began attending Methodist meetings in his teens and soon had a classically evangelical conversion experience. In 1766 he began circuit preaching for John Wesley in England, and in 1771 he volunteered to come to America as a Methodist missionary. When the Revolutionary War broke out, Asbury was the only one of Wesley's official missionaries who remained in America. By the 1780s Asbury had become the recognized leader of American Methodism. Much of his success as a leader had to do with the close contact he maintained with many of the movement's followers. During his administration of American Methodism he rode more than 250,000 miles and crossed the Appalachian mountains some sixty times. For many years he visited nearly every state once a year, traveling more extensively and over a longer period of time in the western backcountry than any other prominent American. One historian estimates that Asbury stayed in ten thousand households.[22] He was more widely recognized than any person of his generation, including such national figures as Thomas Jefferson and George Washington, who did not travel or mingle with common people to nearly the extent that Asbury did.

Asbury first set foot in Ohio in June 1786, though it would be another decade before Methodism had much of a presence in the territory. Once Methodism began to expand into the Ohio Country in the late 1790s, Asbury saw much that encouraged him. Like many Methodist settlers to the state, he was grateful that slavery did not exist north of the Ohio River. He had joined with Thomas Coke and other northern Methodists in the 1780s to enact strict rules against Methodists' owning or selling slaves, but their efforts were blocked by resistance from southern Methodists. At one point in 1784 the church enacted rules requiring all Methodists to gradually liberate all their slaves. But in what is perhaps the best known chapter in early Methodist history, within six months the outcry from southerners led to the indefinite suspension of the 1784 rules. Like the movement's other leaders, Asbury caved in to the pressure of southern slaveholders, but the issue haunted him for the next thirty years. He knew that slavery was morally evil, but he also knew that he could not force southerners to give it up. Ohio represented a reprieve from this dilemma; an opportunity for westward expansion without confronting the curse of slavery.[23]

But the region was not without its temptations. In particular Asbury worried that the availability of good land and the chance to significantly better their economic condition would distract many from spiritual concerns. While traveling near Lexington, Kentucky, in May 1790, he noted that the surrounding land was "the richest body of fertile soil I have ever beheld." While this was exactly what most settlers were looking for, it represented a subtle temptation in Asbury's mind. "Good religion and such good land are not so easily matched together," he wrote while traveling through western Tennessee in April 1796. "I am of opinion it is as hard, or harder, for the people of the west to gain religion as any other," he added the following year, also while in Tennessee. "When I reflect that not one in a hundred came here to get religion, but rather to get plenty of good land, I think it will be well if some or many do not eventually lose their souls."[24]

This seemed to be even more of a problem in Ohio, once it opened to white settlement, than it had been in Kentucky or Tennessee. In fall 1803 as Asbury traveled across southern Ohio for the first time, he was struck by the fertility of the land. "As fine lands as any in America," he wrote. "What will not a little enterprise do for a man in this highly-favoured country!" The next fall Asbury traveled along Braddock's Road in Maryland, which was "crowded with wagons and pack-horses carrying families and their household stuff westward" to Ohio, a state "without slaves, and the better calculated for poor, industrious families. O highly-favoured land!" In fact, land ownership rates were remarkably high in early Ohio. While slightly less than half of all adult males age twenty-six and older owned land, this was still a greater proportion than in Europe at that time. The median size of these farms was 150 acres in 1810, quite adequate considering the quality of the land and greater than would have been the case back East or in Europe. Less than 2 percent of Ohio landowners owned fewer than forty acres. Still, even if Asbury occasionally got caught up in the temporal possibilities Ohio offered, he never completely lost sight of its corrupting potential. At the same time that he was praising the quality of the land in 1803 on his first visit to the state, he could not help but "feel the power of Satan" in the "little, wicked, western trading towns" that were springing up across the state. Writing to Rebekah Ridgley of Baltimore in 1804, Asbury complained that as "our people Emegrate greatly from East, to west," many lost track of their faith in their rush to get ahead.[25]

By 1800 and increasingly during the 1810s and 1820s worldly success became a more common feature of Methodist life. In 1783 Asbury had worried that the end of the American Revolution might work to dampen Methodist zeal. Though Methodists had endured much persecution during the war, he fretted that now that it was over "our preachers will be far more likely to settle in the world; and our people, by getting into trade, and acquiring wealth, may drink into its spirit." This in fact did happen, as the lives of Edward Dromgoole, Edward Tiffin, and (to a lesser extent) Philip Gatch illustrate, though the trend was not readily apparent until the early nineteenth century, just when the Ohio Country was opening up. By preaching on the value of diligence, sobriety, individual initiative, and perseverance in all areas of life, Asbury and his preachers unwittingly helped to create a culture of upward mobility that increasingly eluded their control. Ohio Methodism succeeded spectacularly, but not always in the form that Asbury wished it to.[26]

Even John McLean, who was as politically and socially ambitious as anyone of this period, believed that Methodism had lost some essential element of its earlier zeal in this process. During the 1840s and 1850s McLean edited the journal of Philip Gatch for publication and wrote a biography of John Collins, the preacher who had brought him to conversion. Toward the end of both books McLean could not help but complain about the current state of the church, particularly its preaching. Earlier preachers "did not aim to preach great sermons, but sermons that would reach the heart, and cause it to overflow," McLean noted. "We are becoming a little too refined, and too learned for such exhibitions. . . . What we gain in learning we lose in power." So common were complaints about Methodism's lost zeal by the mid-nineteenth century that critics became known as "croakers," and their number included some of the most distinguished leaders of early Ohio Methodism. Writing at about the same time as McLean, the longtime Ohio preacher James Quinn told the story that at one home in earlier times the "chickens took fright and ran into the weeds and hid themselves" at the sight of a Methodist preacher. But "in these days the most of the preachers appear so much like lawyers that the chickens don't know them." In Quinn's mind conditions in Ohio were fast sinking to the level of those in New England, the land of steady habits but little religious zeal. It is revealing that croakers abounded as much in Ohio, the center of nineteenth-century Methodist success, as anywhere else.[27]

But perhaps this assessment looks too far into the future. For the most part Asbury (who died in 1816) celebrated Methodism's remarkable expansion in Ohio, much as Ohio Methodists themselves did. He had long since realized that mass popular religious movements must accommodate to their cultural settings to some degree if they hoped to be truly popular. There was really no way that Methodism could appeal to large numbers of the settlers pouring into Ohio without making allowances for their drive to succeed financially, socially, and politically. This drive was, after all, a large part of why they came to Ohio.

Ohio is important in part because it was the first place that the new mass religious movements that were reshaping American religion between the Revolution and the Civil War had the opportunity to take root without pressure from the old established colonial denominations and without the presence of slavery. This was particularly true for the Methodists, who roared into Ohio in a way that they had not been able to do even in Kentucky and Tennessee. In Ohio much of the external social and political pressure from established elites and the internal strife over slavery that had held Methodism back in other places was absent. The result was a vibrant form of

American evangelicalism that emphasized a Wesleyan (Arminian) understanding of conversion and spirituality, fostered community support and discipline, encouraged individual initiative in every aspect of life, and rejected slavery as morally corrupt, though not without retaining an element of tacit racism. Ohio Methodism also accepted the workings of the market and popular politics and the strong desire of many to do better in this world, if not for themselves, then for their children. These features would be replicated across middle America for decades to come as the denomination swept west through Indiana, Illinois, Iowa, and parts of Missouri and on into Kansas and Nebraska.[28]

Notes

1. John Campbell Deem, untitled autobiography, manuscript, Beeghly Library, Ohio Wesleyan University, Delaware, Ohio, 1–5. Obituaries of Deem can be found in *Minutes of the 28th Session of the Cincinnati Annual Conference of the Methodist Episcopal Church* (Cincinnati: Methodist Episcopal Church, 1879), 84–86, and *Minutes of the Annual Conference of the Methodist Episcopal Church* (Cincinnati: Methodist Episcopal Church, 1879), 17–18. Deem identifies the preacher who first visited their cabin in Ohio as "Rev. Mr. Helm or Helms." This was probably Thomas Hellums, who began circuit preaching in 1806 on the Red River Circuit in the Cumberland District of Tennessee and had by 1807 moved to the White River Circuit in Ohio. See *Minutes of the Annual Conferences of the Methodist Episcopal Church, For the Years 1773–1828* (New York: T. Mason and G. Lane, 1840), 134, 139, 149 (hereafter *Minutes MEC* [1840]).

2. John Marshall Barker, *History of Ohio Methodism: A Study in Social Science* (Cincinnati: Curts & Jennings; New York: Eaton & Mains, 1898), 126; Matthew Simpson, *Cyclopedia of Methodism. Embracing Sketches of Its Rise, Progress, and Present Condition, With Biographical Notices and Numerous Illustrations* (Philadelphia: Louis H. Everts, 1880), 675; Roger Finke and Rodney Stark, *The Churching of America, 1776–1990: Winners and Losers in Our Religious Economy* (New Brunswick: Rutgers University Press, 1992), 55; C. C. Goss, *Statistical History of the First Century of American Methodism: With a Summary of the Origin and Present Operations of Other Denominations* (New York: Carlton & Porter, 1866), 35–114. Among the recent books that place Methodism in the larger context of the early American Republic are: Dee Andrews, *The Methodists and Revolutionary America, 1760–1800: The Shaping of an Evangelical Culture* (Princeton: Princeton University Press, 2000); Catherine Brekus, *Strangers and Pilgrims: Female Preaching in America, 1740–1845* (Chapel Hill: University of North Carolina Press, 1998);

Richard Carwardine, *Evangelicals and Politics in Antebellum America* (1993; Knoxville: University of Tennessee Press, 1997); Nathan O. Hatch, *The Democratization of American Christianity* (New Haven: Yale University Press, 1989); Christine Leigh Heyrman, *Southern Cross: The Beginnings of the Bible Belt* (Chapel Hill: University of North Carolina Press, 1997); Cynthia Lynn Lyerly, *Methodism and the Southern Mind, 1770–1810* (New York: Oxford University Press, 1998); Kathryn Long, *The Revival of 1857–58: Interpreting an American Religious Awakening* (New York: Oxford University Press, 1998); Philip N. Mulder, *A Controversial Spirit: Evangelical Awakenings in the South* (New York: Oxford University Press, 2002); Christopher Owen, *The Sacred Flame of Love: Methodism and Society in Nineteenth-Century Georgia* (Athens: University of Georgia Press, 1998); Russell Richey, *Early American Methodism* (Bloomington: Indiana University Press, 1991); Lester Ruth, *A Little Heaven Below: Worship in Early Methodist Quarterly Meetings* (Nashville: Abingdon Press, 2000); William Sutton, *Journeymen for Jesus: Evangelical Artisans Confront Capitalism in Jacksonian Baltimore* (University Park: Pennsylvania State University Press, 1998); Beth Barton Schweiger, *The Gospel Working Up: Progress and the Pulpit in Nineteenth-Century Virginia* (New York: Oxford University Press, 2000); John Wigger, *Taking Heaven by Storm: Methodism and the Rise of Popular Christianity in America* (1998; Urbana: University of Illinois Press, 2001). Also see the essays in Nathan Hatch and John Wigger, eds., *Methodism and the Shaping of American Culture* (Nashville: Kingswood Books, 2001).

3. Wigger, *Taking Heaven by Storm,* 21–103; R. Douglas Hurt, *The Ohio Frontier: Crucible of the Old Northwest, 1720–1830* (Bloomington: Indiana University Press, 1996), 284–90. On John Kobler, Lewis Hunt, Henry Smith, and Philip Gatch, see James B. Finley, *Sketches of Western Methodism: Biographical, Historical and Miscellaneous. Illustrative of Pioneer Life* (Cincinnati: Methodist Book Concern, 1854), 154–65, 169–77, 194–99.

4. Philip Gatch, *Sketch of Rev. Philip Gatch. Prepared by Hon. John M'Lean* (Cincinnati: Swormstedt & Poe, 1854), 6–59, 91–108, 127–28; Barker, *Ohio Methodism,* 82–93, 147–50, 173–90; Elizabeth Connor, *Methodist Trail Blazer: Philip Gatch 1751–1834: His Life in Maryland, Virginia and Ohio* (Rutland, VT: Academy Books, 1970); John Lednum, *A History of the Rise of Methodism in America. Containing Sketches of Methodist Itinerant Preachers, from 1736 to 1785, Numbering One Hundred and Sixty or Seventy* (Philadelphia: by the author, 1862), 92–100, 112, 135–39, 145–50, 171–73, 191–92, 225, 283–85.

5. Henry Smith, *Recollections and Reflections of an Old Itinerant* (New York: Lane & Tippett, 1848), 67, 313–14.

6. John Kobler, "Rev. John Kobler Journal, 1789–1799," entries for August 11 and October 23, 1798, and April 14, 1799, Archives of the Baltimore–Washington Conference of the United Methodist Church, Lovely Lane Museum, Baltimore, Maryland; *Minutes MEC* (1840), 86.

7. Gatch, *Sketch,* 102, 189; Smith, *Recollections,* 29; James Quinn, *Sketches of the Life and Labors of James Quinn, Who Was Nearly Half a Century a Minister*

of the Gospel in the Methodist Episcopal Church, ed. John F. Wright (Cincinnati: Methodist Book Concern, 1851), 136.

8. Wigger, *Taking Heaven by Storm,* 198–99. On the development of religion in early Kentucky, see Ellen Eslinger, *Citizens of Zion: The Social Origins of Camp Meeting Revivalism* (Knoxville: University of Tennessee Press, 1999), 187–241; A. H. Redford, *The History of Methodism in Kentucky,* 2 vols. (Nashville: Southern Methodist Publishing House, 1870). On the Baptists in nineteenth-century Kentucky, see Richard C. Traylor, "Born of Water and the Spirit: Popular Religion and Early American Baptists in Kentucky," PhD diss., University of Missouri, 2003. On early Methodism in the Holston region, see R. N. Price, *Holston Methodism. From Its Origins to the Present Time,* 2 vols. (Nashville: M. E. Church, South, 1903). On Methodism in early Ohio and the West, also see William Warren Sweet, *Circuit Rider Days Along the Ohio* (New York: Methodist Book Concern, 1923), 22–42; Sweet, *The Rise of Methodism in the West: Being the Journal of the Western Conference 1800–1811* (New York: Methodist Book Concern, 1920); Samuel W. Williams, *Pictures of Early Methodism in Ohio* (Cincinnati: Jennings and Graham; New York: Eaton and Mains, 1909), 33–214.

9. Dromgoole lived in Brunswick County, Virginia. See 1798 Brunswick County Sheriff's assessment and the 1803 fire insurance policy from the Assurance Society, in Financial and Legal Papers, Edward Dromgoole Papers, Southern Historical Collection, Wilson Library, University of North Carolina at Chapel Hill. On Dromgoole also see *Minutes MEC* (1840), 6, 25, and R. H. Moore, *Sketches of the Pioneers of Methodism in North Carolina and Virginia* (Nashville: Southern Methodist Publishing House, 1884), 76–82.

10. Philip Gatch to Edward Dromgoole, February 11, 1802, in William Warren Sweet, *Religion on the American Frontier, 1783–1840: Vol. IV, The Methodists* (Chicago: University of Chicago Press, 1946), 152–55. Also see pages 159, 160, 171, 172, 175, 178, 184–85, 186, and 196. On migration patterns into Ohio, see Hubert G. Wilhelm and Allen G. Noble, "Ohio's Settlement Landscape," in *A Geography of Ohio,* ed. Leonard Peacefull (Kent, OH: Kent State University Press, 1996), 80–109.

11. Edward Dromgoole Jr. to his parents, June 14, 15, 1807; Peter Pelham to Edward Dromgoole, June 20, July 27, 1807; Frederick Bonner to Edward Dromgoole, July 19, 1807; Bennett Maxey to Edward Dromgoole, July 27, 1807. All: Edward Dromgoole Papers, Southern Historical Collection, Wilson Library, University of North Carolina at Chapel Hill. Edward Dromgoole Jr. married Sarah C. Pelham, daughter of Peter Pelham.

12. Andrew R. L. Cayton, "'Language Gives Way to Feelings': Rhetoric, Republicanism, and Religion in Jeffersonian Ohio," in *The Pursuit of Power: Political Culture in Ohio, 1787–1861,* ed. Jeffrey P. Brown and Andrew R. L. Cayton (Kent, OH: Kent State University Press, 1994), 38–40.

13. There were of course exceptions, places where Federalists and representatives from older denominations held sway. For example, see Andrew R. L. Cayton, "The Contours of Power in a Frontier Town: Marietta, Ohio,

1788–1803," *Journal of the Early Republic* 6 (1986): 103–26; Andrew R. L. Cayton and Paula Riggs, *City into Town: The City of Marietta, Ohio, 1788–1988* (Marietta: Dawes Memorial Library, Marietta College, 1991), 79–101.

14. Dan Young, *Autobiography of Dan Young: A New England Preacher of the Olden Time* (New York: Carlton & Porter, 1860), 202; Alfred Brunson, *A Western Pioneer: Or, Incidents of the Life and Times of Rev. Alfred Brunson, A.M., D.D., Embracing a Period of Over Seventy Years* (1872; New York: Arno Press, 1975), 217–18. As a New Englander, Young found southern Ohio "society very rude and not a little vicious." See Young, p. 202. On the competition between Federalists and Democratic Republicans in early nineteenth-century Ohio, see Ratcliffe, *Party Spirit in a Frontier Republic: Democratic Politics in Ohio 1793–1821* (Columbus: Ohio State University Press, 1998). Also see Jeffrey P. Brown, "The Political Culture of Early Ohio," in *The Pursuit of Power*, ed. Brown and Cayton, 1–14.

15. On voting patterns in early Ohio, see Donald J. Ratcliffe, "Voter Turnout in Early Ohio," *Journal of the Early Republic* 7 (1987): 223–51.

16. Alfred Byron Sears, *Thomas Worthington: Father of Ohio Statehood* (Columbus: Ohio State University Press, 1958), especially chapters 1, 6, and 7; Cayton, "Rhetoric, Republicanism, and Religion," 35–36; Donald J. Ratcliffe, *Party Spirit*, especially chapters 2–5; Hurt, *Ohio Frontier*, 171–72, 278–82; Ella May Turner, "Thomas Worthington," *Magazine of the Jefferson County Historical Society*, 14 (1948): 16–33; Wigger, *Taking Heaven by Storm*, 178; Quinn, *Sketches*, 98. Quinn was an associate judge of the Court of Common Pleas for Fairfield County. In May 1796 Thomas Scott married Catharine Wood, also a Methodist. Thereafter, Scott became a tailor while studying law. In 1801 Scott moved from Kentucky to Chillicothe at the urging of Edward Tiffin. On Scott, see Finley, *Sketches*, 154–62; Smith, *Recollections*, 237, 244.

17. William Edward Gilmore, *Life of Edward Tiffin, First Governor of Ohio* (Chillicothe: Horney & Sons, 1897); Finley, *Sketches*, 260–87; Ratcliffe, *Party Spirit*, especially chapters 2–5; Cayton, "Rhetoric, Republicanism, and Religion," 34–36.

18. Francis Asbury, *Journal and Letters of Francis Asbury*, 3 vols., ed. Elmer T. Clark, J. Manning Potts, Jacob S. Payton (Nashville: Abingdon Press, 1958), 2:575, 576, 614; Jacob Young, *Autobiography of a Pioneer: or, The Nativity, Experience, Travels, and Ministerial Labors of Rev. Jacob Young; with Incidents, Observations, and Reflections* (Cincinnati: Cranston and Curts, [1857]), 144; Smith, *Recollections*, 327; Cayton, "Rhetoric, Republicanism, and Religion," 36. On the conflict between Tiffin and some leaders of Chillicothe Methodism over Tiffin's activities in the Tammany Society in 1811, see Samuel W. Williams, "The Tammany Society in Ohio," *Ohio Archaeological and Historical Society Publications* 22 (1913): 349–70.

19. Francis P. Weisenburger, *The Life of John McLean: A Politician on the United States Supreme Court* (Columbus: Ohio State University Press, 1937); Simpson, *Cyclopedia*, 578; Carwardine, *Evangelicals and Politics in Antebellum*

America, 40–41, 93, 95, 100, 271. On John Collins, see J. B. Wakeley, *The Heroes of Methodism, Containing Sketches of Eminent Methodist Ministers, and Characteristic Anecdotes of Their Personal History* (New York: Carlton & Porter, 1856), 383–92; Finley, *Sketches,* 317–30.

20. Cayton, "Rhetoric, Republicanism, and Religion," 31.

21. On Asbury's early life, see David J. A. Hallam, *Eliza Asbury: Her Cottage and Her Son* (Studley, UK: Brewin Books, 2003); John Wigger, "Francis Asbury," *Biographical Dictionary of Evangelicals,* ed. Timothy Larsen (Leicester, UK: Inter-Varsity Press, 2003), 24–27; Ezra S. Tipple, *Francis Asbury: The Prophet of the Long Road* (New York: Methodist Book Concern, 1916), 37–56; L. C. Rudolph, *Francis Asbury* (Nashville: Abingdon Press, 1966), 13–20; Frederick W. Briggs, *Bishop Asbury: A Biographical Study For Children Workers,* 3rd ed. (London: Wesleyan Conference Office, 1890), 8–26; James Lewis, *Francis Asbury: Bishop of the Methodist Episcopal Church* (London: Epworth Press, 1927), 14–24.

22. Tipple, *Francis Asbury,* 182.

23. Donald G. Mathews, *Slavery and Methodism: A Chapter in American Morality 1780–1845* (Princeton: Princeton University Press, 1965), 3–61; Wigger, *Taking Heaven by Storm,* 125–50; L. C. Matlack, *The Antislavery Struggle and Triumph in the Methodist Episcopal Church* (1881; New York: Negro Universities Press, 1969), 47–74.

24. Asbury, *Journal and Letters,* 1:638; 2:83, 125. While in Philadelphia in September 1790, Asbury wrote that "Our society in the city of Philadelphia are generally poor: perhaps it is well; when men become rich, they sometimes forget that they are Methodists." After reading a portion of John Wesley's journal in February 1793 Asbury noted that he agreed with Wesley "that it is rare—a mere miracle, for a Methodist to increase in wealth and not decrease in grace." Asbury's own commitment, he wrote in March 1800, was to "live and die a poor man." See Asbury, *Journal and Letters,* 1:651, 748; 2:227.

25. Asbury, *Journal and Letters,* 2:405, 406, 445; Francis Asbury to Rebekah Ridgley, August 16, 1804, Methodist Research Collection, General Commission on Archives and History, Drew University, Madison, New Jersey. While riding the New Rochelle Circuit in New York in 1807 and 1808, Billy Hibbard was dismayed to see so many Methodists moving west. "In these times it seems all will move to the Ohio," complained Hibbard. "Great talk about the country, I fear too much." Billy Hibbard, *Memoirs of the Life and Travels of B. Hibbard, Minister of the Gospel, Containing an Account of His Experience of Religion; and of His Call to and Labours in the Ministry for Nearly Thirty Years* (New York: printed for the author, 1825), 294. On landholding patterns in early Ohio, see Lee Soltow, "Inequality Amidst Abundance: Land Ownership in Early Nineteenth Century Ohio," *Ohio History* 88 (Spring 1979): 133–51; Soltow, "Progress and Mobility among Ohio Propertyholders, 1810–1825," *Social Science History* 7 (Fall 1983): 405–26; Ratcliffe, *Party Spirit,* 46, 102, 103.

26. Asbury, *Journal and Letters*, 1:440.

27. Gatch, *Sketch*, 183; Wigger, *Taking Heaven by Storm*, 181–83; Quinn, *Sketches*, 183–84; [John McLean], *A Sketch of the Life of the Rev. John Collins, Late of the Ohio Conference* (Cincinnati: Swormstedt and Power, 1849), 118–21. The Collins biography was published anonymously, but several sources attribute it to McLean. See, for example, Simpson, *Cyclopedia of Methodism*, 578.

28. Edwin Gaustad and Philip Barlow, *New Historical Atlas of Religion in America* (New York: Oxford University Press, 2001), 219–31; Peter Halvorson and William Newman, *Atlas of Religious Change in America, 1952–1990* (Atlanta: Glenmary Research Center, 1994), 130–38.

FOUR

The Evolution of Racial Politics
in Early Ohio

ELLEN ESLINGER

Ohio was the first state admitted to the union (1803) with virtually
no heritage of legal slaveholding. The Northwest Ordinance of 1787
had prohibited slavery in the entire American territory north of the
Ohio River. Both the territorial and the early statehood periods,
however, witnessed repeated efforts to dilute or undermine this prohibition. Although the majority opposed slavery, they wished to preserve Ohio as a white society and therefore supported measures designed to discourage black settlement such as the denial of working
rights and special registration requirements. Yet during the 1820s,
as Ohio's black population began a period of rapid growth, alternative strategies, such as repatriation to Africa by the American Colonization Society, attracted much support across all regions of the
state. By the close of the decade, opposition to black settlers had occasionally become violent.

The efforts to deter black settlement in Ohio did not go unchallenged. Many former New Englanders, as well as southerners,
had migrated to Ohio specifically because land was affordable and
the Northwest Ordinance prohibited slavery. These people formed
a dedicated core of antislavery sentiment. The Underground Railroad wended along multiple routes, and abolitionist societies organized in several communities long before such organizations appeared in other parts of the United States. Ohioans not only read
antislavery publications but also contributed several influential

works that were reprinted for wider consumption. Furthermore, Ohio enjoyed relative proximity to the resources of national reform organizations that were based in the urban centers along the eastern seaboard at the same time that it functioned as a portal to the rest of the Northwest.

Racial issues were also intensified by Ohio's geographical position between two slave states (Virginia and Kentucky) and Canada. In addition to attracting free blacks, it was perhaps inevitable that Ohio would attract fugitive slaves. Harboring fugitives, it was widely feared, would jeopardize the state's economic connections across the Ohio River. Most white Ohioans therefore opposed only the western extension of slavery, ready to let it survive where it already existed. A related geographical problem involved Ohio's appeal as a western state with affordable land. Like most white Americans during this period, even opponents of slavery tended to view a multiracial society as undesirable. Many voters feared that Ohio would be flooded with manumitted slaves from Kentucky and Virginia, as well as from Maryland and farther north. One result was that the American Colonization Society was able to attract support from both proslavery and antislavery contingents of the white population. Although Ohio did not welcome black settlers, many came anyway, driven out of their home states by the hostility toward free blacks common in slave societies and drawn to Ohio by the cheap frontier land.

Hence, more so than others in the nation, early Ohioans repeatedly found themselves forced to examine and re-examine racial policy. Settled initially by the state constitution, the issue resurfaced regularly in the public forum. It underwent particularly close scrutiny in the late 1820s as the free black population swelled. National political controversies such as the Missouri Compromise also elicited strong feeling. Finding a popular consensus sometimes seemed to grow ever more elusive. By the 1830s, however, Ohio was emerging as an important antislavery ground, one whose roots had been established through several decades of public debate about the peculiar institution and its wider effects.

Ohio ranks as a pivotal state in the national story of the antebellum antislavery movement. Its course—prohibiting slavery while offering people of color restricted privileges—was followed by most of the other states later admitted to the Union from the Northwest Territory. This pattern established an important foundation for opposing the extension of slavery in the territories farther west, particularly those that lay in the same latitudes.

The Northwest Ordinance's prohibition on slavery had been a controversial issue, and efforts to compromise it commenced almost immediately.[1] Eliminating slavery completely was a virtual impossibility. Slavery already existed in the Northwest Territory, primarily in the French settlements of the Illinois region. Governor Arthur St. Clair adopted a policy protecting slavery where it existed prior to 1787, signaling hope for slaveholders. A group of prospective settlers to Virginia's huge military tract in Ohio, which had been set aside for Revolutionary War veterans, for example, perceived this as an opportunity and petitioned for a special exemption.[2] Although the Northwest Territory was not a region conducive to the production of staple crops, the task of clearing and fencing land for agriculture demanded much unskilled labor. Free whites were seldom available for hire. It was a "common complaint," noted a visitor to Ohio, "in all the western non-slave-holding States. Nearly all the people are landowners, and few can be induced to act in the capacity of servants, unless extravagant wages are given." Slavery and its cousin, indentured servitude, therefore offered tantalizing options on the Ohio frontier.[3]

Territorial records, not surprisingly, include a number of instances where white Ohioans attempted to defy the prohibition on slavery. In Marietta, for example, a grand juror from New England named Thomas Wallcut objected in 1790 to the recent local sale of two blacks, one only seven years old, to a new owner in Virginia and pressed that a specific law be adopted prohibiting the buying and selling of slaves. He followed this action with a petition to the governor. "This atrocious crime, we presume, is against the divine and moral, as well as (according to Judge Blackstone) the Jewish code, the common law of England, and the ordinances of Congress for the government of the Territory." According to an early visitor, "Many persons in this State have coloured people, which they call *their property*. The mode in which they effect this perpetuation of slavery, in violation of the spirit of the Ohio constitution, is to purchase blacks, and have them *apprenticed* to them. Some are so base as to take these Negroes down the river at the approach of the expiration of their apprenticeship, *and sell them at Natchez for life!*"[4]

The prohibition against slavery in the Northwest Ordinance did, however, exert a special attraction for some people. Article VI of the ordinance had been the product of the New England–based Ohio Company, and settlers from New England generally shared the company's antipathy regarding slavery.[5] Article VI also attracted some southerners who opposed slavery. The most conspicuous of these were Quaker. A stream of southern Quakers, particularly from North Carolina, began early. Already by the end of 1800 an estimated eight hundred Quaker families had reached Ohio. Some eight thousand resided in the eastern counties of Belmont, Jefferson, Harrison, and Columbiana by 1826.[6] Opposing slavery on moral grounds, early Ohio Quakers worked to reduce racial prejudice and often aided fugitive slaves. They also engaged in educating black neighbors. As a result of Quaker aid and assistance, some of Ohio's largest African American enclaves were situated amidst or adjacent to Quaker communities. Quakers also founded the state's first antislavery organization, the Union Humane Society, in 1816. Quakers were also conspicuous in organizing local antislavery societies during the 1820s. Their newspaper, *The Philanthropist,* published arguments against the slave trade and decried the breakup of black families and inhumane treatment by masters. Sometimes at personal risk, Ohio's Quaker pioneers were among the most outspoken protestors concerning the western expansion of slavery.[7]

Other religious southerners also figured prominently among Ohio's antislavery activists. The early-nineteenth-century Methodists, Baptists, and Associate Reformed Presbyterian denominations all disapproved of human bondage on Christian principle and struggled to devise a workable course of action to eradicate an evil already poisoning the church body. One result was that official church positions occasionally shifted over time and between local congregations. The difficulty of pursuing racial justice without sowing discord and division defied lasting solution. Race and slavery remained a tinderbox issue.

Despite the divisive effects upon infant congregations, a few religious leaders openly opposed slavery. The first Methodist congregation in Ohio was established in 1795 by Francis McCormick, who had abandoned his home in Kentucky because that new state's constitution explicitly protected slavery. McCormick was not alone. Rev. Phillip Gatch, who had inherited slaves from his father-in-law, liberated them before moving to Ohio in 1798. His brother-in-law, Rev. James Smith, had first considered moving to Kentucky but chose Ohio specifically because of the prohibition against slavery. In 1812 the Ohio Annual Methodist Conference ordered the expulsion of any church member who sold a slave unless done to keep a family together. Purchases were limited to benevolent purposes and a specific term of service. In 1816 the Methodist General Conference adopted a nationwide resolution that "no slaveholder shall be eligible to any official station in our Church hereafter, where the laws of the state permit the liberated slave to enjoy freedom."

The issue of slavery also troubled Baptist congregations. In 1812 the Indian Creek congregation resolved to bar from membership persons who believed that the Bible defended slavery. Congregations struggled to resolve religious principles with political practice. Such concerns prompted the Presbyterian Synod of Ohio to petition the church's national governance body in 1814 to consider measures to rid American Presbyterians from the "sins" of slave owning, the slave trade, and "manstealing." Several ministers were particularly active in promoting the antislavery cause. Rev. Dyer Burgess was a leading figure in the Miami Presbytery's agitation for the Presbyterian Church to adopt a stronger opposition to slaveholding, slave trafficking, and related practices. Rev. James Gilliland left South Carolina in 1804 for Brown County, Ohio, because the presbytery and synod had ordered him to be silent on the topic of emancipation. Another leading Presbyterian activist was the Reverend Samuel Crothers, ordained in 1810 as pastor of the Chillicothe and Hope Run congregations in Ross County. Crothers gained a reputation as an eloquent voice in demonstrating how slavery was contrary to biblical principles.[8]

The most infamous religious activist was probably Presbyterian minister John Rankin, pastor at the Ohio River town of Ripley, directly across from Maysville, Kentucky. His house, built in 1828, stood on a hill overlooking town and river, and he reportedly kept a lamp in a window at night as a beacon to fugitives as they crossed to the Ohio shore. An early historian of the Underground Railroad declared that Rankin "did more to propagate practical abolitionism in Ohio than any other citizen of the state."[9]

Ohio also attracted other southerners who opposed slavery. Some believed, as did political leader Thomas Worthington, that the institution should be abolished. "I was decidedly opposed to slavery long before I removed to the territory—the prohibition of slavery in the territory, was one cause of my removal to it." Their reasons varied. Some certainly held benevolent feelings, but others opposed slavery because they thought it "unrepublican" and inappropriate for a nation founded upon principles of liberty. Worthington and other southern opponents of bondage usually had manumitted their slaves, a significant portion of whom followed their former masters to Ohio, prior to migration. Had Ohio not attracted such influential and eloquent people, slavery could conceivably have attained a very important foothold.[10]

Yet Ohio's agricultural potential also attracted a significant number of southerners who supported or were ambivalent toward slavery.[11] They saw a practical need to alleviate the shortage of unskilled labor. Nothing was more essential than labor in opening a frontier farm. Some proslavery people hoped, at least in this early period, that Ohio's admission to the Union as a state would provide an opportunity to reverse the ordinance's prohibition. During the 1802 state constitutional convention and later in the state legislature, the proslavery representatives repeatedly sought to get slavery, or some form of African bondage, legalized. This segment of Ohioans also sympathized with southern owners pursuing fugitive slaves. Others acted not on principle but for the reward money offered for apprehending fugitives. Ohio newspapers regularly carried advertisements for runaways.[12]

Early Ohio's diverse population made for an ambivalent legislative record on racial issues. Slavery dominated the 1802 constitutional convention. Although the prohibition of slavery was preserved in the new state, blacks were not treated as equal citizens. The majority of white Ohioans viewed people of color as inherently inferior and unworthy of voting privileges and the right to hold public office.[13] African American rights were reduced further by subsequent legislative enactments, two of which followed shortly afterward. In 1804, primarily to deter future black settlement, the state legislature passed a law requiring all African American immigrants to the state to possess a certificate of freedom. They and all other resident African Americans were to register this document with the local county clerk. Anyone employing blacks unable to produce evidence of free status was subject to a heavy fine. As an inducement, informers were to receive half of the fine. These restrictions were strengthened in 1807, with an additional restriction prohibiting blacks from giving court testimony in cases involving whites. Furthermore, African American immigrants to Ohio were required to post a five-hundred-dollar surety bond with the local court, a requirement intentionally beyond the means of most people but designed principally to deter further black immigration.[14] As this legislation indicates, the majority of white Ohioans may have opposed slavery (or its extension), but they did not desire a multiracial society.

The "Black Laws," as these statutes came to be known, not only disappointed many opponents of slavery but also frightened some of Ohio's black pioneers into leaving for the protection of British Canada. An early black settler named George Williams recalled, "I had a farm in Ohio, and was doing well, but a law was then passed requiring security [bond] for good behavior." Unfortunately for Williams, "a white man represented it worse than it was, so as to take advantage, as myself and two others had a heavy crop standing. I lost by coming off before harvest." According to a black resident of Cincinnati, many of the approximately three thousand black residents of Cincinnati, few of whom could post the required bond, "were thrown out of employment" when the city decided in 1829 to enforce the Black Laws. This individual, who had been earning by his own calculations about six hundred dollars annually, could have afforded to give bond but "refused" to do so on principle. At a community meeting it was decided to send several delegates to Canada to explore the possibility of finding asylum there. Although many more had expressed interest, only about five hundred black Cincinnatians actually made the move. The main reason was that the Black Laws had quickly again become inoperative, "and the colored people wrote me, that they could now walk without being pushed off the side-walks, were well-used, and were living in clover." David Grier explained his move to Canada, stating, "From Ohio, I came here on account of the oppressive laws demanding security for good behavior,—I was a stranger and could not get it." Eli Artis likewise bitterly explained his departure for Canada: "I suffered from mean, oppressive laws in my native state, Ohio."[15]

Although the racial prejudice that had inspired Ohio's Black Laws was real, enforcement proved almost universally lax. The failure to enforce registration requirements was, however, not unique to Ohio or even unusual. Southern states such as Virginia and Kentucky also passed registration laws in the early nineteenth century, not only to deter free black population growth but also to control free black influence upon the slave population. Even in these slave states, enforcement was notoriously lax. Until the middle of the nineteenth century, strict enforcement in Ohio, as in the South, was usually reserved for vagrants, suspected runaways, and petty crimi-nals.[16] Although Ohio's failure to enforce the laws for registration and bond has sometimes been interpreted as symptomatic of the an-tislavery movement's emerging strength, the wider context indicates a more ambivalent attitude. Selective enforcement of the registra-tion laws allowed white communities to expel undesirable free blacks while retaining a cheap source of menial labor.

Since Ohio was not a slave state, however, registration operated a bit differently there than in the South. From the outset, the pri-mary intent of the 1804 and 1807 Black Laws was to deter future im-migration rather than to expel those African Americans who were al-ready residents. Local government bodies therefore felt little inclined to vigorously enforce the Black Laws, particularly since most black communities remained rather small during the early nineteenth century. Moreover, most black immigrants to Ohio, particularly those who traveled through slave states, did carry official proof of their free status for fear of being detained as runaways. Their failure to register probably reflected a desire to avoid paying recording fees and posting the oppressive surety bond. Thus Ohio's 1804 registra-tion requirement posed a problem primarily for blacks already in the state and for fugitives from slavery. The 1807 bond requirement was more problematic because it required that a person have friends in Ohio who were willing to undertake a substantial financial risk, but, paired as it usually was with registration, the bond requirement typically met the same fate.

Over time, however, Ohio's Black Laws appear to have changed in function. Whereas initially most Ohio blacks registered in order to establish their exemption from the bond requirement, by the 1820s the overwhelming number of registrations being recorded were by former slaves confirming their free status. Black immigrants who had been born free could usually produce registration papers from their home state on demand. Former slaves perhaps had greater concern about their legal status, particularly a fear of kid-napping. Most probably carried some sort of "freedom papers," but these sometimes were in the form of a private document from the person who had granted their freedom. Although filing a deed of manumission with the local court offered protection against lost or stolen documents, it was optional. Many newly freed African Ameri-cans chose to avoid the recording fees and rely upon patrons or witnesses to vouch for them. In Ohio, however, they were among strangers, making a court record more important.[17] Local government records bear out this pattern.

In Ross County, home of the first state capital, legal compliance with the law might be expected to have been high. It was located in the midst of the Virginia Military District, was peopled by many former southerners, and had more free people of color than any other county (125 in 1800) save Hamilton, where the booming town of Cincinnati offered exceptional wage-earning opportunities. Yet the earliest black registrations seem more often concerned with establishing individual exemptions from the 1804 and 1807 statutes than with submitting to them. To take but one example, longtime Ohio residents Billy and Rachel Miles recorded their freedom in 1812—the date itself indicates lax enforcement—and the record was witnessed by Nathaniel Massie, a prominent pioneer and speculator who testified that they had been residents during the territorial period and were therefore exempt from the legislative requirements. The other free black registrations recorded in this early period appear to have been directed toward similar ends. Despite Ross County's comparatively large black population, authorities there never prosecuted anyone for failure to register. Neither did they prosecute free blacks arriving after 1807, who were also subject to posting the five hundred dollar bond. Rather, the Ross County Court of Common Pleas appears to have enforced these requirements selectively. Although Sally Hill, for example, entered a bond in 1812, this aspect of the law was not applied to Perry Coin.[18]

Lax or sporadic enforcement was also the reigning pattern in other counties with early records. In Belmont County, in eastern Ohio, the Court of Common Pleas took a more explicit position. Not only did it seldom enforce the state's five-hundred-dollar surety bond, it sometimes formally suspended the bond requirement altogether contingent upon good behavior and self-support. This was done on behalf of a former slave named Jack Blair in 1812, for example, and for John Moxley in 1815. The court acted likewise for Moses William and his wife Mariah in 1830. In other cases, immigrants of color settling after 1807 merely recorded their freedom papers without the Belmont Court ever addressing the matter of posting the stipulated bond.[19] Voiding the bond requirement exceeded the court's authority but was apparently never challenged. As in Ross County, the Belmont County Grand Jury did not pursue unregistered black residents. Of eighteen black household heads counted in the 1820 census, only two had registered. A similar situation appears to have existed in Champaign County, where the 1820 census enumerated twenty-nine black families but only four individuals, including one wife, had registered. Although court records and registrations survive for few Ohio counties during this early period, no reason exists to believe that the situation was different elsewhere.[20] And like elsewhere, the lax enforcement in Ohio probably had more to do with self-interest among whites than with benevolent concern for black welfare.

A parallel ambivalence appears to have operated also regarding the prohibition against slavery. In 1812 a Highland County man named James D. Scott sued Beverly Milner for violating the 1807 law by employing a woman of color named Lydia, "alias Phebe." Scott also sued William Daley in regard to a man named Bob Cox, whom Daley "did hire, employ, harbour & conceal." Scott also sued Thomas Terry, as well as Pheneas Hunt, for the same offense. In all of these cases, significantly, the jury found for the defendant and the judges held Scott liable for the court costs. Scott's motives in bringing these suits is unclear. Scott would have been entitled to half of each fine had he won, but it is also possible that he wished to attack thinly veiled forms of bondage. Unfortunately, court records reveal little detail for any of these suits.[21] All that can be said is that some blacks in Highland County lived under conditions that provided some basis for bringing suit, although the jurors selected from the community viewed the situation differently.

Montgomery County witnessed a different type of challenge. Robert Patterson, a Presbyterian elder from Kentucky, had freed slaves prior to his move but like many other early white Ohioans met his labor needs in Ohio by hiring Kentucky slaves. In 1804 he was prosecuted for restraining the liberty of Edward Page and his wife Lucy, hired from Andrew McCalla of Lexington and purportedly about to be returned to their owner and sold. Another slave, Moses, the property of William Lindsey of Scott County, Kentucky, had been hired by Patterson to help move his household effects to Ohio. The court granted the Pages their liberty, while Moses liberated himself by running away before the verdict. Having lost in court, Patterson attempted to thwart the verdict by having the Pages kidnapped and returned to their Kentucky owner. A number of ethnic German neighbors, however, successfully intervened. As the legal cases in Montgomery and other counties indicate, the conditions of service could be ambiguous and subject to local social pressures.[22]

The Black Laws remained in effect until their repeal in 1849, but they certainly did not have the intended effect of deterring black immigration. Ohio's black population increased from a minuscule 337 in 1800 to 1,890 in 1810. In 1820, the federal population census counted 4,723 people of color, and this nearly doubled in the ensuing decade. This was still an extremely small proportion of the state population, well under one percent, but the failure of the Black Laws to deter immigration was so obvious that as early as 1816 the legislature considered a bill to abolish the two laws.[23] It would be a mistake, however, to conclude that the Black Laws were irrelevant. Although the Black Laws were seldom enforced, government authorities could resort to them at their discretion at any time. This possibility alone, while impossible to measure, must have exerted some deterring effect. A second, unintentional effect was that the laws benefited Ohio's black population by providing some legal protection. Blacks resident prior to 1807 could establish their right to exemption from the new bond requirement, which applied only to more recent immigrants. Those finishing an indenture could legally record their new free status. Black parents could register children as free Ohio natives.

As the Black Laws proved an insufficient deterrent to black immigration, interest began turning to a new strategy for making Ohio a white society: repatriation to Africa. The American Colonization Society (ACS), founded in 1816, initially attracted both opponents and defenders of slavery. It might well be described as trying to be everything to everybody. Proponents of repatriation argued that in the South the institution of slavery would be protected from the influence of what was deemed a dangerous and undesirable sector of the population (free persons of color). Northern states such as Ohio would be protected from an influx of manumitted southern slaves, who would instead be shipped to Africa. African colonization appealed to a broad spectrum of white Ohioans, some for humanitarian reasons and others due to racial prejudice. Four counties soon petitioned the state legislature that "measures may be taken to effect the emancipation and colonization of people of color." The legislature responded positively, an indication of the colonization movement's growing popular support, and urged Ohio's senators and representatives in Congress to pass national legislation aiding the

ACS and its goals. In 1824 the Ohio legislature circulated to the governors of other states a set of resolutions urging them to lend support to a national colonization plan, as well as a plan for gradual emancipation for those slave owners consenting to foreign colonization. Although endorsed by most northern states, the plan was repudiated by most of the South.[24] Nonetheless, an influential core of Ohioans believed that African colonization presented the most humane and effective solution for ridding the state of present black residents as well as helping to prevent further immigration.

Meanwhile, as the number of African Americans in Ohio swelled during the 1820s, public hostility increased. "Immense numbers of mulattoes are continually flocking by tens and by hundreds into Ohio," declared the Columbus *Ohio State Journal* in 1827. "Their fecundity is proverbial.—They are worse than drones to society, and they already swarm in our land like locusts." White citizens tended to perceive colonization as but a partial solution; the legislature also needed to enact more effective deterrents to further immigration.[25] State Representative Anthony Walker of Ross County declared before the House that "although they are nominally free, that freedom confers only the privilege of being more idle and vicious than slaves." Governor Allen Trimble concurred in his address to the legislature in 1827, stating, "Their rapid increase has already given serious alarm to many of our citizens." Consequently, it might soon "be necessary for us (in self defense) to adopt some measure to counteract the policy of slave states which tends to throw from themselves upon us, the whole mass of their free colored population."[26]

The growing hostility toward free blacks by the late 1820s in Ohio (as well as elsewhere in the Old Northwest) inspired the ACS's national leaders to send agents to organize local chapters. The years 1826 and 1827 witnessed the appearance of at least thirty auxiliaries. Most were located in the state's southern counties, where the black population was most concentrated, but local auxiliaries embraced all sections of Ohio, including the Western Reserve. In December 1827 the local chapters organized under a state auxiliary of the national ACS, the Ohio State Colonization Society, with former governor Jeremiah Morrow as president. Other prominent political leaders were also among the society's early members.[27]

A major part of the ACS's appeal was its position that people of African descent remained an alien element in American society. In addressing the citizens of Ohio, the society argued that colonization to Africa would benefit African Americans, who would inevitably remain a "degraded" caste in the United States. Although free, a black American "remained a Negro still, and must always continue in a state of political bondage; and it is obvious that he who is deprived of the inherent rights of a citizen can never become a loyal subject." Moreover, although Ohio law prohibited slavery, slavery still threatened the republican character of Ohio society. Several southern states had adopted laws requiring manumitted slaves to depart, and many of these former slaves could be expected to head for the Old Northwest. Especially conspicuous were several instances where southern planters had liberated all of their slaves and purchased land for their resettlement in Ohio.[28] Consequently, a growing number of Ohioans came to agree that manumission came "at the expense of *our* safety and happiness in this and other free states."[29] For white Ohioans, as for those living in other regions of the country, the primary appeal of repatriation to Africa was self-interest rather than benevolence.

Despite the colonization movement's positive reception, no black Ohioans are known to have emigrated to the new African colony of Liberia before 1833.[30] A major problem was a lack of funding. Equally important was the lack of volunteer immigrants (the ACS insisted that the decision be voluntary). The ACS nonetheless exerted a considerable effect. In the course of its efforts to muster support for African colonization, the society inflamed popular feeling against free blacks. The high rate of black immigration to the state in the 1820s made this all the easier to accomplish. Although only a few years earlier the Ohio assembly had considered abolishing the Black Laws, it instead passed further restrictions in 1829. These statutes made blacks ineligible for public poor relief and excluded children of color from attending public schools with whites. In every respect possible, blacks were effectually cut off from the full rights of citizenship.[31]

Although the Black Laws were still not being fully enforced, by the end of the 1820s life had become increasingly difficult for the black people of Ohio. John Malvin, a man of color from Virginia who emigrated to Ohio in 1827, remarked, "I thought upon coming to a free state like Ohio that I would find every door thrown open to receive me, but from the treatment I received by the people generally, I found it little better than in Virginia." Malvin's experience was not exceptional. A free black woman who emigrated to Canada came to a similar conclusion and declared, "I lived in Ohio ten years, as I was married there,—but I would about as lief live in the slave States as in Ohio." According to a former Ohio resident named George Williams, "I suffered on account of my color. Many looked on me with contempt because I was colored." William Lyons found employment in Columbus, but "the journeymen all left the shop—wouldn't work in the shop with a colored man."[32]

This hostile racial environment culminated in a destructive riot in Cincinnati in 1829. The city had experienced conspicuous growth in its black population in the preceding few years. Unofficial estimates count 690 blacks in 1826 and 2,258 in 1829.[33] Although these men and women fulfilled a vital economic role, the city's white citizens held them in low esteem. As early as 1808 an ordinance had addressed as a problem "black and mulatto persons of idle lives and vicious habits" who engaged in "Riots, quarrels and disturbances."[34] Such sentiments intensified by the mid-1820s. Cincinnati's local chapter of the ACS, organized in 1826, quickly boasted some 120 members. In 1828, citizens petitioned the city "to take measures to prevent the increase of the Negro population within the city."[35] Cincinnati authorities finally responded by announcing in July of the following year that they would begin aggressively enforcing the Black Laws of 1804 and 1807. An untold number of black Cincinnatians were fugitives without freedom papers, and the five-hundred-dollar bond requirement was beyond the means of many black residents who did possess documents of freedom. Some blacks responded by investigating prospects for colonization in Canada, but frustrations among certain whites erupted in spontaneous violence before anything could be effected. Throughout the weekend of August 22 and 23, 1829, a mob of white residents rioted against their black neighbors and competitors for menial employment. By the end of the year, approximately half of Cincinnati's black population had departed. Ironically, many of those who departed belonged to the "sober, honest, industrious and useful" portion of Cincinnati's black population—the more impoverished lacked the financial means to relocate.[36]

At about the same time, the surge of racial hostility in Cincinnati and elsewhere in Ohio began generating an opposite reaction. By this point few opponents of slavery still viewed African colonization as a benevolent cause, and a small but dedicated core of abolitionists began to emerge. Some became active in organizing black schools, believing this to be the best means for blacks, once free, to escape menial labor and its accompanying poverty. Others plunged into deeper waters. The Emancipation Society of Zanesville, established in 1826, declared as its mission the "total extinction of slavery in the United States at the earliest practiceable period." The Aiding Abolition Society in Monroe County, organized the same year, advocated the "entire abolition of slavery." It promoted boycotting produce grown by slave labor, disseminated antislavery literature, and petitioned the state legislature to repeal Ohio's Black Laws. Members were required to declare themselves not only opposed to slavery but also ready to work "consistently, towards the immediate abolition of slavery." Furthermore, membership required according free people of color all the rights and privileges of citizenship enjoyed by the white population. The Columbiana Abolition Society, organized in 1827 and dedicated to "abolition, without condition or qualification," reportedly attracted more than five hundred members in its first year of existence. The same year saw other efforts to organize abolition societies. A group of free blacks undertook to establish a similar organization in Belmont County. Abolitionist organizations also appeared in Jefferson and Stark counties. Whereas Ohio's earlier antislavery advocates had generally been content to allow slavery to continue in states where it already existed, an influential sector now adopted complete abolition as its goal.[37]

Many members of these organizations, as well as the denominationally based networks created by John Rankin and others, became actively engaged in what later became famous as the Underground Railroad.[38] The majority of fugitives lacked reliable knowledge of the route to Canada, much less of how to evade slave catchers and Ohioans who were eager to collect the monetary rewards offered to those who apprehended runaways.[39] With slave states to the south and Canada directly north, Ohio may well be the state whose citizens most extensively engaged in aiding fugitive slaves.

Early fugitive assistance tended to be isolated and spontaneous. In 1812, for example, in the town of Worthington, an enraged group of citizens took an alleged fugitive who had been captured and bound with ropes and forced to walk behind his mounted master before a sympathetic local justice. After being declared free, he was promptly sent with a military wagon headed north to Sandusky. By the time the master returned with a writ to reclaim the man, he was already well on his way.[40] Some other communities encountered similar situations. A Franklin County newspaper, for example, reported in 1821 that an apprehended runaway from Kentucky had been liberated from custody by an unknown party of local citizens "a few days since . . . and was set at liberty."[41] In Montgomery County during the late 1820s, the children of a farmer named Peter Sutherland discovered a black man cooking in the nearby woods. The Sutherlands took the man, a fugitive from Kentucky, into their care. Unfortunately, a visitor recognized the fugitive and revealed his location to his purported owner, who soon came to reclaim him. Surprised by the appearance of the owner one day, Peter Sutherland grabbed a corn cutter and yelled a warning to the fugitive, who successfully escaped across the countryside. According to a white inhabitant who grew up near the town of Lebanon, "My first recollection of the [Underground Railroad] business dates back to about 1820, when I remember seeing fugitives at my father's house, though I dare say it had been going on long before that time."[42]

Most of the aid in this early period came from people of color, many of whom had witnessed the effects of slavery or were themselves former slaves and therefore reliably sympathetic. Speaking of Cincinnati, Levi Coffin, a leading organizer of the Underground Railroad, recalled, "The fugitives generally took refuge among the colored people." According to one of the Underground Railroad's first historians, the African American communities in Cincinnati and rural Jackson and Brown counties actively assisted fugitives.[43] Unfortunately, not only were Ohio's black communities the first place slave catchers tended to search, most were isolated and could do little to forward fugitives toward a safe haven. Coffin and other activists, valuing the racial connection, integrated Ohio's free black communities into a more extensive network as the Underground Railroad developed in the 1820s. As a point of first contact for fugitives, Ohio's black communities remained integral. As one historian stated, "To a Negro Abolitionist, few things could be so satisfying as helping a runaway."[44]

Early assistance from white people in Ohio's Underground Railroad seems to have come mainly from those of religious backgrounds. The tightly knit Quaker communities have been most closely associated with aiding fugitive slaves, but they did not act alone. Rev. John Rankin at Ripley and his Presbyterian network is said to have assisted an estimated one thousand slaves by 1817.[45] As early as 1825, people in at least sixteen Ohio counties are believed to have been assisting fugitives northward.[46] Southern slave owners placed advertisements for their runaways in newspapers throughout the state, often offering generous rewards. Sometimes this bait worked. But a core of true believers successfully escorted an impressive number of fugitives out of the country. This illicit network would escort thousands more in the years preceding the Civil War.

Historians of racial relations in antebellum Ohio have tended to emphasize the three dramatic and well-documented decades of abolitionist agitation that preceded the Civil War. Without question, however, Ohio's first three decades as a state deserve equal attention. The politics of race during these decades forced Ohio citizens to examine and re-examine their personal morals, explore various alternative solutions, and consolidate with like-minded residents. Due to Ohio's strategic political and geographic position, people were compelled to a greater degree than elsewhere in the nation to declare themselves and formulate the rationale for whatever position they eventually chose. The ambiguity that had marked Ohio's first decade gave way to an increasingly polarized situation by 1830. From a broadly embraced desire to restrict further black immigration at the beginning of the century, racial politics had split the electorate into two distinct factions. One was dedicated through means such as the Black Laws and the colonization movement to not only deter black immigration but ideally to expel the black population already in Ohio. Others found governmental measures inadequate and began undertaking illicit personal action such as offering harbor and aid for fugitive slaves. By 1830, the middle ground of moderation had shrunk and Ohio would quickly emerge as the vortex of the national dilemma.

Notes

1. On the Northwest Ordinance, see Jay Amos Barrett, *The Evolution of the Ordinance of 1787* (New York: Arno Press, 1971); Peter S. Onuf, *Statehood and Union: A History of the Northwest Ordinance* (Bloomington: Indiana University Press, 1987); and Frederick D. Williams, ed., *The Northwest Ordinance: Essays on Its Formulation, Provisions, and Legacy* (Lansing: Michigan State University Press, 1989). On the Northwest Ordinance and the issue of slavery, see David Brion Davis, *The Problem of Slavery in the Age of the Revolution, 1770–1823* (Ithaca: Cornell University Press, 1975) and Paul Finkelman,

Slavery and the Founders: Race and Liberty in the Age of Jefferson (London: M. E. Sharpe, 1996).

2. Governor Arthur St. Clair to President George Washington, May 1, 1790, in Clarence Edwin Carter, ed., *Territorial Papers of the United States,* 27 vols. (Washington, DC: Government Printing Office, 1934), 2:248. See also Richard Frederick O'Dell, "The Early Antislavery Movement in Ohio" (PhD diss., University of Michigan, 1948), 71–73; Finkelman, *Slavery and the Founders,* 53–54; and Eugene H. Berwanger, *The Frontier against Slavery: Western Anti-Negro Prejudice and the Extension of Slavery Controversy* (Urbana: University of Illinois Press, 1967), 19–20.

3. Frederick Hall, *Letters from the East and from the West* (Washington, DC: F. Taylor and William M. Morrison, 1840), 93. The 1802 state constitution prohibited involuntary servitude, except under the same conditions as pertaining to white inhabitants, such as apprenticeship. Adults of color could enter into a term of indenture if they were free and paid consideration for their services, with the term of indenture not to exceed one year. Agreements made outside Ohio were invalid. On indentured servitude in the region, see O'Dell, "Early Antislavery Movement in Ohio," 82–86, 137–42, and Emma Lou Thornbrough, *The Negro in Indiana: A Study of a Minority,* Indiana Historical Collections, vol. 37 (Indianapolis: Indiana Historical Bureau, 1957), 1–30.

4. "Journal of Thomas Wallcut," *Proceedings of the Massachusetts Historical Society* 17 (1879–80): 181–83; Henry B. Fearon, *Sketches of America* (London: printed for Longman, Hurst, Rees, Orme and Brown, 1818), 224.

5. Lois Kimball Mathews Rosenberry, *The Expansion of New England: The Spread of New England Settlement and Institutions to the Mississippi River, 1620–1865* (Boston: Houghton Mifflin, 1909), 178–86; William S. Kennedy, *The Plan of Union, or a History of the Presbyterian and Congregational Churches of the Western Reserve* (Hudson, OH: Pentagon Steam Press, 1856), 60–65, 79; O'Dell, "Early Antislavery Movement in Ohio," 43–47; Virginia E. McCormick and Robert W. McCormick, *New Englanders on the Ohio Frontier: The Migration and Settlement of Worthington* (Kent, OH: Kent State University Press, 1998).

6. James L. Burke and Donald E. Bensch, "Mount Pleasant [Jefferson County] and the Early Quakers of Ohio," *Ohio History* 83 (1974): 220–55; J. A. Caldwell, *History of Belmont and Jefferson Counties, Ohio* (Wheeling: The Historical Publishing Co., 1880), 544–45; H. E. Smith, "The Quaker Migration to the Upper Ohio, Their Customs and Discipline," *Ohio Archaeological and Historical Society Publications* 37 (1928): 35–85.

7. Stephen B. Weeks, *Southern Quakers and Slavery* (Baltimore: Johns Hopkins University Press, 1896); O'Dell, "Early Antislavery Movement in Ohio," 190–230, 381–88; Annetta C. Walsh, "Three Anti-Slavery Newspapers Published in Ohio Prior to 1823," *Ohio Archaeological and Historical Society Publications* 31 (1922), 172–212; Smith, "Quaker Migration to the Upper Ohio," 41–45; Thomas E. Drake, *Quakers and Slavery in America* (New

Haven: Yale University Press, 1950); Merton L. Dillon, *Benjamin Lundy and the Struggle for Negro Freedom* (Urbana: University of Illinois Press, 1966); Randall M. Miller, "The Union Humane Society," *Quaker History* 61 (1972): 91–96; Harlow Lindley, "The Quaker Contribution to the Old Northwest," in *Children of Light, In Honor of Rufus M. Jones*, ed. Howard H. Brinton (New York: Macmillan, 1938), 307–30; Burke and Bensch, "Mount Pleasant," 230; A. D. Adams, *The Neglected Period of Anti-Slavery in America, 1808–31* (Boston: Ginn, 1908), 108. Missouri's admission as a slave state was an extremely controversial topic in Ohio, where most people opposed the western extension of slavery. See Donald J. Ratcliff, "Captain James Riley and Antislavery Sentiment in Ohio, 1819–1824," *Ohio History* 81 (1972): 81–85.

8. Wilbur H. Siebert, *The Underground Railroad from Slavery to Freedom* (1898; New York: Russell and Russell, 1967), 94–96; John M. Barker, *History of Ohio Methodists: A Study in Social Science* (Cincinnati: Curt and Jennings, 1898); I. F. King, "Introduction of Methodism in Ohio," *Ohio Archaeological and Historical Society Publications* 10 (1901): 181–82; *History of Clermont County, Ohio, with Individual and Biographical Sketches* (Philadelphia: Louis H. Everts, 1880), 181, 462–63; A. H. Dunlevy, *History of the Miami Baptist Association; From Its Organization in 1797 To a Division in That Body on Missions, Etc., In the Year 1836*, 16–17, 147–57; Josiah Morrow, "Sketch of Rev. James Smith," *Ohio Archaeological and Historical Society Publications* 16 (1907): 348–52; Ophelia D. Smith, "The Beginnings of Presbyterianism in Butler County, Ohio," *Ohio Presbyterian Historical Society Proceedings* 4 (1953): 29; Andrew Ritchie, *The Life and Writings of Rev. Samuel Crothers, D.D., being extracts from his writings illustrative of his style* (Cincinnati: Moore, Wilstock, Keys, 1857); O'Dell, "Early Antislavery Movement in Ohio," 47–65, 181–90, 358–61; Fred H. Eastman, "The Planting and Development of Presbyterianism in Southern Ohio," *Ohio Presbyterian Historical Society Proceedings* 1 (1938): 6–19; and R. G. Galbraith Jr., *The History of Chillicothe Presbytery, From Its Organization in 1799 to 1889* (Chillicothe, OH: H. W. Guthrie, Hugh Bell, and Peter Platter, Committee on Publications, 1889), 144–45.

9. Wilbur H. Siebert, quoted in J. Blaine Hudson, *Fugitive Slaves and the Underground Railroad in the Kentucky Borderlands* (Lexington: University Press of Kentucky, 2002), 153; Larry Gene Willey, "The Reverend John Rankin: Early Ohio Antislavery Leader," (PhD diss., University of Iowa, 1976); Ann Hagedorn, *Beyond the River: The Untold Story of the Heroes of the Underground Railroad* (New York: Simon and Schuster, 2002). Rankin's influence extended far beyond rendering aid to fugitives through the publication of letters to his brother Thomas, who lived in Virginia and had purchased slaves (*Letters on American Slavery, Addressed to Mr. Thomas Rankin* [Boston: Garrison and Knapp, 1833]) and through his friendship with Harriet Beecher Stowe and her family. Portions of her novel *Uncle Tom's Cabin* were purportedly inspired by Rankin's relation of daring fugitive escapes, including a woman's hairbreadth escape across the partially frozen Ohio River in 1838. See O'Dell, "Early Antislavery Movement in Ohio," 365–67, and Forrest Wilson,

Crusader in Crinoline: The Life of Harriet Beecher Stowe (New York: J. B. Lippincott, 1941), 144–47. Rankin worked closely with an African American named John P. Parker, who at great personal risk ferried countless fugitives across the Ohio. See John P. Parker, *His Promised Land: The Autobiography of John P. Parker, Former Slave and Conductor on the Underground Railroad*, ed. Stuart S. Sprague (New York: Norton, 1996).

10. Worthington's statement is from the *Chillicothe Scioto Gazette*, August 28, 1802. Smith, *A Political History of Slavery*, 501–2, 494; Henry Howe, *Historical Collections of Ohio: Containing Collection of the Most Interesting Facts . . . Relating to Its General and Local History*, 3 vols. (1847; Cincinnati: Robert Clarke, 1849), 97, 284–85, 613, 634–37, 646–47; *History of Clermont County*, 337.

11. John D. Barnhart, "Sources of Southern Immigration into the Old Northwest," *Mississippi Valley Historical Review* 22 (1935): 49–62; Robert E. Chaddock, *Ohio before 1850: A Study of the Early Influences of Pennsylvania and Southern Populations in Ohio* (New York: Longmans and Green for Columbia University, 1908); O'Dell, "Early Antislavery Movement in Ohio," 38–40.

12. The exception was the *Steubenville Herald*, which declined to publish advertisements for runaways and unsuccessfully urged the other editors of Ohio newspapers to follow suit. See *Chillicothe Scioto Gazette*, June 15, July 13, August 17, August 31, 1820.

13. General studies of the Ohio Constitutional Convention of 1802 include Charles Thomas Hickok, *The Negro in Ohio, 1802–1870* (Cleveland: Western Reserve University, 1896); O'Dell, "Early Antislavery Movement in Ohio"; Frank U. Quillin, *The Color Line in Ohio: A History of Race Prejudice in a Typical Northern State* (Ann Arbor: G. Wahr, 1913); James A. Rodabaugh, "The Negro in Ohio," *Journal of Negro History* 31 (1946): 12–17; and Julia Perkins Cutler, *Life and Times of Ephraim Cutler: Prepared from His Journals and Correspondences* (Cincinnati: R. Clarke, 1890). Convention voting patterns are closely analyzed in Helen M. Thurston, "The 1802 Constitutional Convention and Status of the Negro," *Ohio History* 81 (1972): 15–37.

14. *Journal of the House of Representatives of the State of Ohio*, 2nd sess., 1803–4, 2:43, 4; *Journal of the Senate of the State of Ohio*, 2nd sess., 2:68; Salmon P. Chase, ed., *The Statutes of Ohio and of the Northwestern Territory, . . . from 1788 to 1833*, 3 vols. (Cincinnati: Corey and Fairbank, 1833–35), 1:393–94, 555–56. See also Stephen Middleton, *The Black Laws in the Old Northwest: A Documentary History* (Westport, CT: Greenwood Press, 1993); William Henry Smith, *A Political History of Slavery: Being an Account of the Slavery Controversy from the Earliest Agitation*, 2 vols. (1903; New York: Frederick Unger, 1966); and Hickok, *The Negro in Ohio*, 40–43. Governor Thomas Worthington, who opposed slavery and had manumitted his slaves, shared the widespread fear that Ohio might become a haven for "vagabonds or even criminal [fugitive] slaves" and facilitated enactment of the 1807 statute. Sarah Ann Worthington King, *Private Memoir of*

Thomas Worthington, Esq. Of Adena, Ross County, Ohio, Senator, Governor, etc. etc. by His Daughter (Cincinnati: Robert Clarke, 1882), 71–72.

15. Benjamin Drew, *The Refugee: A North-side View of Slavery* (1856; Reading, MA: Addison-Wesley, 1969), 242, 172, 262, 263.

16. See for example, John Hope Franklin, *The Free Negro in North Carolina, 1790–1860* (Chapel Hill: University of North Carolina Press, 1943); Ira Berlin, *Slaves without Masters: The Free Negro in the Antebellum South* (New York: Random House, 1974), 327–32; Brenda E. Stevenson, *Life in Black and White: Family and Community in the Slave South* (New York: Oxford University Press, 1996); and Sherrie S. McLeRoy and William R. McLeRoy, *Strangers in Their Midst: The Free Black Population of Amherst County, Virginia* (Baltimore: Heritage Books, 1993), 13. Despite the generally lax enforcement, government authorities could invoke the Black Laws at any time. The most renowned instance was in Cincinnati in 1829, precipitating riots there against the black community. See Middleton, *Black Laws in the Old Northwest,* 5–6, and Marilyn Baily, "From Cincinnati, Ohio, to Wilberforce, Canada: A Note on Antebellum Colonization," *Journal of Negro History* 58 (1973): 427–40.

17. The kidnapping of free black residents of Ohio was serious enough to elicit protective legislation in 1819. See Wilbur H. Siebert, "Beginnings of the Underground Railroad in Ohio," *Ohio Archaeological and Historical Quarterly* 56 (1947): 75. See also Minnie Shumate Woodson, "Black and Mulatto Persons in Jackson County, Ohio," *The Journal of the Afro-American Historical and Genealogical Society* 5 (1984): 5–7; and Carol Wilson, *Freedom at Risk: The Kidnapping of Free Blacks in America, 1780–1865* (Lexington: University Press of Kentucky, 1994).

18. Joan Turpin, *Register of Black, Mulatto and Poor Persons in Four Counties, 1791–1861* (Baltimore: Heritage Books, Inc., 1985), 15–28. Gender may have been a factor, since lower wages made women more likely to become public charges.

19. Irene M. Ochsenbein and Catherine F. Fedorchack, *Belmont County, Ohio, Before 1830* (n.p.: the authors, 1977).

20. Sheila J. Farmer Clay, *Black Legacy: African Americans of Champaign County, Ohio* (Trotwood, OH: the author, 1996), 11–12.

21. Highland County Court of Common Pleas, vol. 2, 45–46, 48–49, 57–58, 60–61.

22. Rose Shilt and Audrey Gilbert, *Montgomery County, Ohio Common Pleas Law Record, 1803–1849* (Dayton: Craftmasters Book Bindery, 1980), 62, 79; "Record of Blacks [Greene, Logan, Miami, and Montgomery Counties]" (microfilm), Ohio Historical Society, Columbus, Ohio; O'Dell, "Early Antislavery Movement in Ohio," 136, 144; Charlotte Reeve Conover, ed., *Concerning the Forefathers* (New York: Lewis Historical Publishing Company, Inc., 1932), 312–14. Perhaps as many as two thousand slaves were hired from the neighboring states of Kentucky and Virginia during this early period, usually on an annual basis.

23. Federal census figures for Ohio in the early nineteenth century are compiled in Chaddock, *Ohio before 1850*, 82.

24. These campaigns are succinctly summarized in Barbara A. Terazian, "'Effusions of Folly and Fanaticism': Race, Gender, and Constitution-Making in Ohio, 1802–1923," PhD diss., Ohio State University, 1999, 139–41. See also P. J. Staudenraus, *The African Colonization Movement, 1816–1865* (New York: Columbia University Press, 1961), 136–49; O'Dell, "Early Antislavery Movement in Ohio," 294–303; and Thomas D. Matijasic, "The Foundations of Colonization: The Peculiar Nature of Race Relations in Ohio During the Early Ante-Bellum Period," *Queen City Heritage* 4 (1991): 23–30.

25. The *Columbus Ohio State Journal,* July 12, 1827.

26. The *Columbus Ohio State Journal,* February 1, 1827, and September 18, 1828, quoted in Matijasic, "Foundations of Colonization," 25.

27. Staudenraus, *African Colonization Movement,* 136–49; O'Dell, "Early Antislavery Movement in Ohio," 317.

28. The most prominent case of group resettlement during the period before 1830 concerns the slaves of Samuel Gist, a Virginia planter who in his will manumitted nearly three hundred slaves. In 1818 Gist's executor settled one group in Brown County, Ohio, but hesitated to send the others at that time due to anticipated racial hostility (they were settled more than a decade later). For the best summary of the Gist bequest and the problems it entailed, see Philip J. Schwarz, *Migrants against Slavery: Virginians and the Nation* (Charlottesville: University Press of Virginia, 2001), 122–48. See also Michael Trotti, "Freedmen and Enslaved Soil: A Case Study of Manumission, Migration, and Land," *Virginia Magazine of History and Biography* 104 (1996): 455–80; Quillin, *The Color Line in Ohio;* C. G. Woodson, "The Negroes of Cincinnati Prior to the Civil War," *Journal of Negro History* 1 (1916): 1–7; William Buckner McGroarty, "Exploration in Mass Emancipation," *William and Mary Quarterly,* 2nd ser., 21 (1941): 208–17; "Transplanting Free Negroes to Ohio," *Journal of Negro History* 1 (1916): 302–17; William H. Pease and Jane H. Pease, *Black Utopia: Negro Communal Experiments in America* (Madison: State Historical Society of Wisconsin, 1963), 24–26; and O'Dell, "Early Antislavery Movement in Ohio," 158–61, 318–22.

29. "A Brief Exposition of the Views of the Society for the Colonization of Free Persons of Colour, in Africa," reprinted in *Quarterly Publications of the Historical and Philosophical Society of Ohio* 7 (1912): 81–87.

30. *Roll of Emigrants That Have Been Sent to the Colony of Liberia, Western Africa, by the American Colonization Society and Its Auxiliaries, to September 1843, and etc.,* Senate documents, 28th Cong., 2nd sess., 1844, 9:152–301. See also Chaddock, *Ohio before 1850,* 94–95.

31. 27 Laws of Ohio 72–73 (1828–29) and 29 Laws of Ohio 320 (1829). See also Terazian, "Effusions of Folly and Fanaticism," 113–17; Middleton, *Black Laws in the Old Northwest,* 34; and O'Dell, "Early Antislavery Movement in Ohio," 320–23.

32. John Malvin, *Autobiography of John Malvin* (1877; Kent, OH: Kent State University Press, 1988), 38–39; Drew, *The Refugee*, 233, 242, 252.

33. B. Drake and E. D. Mansfield, *Cincinnati in 1826* (Cincinnati: Morgan, Lodge, and Fisher, 1827), 57; *Cincinnati Directory for the Year 1829: To Which are Appended, Lists of State, County, & City Officers* (Cincinnati: Robinson and Fairbank, 1829), 158.

34. Town of Cincinnati, *Ordinances,* March 22 and September 20, 1808. See also Richard C. Wade, "The Negro in Cincinnati, 1800–1830," *Journal of Negro History* 39 (1954): 43–57, and Woodson, "Negroes of Cincinnati Prior to the Civil War," 6–7.

35. Cincinnati City Council, *Minutes,* November 19, 1828. Although Ohio's black population was distributed in small numbers in the rest of the state, more than two thousand blacks (approximately ten percent of the city's population) resided in Cincinnati by the end of the 1820s. Many were clustered in the neighborhood known as "Little Africa." See Drake and Mansfield, *Cincinnati in 1826,* 57; Berwanger, *Frontier against Slavery,* 34; and Wade, "Negro in Cincinnati," 44.

36. *Cincinnati Gazette,* September 17, 1829, quoted in Wade, "Negro in Cincinnati," 56–57. See also Baily, "From Cincinnati, Ohio to Wilberforce, Canada."

37. Carter G. Woodson, *The Education of the Negro Prior to 1861* (New York: G. P. Putnam and Sons, 1915), 245, 328, 329; O'Dell, "Early Antislavery Movement in Ohio," 383–88; C. B. Galbreath, "Anti-Slavery Movement in Columbiana County," *Ohio Archaeological and Historical Quarterly* 30 (1921): 359.

38. Most of what is known with confidence about the Underground Railroad dates to the period after 1830. Key works include William Still, *The Underground Railroad* (1872; New York: Arno Press and the New York Times, 1968); Levi Coffin, *Reminiscences of Levi Coffin, Reputed President of the Underground Railroad* (New York: Russell and Russell, 1898); Siebert, *Underground Railroad;* and Larry Gara, *The Liberty Line: The Legend of the Underground Railroad* (Lexington: University Press of Kentucky, 1961).

39. Gara, *Liberty Line,* 35–46.

40. Siebert, "Beginnings of the Underground Railroad," 71.

41. Advertisement for runaway quoted in McCormick and McCormick, *New Englanders on the Ohio Frontier,* 214–16.

42. Janet Smith Thobaben, "A History of Blacks in Centerville and Washington Township" (Centerville, OH: Centerville Historical Society, 1977), 7–8; R. C. Corwin is quoted in Siebert, *Underground Railroad,* 39 (pages 87–88 provide additional examples of early fugitive aid).

43. Coffin, *Reminiscences,* 297–98; Siebert, *Underground Railroad,* 32. See also O'Dell, "Early Antislavery Movement in Ohio," 236–37.

44. Benjamin Quarles, *Black Abolitionists* (New York: Da Capo Press, 1969), 167. See also Hudson, *Fugitive Slaves,* 40, 91–94. This was the case also in other regions. See, for example, James O. Horton*, Free People of Color:*

Inside the African-American Community (Washington, DC: Smithsonian Institution Press, 1993).

45. O'Dell, "Early Antislavery Movement in Ohio," 236–40.

46. Siebert, *Underground Railroad;* Wilbur H. Siebert, "The Underground Railroad in Ohio," *Ohio Archaeological and Historical Quarterly* 4 (1895): 44–63.

FIVE

How Colleges Shaped a
Public Culture of Usefulness

KENNETH H. WHEELER

At the end of the nineteenth century, John Patterson, the head of National Cash Register in Dayton, Ohio, learned that a bar was going to open in a building near his factories. Patterson preempted the situation; hc purchased the building himself and made it into a chapel, a meeting place for his employees, and a kindergarten for their children. Action of this sort was not uncommon for Patterson, who personified Progressive Era corporate welfare notions, but the name of the house is significant—Patterson called it "the House of Usefulness."[1] The term *usefulness* arises repeatedly when one studies nineteenth-century Ohio, and this essay contends that denominational colleges, chartered liberally by the state, helped to form a culture of usefulness in Ohio, especially through productivity, practicality, and piety. People affiliated with these colleges demonstrated these cultural values by supporting manual labor programs, alternative curricula, coeducation, and religious revivalism. The long-term significance of these publicly chartered but privately funded and organized colleges was the spread of this culture of usefulness to the public arena, a change exemplified by reform movements during the late nineteenth century and by the reform efforts of the Progressive Era.

In 1990 Andrew Cayton and Peter Onuf argued in *The Midwest and the Nation* that by the 1850s the Old Northwest had become dominated by a hegemonic bourgeois class. For Cayton and Onuf, bourgeois culture embraced a capitalistic market economy, encouraged gender roles that separated men and women, and was preoccupied with the self through self-development and self-control. If Cayton and Onuf were correct, then much of higher education in the Old Northwest represented a countervailing tradition. College after college in the region demonstrated ambivalence about the market economy by adopting and instituting manual labor programs that provided not wages but credit with an institution for whose good all were working. Historian Paul Goodman has written that manual labor combated bourgeois ideals and contained "radical implications for class, gender, and race relations" that, among other things, helped to question separate spheres for men and women. Another development that more directly eschewed gender separation, collegiate coeducation, was a product of the Old Northwest. And the culture of usefulness, hostile to the emphasis on the self, retained great power within Old Northwest higher education. In Ohio and the Old Northwest, manual labor, collegiate coeducation, and other deviations from educational norms represented the beginnings of a regional culture that despite inheritances from other places also became something new and unique, with significant implications for the developing nation.[2]

Prior to the mid-1820s, Ohio state legislators chartered four colleges, including two public universities, none of which amounted to much before 1825. About 1825, though, state legislators began chartering numerous denominational colleges; so many, in fact, that by 1860 Ohio had more colleges than any other state—more than twenty functioning colleges. State legislators recognized that the state simply did not have the financial resources to support public higher education, the bureaucratic apparatus to oversee these institutions, or the educational expertise to manage them. The state turned Ohio and Miami universities, both public, over to the Presbyterians and let the Presbyterians run the schools. But soon politicians decided to be even less in control and let churches and local communities provide the financial support, decide where to locate a college, operate it daily, and take the risks besides. This plan was not the norm in the nation. Compare Ohio to South Carolina, for example, which refused to charter any private colleges prior to the 1850s; or to Michigan, which, until the mid-1850s, saw private colleges as a threat to a comprehensive school system that culminated in the University of Michigan; or to Massachusetts, which had only four colleges by 1860, a legacy of its established religious past.[3] Unlike these states, where politicians retained much greater control over higher education, in Ohio the state willingly accepted a partnership with religious denominations to help create a civil society. State leaders did not abdicate their role in building civil society in Ohio, nor did they cynically maneuver to create that best government which governs least. Rather, they sought to contribute to the public good despite the limitations of their own power. They created institutions outside the authority of the state and not financially dependent on the state but also complementary to the goals of the state. The resulting variety of schools shaped the daily lives of Ohioans and informed Ohio, Old Northwest, and midwestern culture into the early twentieth century.

At the same time Ohioans were founding these colleges, they and other Old Northwest residents articulated ways in which they were distinct from other Americans, particularly from easterners. Some of them thought of themselves as "Buckeyes," but however they named themselves, their preoccupations were with distinguishing their differences. In 1835, for example, Eliza Dana wrote from Athens, Ohio, to a relative that a mutual acquaintance had "gone on to the East." Dana suspected the woman would be *"yankeyfied"* there and admitted, "I have got so sick of yankies that I don't want to see one, although my ancestors sprung from that *noble race*. I boast myself in being a true blooded Buckeye. . . . I admire an independent spirit and not one that will be governed by laws made by those over-bearing yankies." To Dana, the Yankee placed too much emphasis on laws and attempted to restrain people. Dana would have agreed with the observation of Unitarian clergyman James Freeman Clarke, who in 1833 found "the West to be a place where freedom of thought prevails. I say things constantly with effect that if lisped in New England would be overborne at once by the dominant opinions."[4]

Educators also testified to these regional differences. In 1834 Daniel Drake, noted Ohio Valley scientist, physician, and educational leader, addressed the members of the Union Literary Society of Miami University on the "History, Character, and Prospects of the West." Drake spoke about how educational environments shaped persons. Children "born in old and compactly organized communities," observed Drake, were "surrounded" by books, good schools with fine teachers, "ingenious toys," and "public lectures in lyceums."

As a result, Drake argued, "these children became "the objects of a sleepless superintendence" that "lays down the rules by which their growth in intellect shall proceed." These children "acquire[d] a copious and varied learning," and as adults displayed "a conformity more or less striking." Drake's characterization of the educational process in long-settled areas was at once complimentary and critical. Drake did not deny the advantages, but he also portrayed the adults who came out of this educational process as conformists, overly bound by laws.[5]

In contrast, Drake posited that the children of a "new country" had different opportunities. In the new country, the "want of arts and inventions" to solve problems led people to "invent and substitute others," which engendered "a spirit of self-dependence." Drake cited the "many opportunities for bold enterprize" and argued that the problems people faced "call forth ingenuity." Similarly, two years later, the incoming president of Wabash College, Elihu W. Baldwin, asked in his inaugural address "whether the unprecedented growth and other marked peculiarities of the West, do not call for a new style of education, and consequently for Colleges founded on some new and improved plan." Baldwin believed the new region indeed called for distinctive collegiate institutions. Educators, continued Baldwin, must consider "the unimproved state of a new county, . . . the heterogeneous character of the population, and the hardy, active and impatient spirit, by which young communities, made up of enterprising adventurers, are always distinguished." "Greater rapidity and energy in decision," asserted Baldwin, "and a more extempore method of doing things, a freer and bolder eloquence, now obtain here, than amidst the restraints and leadings of established forms and usages of the East."[6]

A lack of specialization was a marked characteristic of the West; while inhabitants would not attain the degree of perfection of the specialist, the varied demands of the region expanded the intellect. This same theme received a more extended exposition in 1838 from Andrew Wylie, president of Indiana University, who told an audience at Wabash College that the "division of labor . . . affords some striking illustrations of the effect which confinement to a narrow circle of thought has in producing mental imbecility." Wylie offered the example of a mechanic whose life consisted of pointing pins. Place the specialized mechanic alongside "the most unlettered, uncouth stripling you can find in the woods of Indiana," put the two of them in a predicament, and one would see who was more *"liberally educated."* "The man of pins is confounded and paralized. But the Hoosier, who has rambled over mountain and forest, and met, every day of his life, with some new object to awaken his attention, or some new adventure to sharpen his wit, and who . . . has tried his hand at almost everything, . . . gathers up his thoughts in a moment, and . . . extricates both himself and his astounded companion."[7] Drake, Baldwin, and Wylie agreed that the Old Northwest provided the most liberal of educations.

This liberal learning proceeded from the institutional structure of the region. Institutionally, according to Drake, the West lacked "the restraints employed by an old social organization." Drake told his listeners that "a thousand corporations,—literary, charitable, political, religious, and commercial, have not combined into an oligarchy" to erect "one set of artificial and traditional standards." One senses in Drake's words hostility to eastern norms and a desire that western schools be able to work outside the "oligarchy" in new ways. While some comments may betray a sense of inferiority or insecurity about not matching eastern patterns, Old Northwest college founders also consciously defended the reasons their colleges would differ from eastern expectations. "There are many in the Eastern States who are determined that every thing at the West shall be modeled after the traditions of the fathers," wrote a founder of Oberlin in 1837: "But let us inquire what kind of institutions are needed at the West."[8]

As for "usefulness," the idea was not limited to the Old Northwest. E. Anthony Rotundo, in studying American manhood in the East, found that eighteenth-century American men used the phrase "usefulness" constantly as a reminder about the obligations that individuals had to God and to the community. Fathers encouraged sons to be useful, and heroes were measured by their "publick usefulness." But Rotundo found that the term "usefulness" dropped out of favor at the beginning of the nineteenth century and was replaced by "self": self-improvement, self-mastery, self-cultivation.[9] The emphasis shifted from working in God's world to developing oneself. This change may be true of the East, but in the Old Northwest, usefulness remained central.

An integral quality of usefulness was productivity, and manual labor programs manifested this quality in Old Northwest colleges.

The manual labor movement was a national movement in the late 1820s and 1830s that was propagandized by Theodore Dwight Weld (1803–95) of the Oneida Institute in New York. Manual labor meant mostly that college students defrayed the cost of tuition by working, usually about four hours each day, on a college farm or in a college shop that made items that could be used at the college or sold for profit. The movement, though important, was short-lived, mostly because it proved universally unprofitable. By 1838 manual labor had disappeared from New England colleges; only a handful of programs persisted in colleges outside Old Northwest states. A year earlier, in 1837, a New England college student stated that he hoped to transfer to Oberlin because he had no opportunity for exercise beyond walking. He reported that many of his fellow students complained of "declining" health, "so that probaly [sic] many after haveing completed there [sic] Studies will not be fit for usefullness." Manual labor programs in the South also perished. At Kentucky's Centre College, students called the two college farms "Do Little" and "Do Less." The program soon ended. At Emory and Oglethorpe in Georgia, trustees discontinued manual labor within a year.[10]

North Carolina's Wake Forest, a Baptist institution, was more dedicated to manual labor, but at Wake Forest manual labor was controversial from the start. Supporters of the program recognized that opponents associated manual labor with degradation in their slave-based society. The *Baptist Weekly Journal* declared in 1832 that "one of the grand objects of the institution is to overcome southern habits and prejudices against manual labor and to promote habits of economy and industry." The experiment at Wake Forest lasted longer than at most other southern schools, but even at Wake Forest manual labor disappeared after five years' time in 1838. At Davidson College in North Carolina, students, led by the most wealthy among them, vigorously subverted the manual labor program through pranks and destruction of property. These students, many of whom were sons of plantation owners, had little acquaintance with manual labor and associated manual labor with enslavement or a low class status. A striking example of the meaning that many southerners ascribed to manual labor comes from a visit paid in 1839 to Jubilee College in Illinois by South Carolinian Robert S. Bailey, a medical doctor who reported about his visit in an Episcopal publication. The head of Jubilee, Philander Chase, escorted Bailey around the college. Bailey was particularly interested in the banks of coal that Chase was mining and mentioned encountering "a young man with a cart load of the coal." After the man passed, Chase explained that the fellow "was qualifying himself for the ministry, and . . . although we saw him so employed, he was nevertheless a gentleman that possessed talents of the first order." Chase was familiar with elite southern culture. He knew what Bailey and his readers would presume about a student who mined coal, thus Chase stated explicitly that "although" a student performed manual labor, he was "nevertheless" a talented gentleman.[11]

In the Old Northwest states, manual labor remained vital, and the rhetoric in support of manual labor continued. In 1854 Horace Mann of Antioch College knew his Cincinnati audience when he admonished, "We must pay far more attention to the health of the students." Mann claimed that the faculty believed in manual labor; the professors "encourage manual labor in every practicable way; and if a liberal public, or a liberal individual, would give us land for agricultural, or even for horticultural purposes," said Mann, "we promise them that the old injunction, *to till the ground and dress it,* shall not be forgotten." The manual labor program lasted into the 1850s at Oberlin College, and in that decade the United Brethren actually began manual labor programs at colleges they founded in both Ohio (Otterbein) and Iowa (Western).[12]

In the South, military drill replaced manual labor. The earliest prominent southern example of collegiate military instruction was the University of Virginia. Thomas Jefferson recommended that the school include military drill for its students. When the university opened in 1824 the board of trustees required that all students perform military drill weekly under the direction of a military instructor. Military instruction, military companies, and drill characterized many southern colleges, especially during and after the 1840s. Southerners particularly liked military training because they believed such training would encourage discipline, which contemporaries claimed was lacking in many southern males. Another virtue of military groups, according to proponents, was their tendency to make students equal, especially through military uniforms.[13] But although such uniforms may have made *students* equal to each other as gentlemen and men of honor, they severely distinguished the students from nonstudents, especially persons of a lower social class. By way of comparison, students who worked at manual labor were made equal not only to each other but also to other laborers.

In the Northeast, some colleges had military programs. West Point was, of course, a military academy. Still, in comparison to the South, schools in New England and elsewhere in the East adopted military companies and curricula at a slow rate. It was more common in the East for schools to replace manual labor with gymnastics. Gymnastics did not extend farther south than Virginia, where both the University of Virginia and Randolph-Macon College had gymnastics. A lithograph of the Randolph-Macon campus on a diploma from 1860 includes parallel bars, rings, and other bars. Georgetown University in Washington, D.C., had students who fenced and boxed, performed chin-ups, and threw weights, although handball was the favorite exercise. Other eastern schools that had introduced gymnastics by the end of the antebellum period included Princeton, Yale, Dartmouth, Middlebury, Bowdoin, and Amherst.[14]

Military drill and gymnastics are forms of exercise, but they are unproductive forms of exercise and were almost entirely absent from Old Northwest colleges prior to the 1860s. Old Northwesterners were most likely to stick with manual labor because they were producers—they believed in making things. So while some college students carried firearms on the parade ground and others dangled from rings and bars, Old Northwest students swung axes, turned the lathe, and milked the cows.

A related aspect of productivity was an action orientation. The idea that Old Northwesterners were active was commonplace. In 1840 Lewis Clarke, a seminary student at Andover Theological Seminary in Massachusetts, wrote to his brother in Ohio that Lyman Beecher of Lane Seminary in Cincinnati had come to Andover for a few days. Beecher had encouraged the Andover students to serve as ministers in the West, and Clarke confessed, "I have sometimes been half sorry I did not go to Lane Sem. instead of coming here—This is the better place for study:—that for making active, efficient men." In 1848 one Ohio student wrote to a friend, "I tell you what, the Ohioans learn faster, live faster, arive faster, & die faster than Pennsylvanians." This trait was reportedly not confined to the colleges. A New Englander who visited Ohio in 1850 framed the differences between New Englanders and Ohioans this way: "A Yankee takes every thing coolly and sits down and calculates the exact issue of his plans and projects. . . . But the Buckeye dives right into things with all his might, and begins to pull and haul, very much like a fractious horse hitched to a heavy stone."[15] Old Northwest colleges encouraged this bent toward action and productivity when they stuck with their manual labor programs longer than colleges in other regions.

A second element in this culture of usefulness was practicality. Old Northwest students were, on average, the oldest college students in the nation. When a Kenyon College student reported in 1830 that in his college "there [we]re many between twenty and thirty years of age, and even older," he was identifying a regional trend. For example, the average age at graduation from Oberlin during the antebellum period was twenty-five years; fewer than 5 percent of entering Oberlin students were under age seventeen during the 1840s and 1850s. By way of contrast, almost half of incoming college students at Harvard in the 1830s were under age seventeen. At other mid-Atlantic schools, such as Columbia and the University of Pennsylvania, over 60 percent of entering college students were under seventeen in both the 1830s and 1850s. Even more youthful, southern college students had the lowest average ages among students of all regions. Partly because Old Northwest students were, on average, older, they knew what they wanted to study; consequently the curricula in Old Northwest colleges were often designed for utility rather than gentility. Old Northwesterners sometimes modified the classical education of most eastern and southern colleges, substituting Latin with Hebrew, thus making ancient language study conducive to reading the Old Testament, rather than Roman authors, in the original language. Other students dispensed with ancient languages altogether and took what people called the "scientific" course of study. Farmers' College outside Cincinnati designed a curriculum in scientific agriculture in the late 1840s. This Old Northwest collegiate landscape of "mental, moral, and physical" education contrasted sharply with the classical model that dominated the East and South.[16]

Coeducation was another departure from the norm. Oberlin, as is well known, first established "joint education" of the sexes, but it is less well known that coeducation flourished in the Old Northwest and farther west. By 1860 a score of colleges were coeducational—more in Ohio than in any other state. No coeducational colleges existed in New England and the South, where women attended single-sex colleges, most of which taught a curriculum centered upon the ornamental or genteel.[17]

The Old Northwest nurtured collegiate coeducation for a variety of reasons. First, Ohio politicians, and those of most of the other Old

Northwest states, created the conditions in which coeducation could flourish when they handed out charters to literally dozens of different denominations and then exerted almost no oversight (or pressure) on these groups to conform to certain norms. The one attempt to take away an Ohio college charter (an attack on Oberlin because of its abolitionist character) failed. Thus these colleges operated within a mostly unrestricted environment as long as the supporters were satisfied. Also, many of the denominations that started coeducational colleges were splinter groups and marginal religious groups. These churches tended to have members who were rural, not highly educated, and not terribly concerned about being respectable in the eyes of educated elites. The much larger Methodist church, which partially shared these characteristics, also founded a number of coeducational colleges in the Old Northwest. One consideration that held back collegiate coeducation elsewhere was that people feared that a coeducational school would be seen as the equivalent of an academy, where boys and girls acquired rudimentary education, and therefore as not sufficiently rigorous. Founders of coeducational colleges were more interested in results than in appearances. Furthermore, these college leaders often came out of a rural and evangelical Protestantism that called for people to reform society. Women were no less responsible for reform than men, and people in the Old Northwest widely recognized the college as a place where one could become useful through greater knowledge and learning. Thus Old Northwest practicality is found in the belief that if women could become useful by going to college with men, they should go to college. Finally, almost no evidence exists that Old Northwest men minded going to college with women, a far different situation from that which obtained in the East and South, where male college students were much more insistent that they have only males as college classmates. Old Northwest gender norms meant not only that male Old Northwest college students preferred manual labor to military drill and gymnastics but also that they were accustomed to a rural heterogeneity that made them more receptive to having women as fellow students.[18]

A third quality of usefulness was piety. Charles Grandison Finney (1792–1875), the great evangelist who joined the Oberlin faculty in 1835, told converts "to *aim at being useful in the highest degree possible*," which meant *"usefulness in religion."* Many Old Northwest college students took these considerations seriously. Nineteen-year-old Aaron

Sadner Lindsley was working at a newspaper press in Illinois in 1837 when he introduced himself to Charles Finney of Oberlin College by writing, "I am a poor young man, endeavoring to enter the gospel ministry." Lindsley explained that the year before, "at a camp meeting, I believe I gave my heart to God; and I now desire to become a useful man." One Old Northwest college student who agonized over what vocation to pursue concluded in 1846 to embrace "duty," which meant to him, "'Obey and serve you[r] God, and do all you can for the benefit of your *Country* and the *Human race* in general.'" Females also heard this call to piety. In 1836 forty-three young Oberlin women recorded their intentions for the future. Most wanted to teach or become missionaries. Nine expected to "prepare for whatever station the Lord directs" or enter "some sphere of Christian usefulness." Most of these women expected to use their education to enhance their religious calling. They were similar to the well-wisher who in 1855 instructed a student at the Ohio Wesleyan Female College, "'We should measure our lives by usefulness, not by years.' May you prepare for usefulness by earnestly cultivating both mind and heart. Then live for some high and holy purpose."[19]

A chief instrument of inculcating piety in Old Northwest colleges was the religious revival. Most Ohio colleges had revivals annually; classes were often suspended for days or even weeks to allow religious feeling to have full sway. Revivals on college campuses were not exclusive to the West, but they were more common in the West than in the East. In 1837 a Middlebury student desired to transfer to Oberlin to protect his piety because everyone at Middlebury concurred "that as a general thing, students come out of college with less religion or piety than they had when they went in." Ohio students never complained similarly. If anything, they protested that the moral and religious influences of the college were too strong. In 1839 Rutherford B. Hayes was among only ten students not "changed" when a revival swept through Kenyon College in Ohio. Hayes complained, "Every single one of my best friends are 'gone,'" converted by the revival. Through these revivals and the unremitting efforts of college leaders to produce piety among their students we see how this part of the culture of usefulness shaped students as they considered their life goals and vocations.[20]

In 1883, in the *North American Review*, a writer discussing women in higher education commented that collegiate coeducation "was an innovation that would scarcely been possible, except in a new country where social prescription had no existence, where manual labor was almost a necessary adjunct to study, and where economy made it advisable. . . . It was natural that the example thus set [at Oberlin] should be followed, first in the great West, amid a population that was remarkable for its freshness and physical vigor, its passion for progress, and consequently its disregard for conventionality." Ohio was the fountainhead of the culture of usefulness that this observer so accurately described. Political leaders encouraged the growth of usefulness and thus paved the way for an incipient regional culture by chartering numerous denominational colleges; in the process, they revealed ways that nineteenth-century state governments could be important without relying on a twentieth-century bureaucracy. As Ohioans and others in the Old Northwest built regionally appropriate institutions, the distinctiveness of their colleges reflected and shaped their action-oriented culture through manual labor, evolving curricula, coeducation, and religious revivalism. As students roomed and boarded in townspeople's homes and taught winter schools, as graduates dispersed, and as townspeople interacted with college personnel and heard sermons and lectures, the college influence spread. This culture underlay the participation of later midwesterners in areas as diverse as temperance, laboratory science at land-grant colleges, and the invention and reform of the Progressive Era that produced a John Patterson and his House of Usefulness.[21] If we are to understand that Midwest, we must note the culture of usefulness that Ohioans in the early republic built with the crucial participation of and contributions from colleges.

Notes

1. Raymond Boryczka and Lorin Lee Cary, *No Strength without Union: An Illustrated History of Ohio Workers, 1803–1980* (Columbus: Ohio Historical Society, 1982), 155; and Samuel Crowther, *John H. Patterson: Pioneer in Industrial Welfare* (Garden City, NY: Doubleday, Page, 1923).

2. Andrew R. L. Cayton and Peter S. Onuf, *The Midwest and the Nation: Rethinking the History of an American Region* (Bloomington: Indiana University Press, 1990), especially xvii–xviii, 45, 51, 54, 56–57, 63; Paul Goodman, "The Manual Labor Movement and the Origins of Abolitionism," *Journal of the Early Republic* 13 (1993): 355–88 (quotation, 388).

3. On Ohio higher education prior to 1825, see William T. Utter, *The Frontier State: 1803–1825,* vol. 2 of *The History of the State of Ohio,* ed. Carl Wittke (Columbus: Ohio State Archaeological and Historical Society, 1942), 411–13. Beyond Ohio (1804) and Miami (1809) Universities, Ohio chartered Cincinnati University (1809) and Worthington College (1819). The charters for educational institutions issued by the Ohio state legislature are listed in Edward A. Miller, "The History of Educational Legislation in Ohio from 1803 to 1850," *Ohio State Archaeological and Historical Quarterly* 27 (1919): 117–18. On Presbyterian control of Ohio and Miami Universities, see "Report of the Ohio Conference on Education," *Western Christian* Advocate, October 18, 1842. On antebellum colleges in each state, see the appendices in Colin B. Burke, *American Collegiate Populations: A Test of the Traditional View* (New York: New York University Press, 1982). On South Carolina, see Daniel Walker Hollis, *South Carolina College,* vol. 1, *University of South Carolina* (Columbia: University of South Carolina Press, 1951), 172–73. On Michigan, see Willis Dunbar, "Public versus Private Control of Higher Education in Michigan, 1817–1855," *Mississippi Valley Historical Review* 22 (1935): 388–91.

4. Eliza Dana to Mary B. "Polly" Dana, October 19, 1835, Box 1, Folder 9, MSS 181, Dana Family Papers, Ohio Historical Society (hereafter OHS; emphasis in original); James Freeman Clarke to Margaret Fuller, December 19, 1833, quoted in John W. Thomas, *James Freeman Clarke: Apostle of German Culture to America* (Boston: John W. Luce, 1949), 58.

5. Daniel Drake, "Discourse on the History, Character, and Prospects of the West: Delivered to the Union Literary Society of Miami University, Oxford, Ohio, at their Ninth Anniversary, September 23, 1834. By Daniel Drake, M.D." (Cincinnati: Truman and Smith, 1834), reprinted in *Physician to the West: Selected Writings of Daniel Drake on Science & Society,* ed. Henry D. Shapiro and Zane L. Miller (Lexington: University Press of Kentucky, 1970), 240–59 (quotations on 242).

6. Drake, "Discourse," 244; Elihu W. Baldwin, "An Address Delvered in Crawfordsville, Indiana, July 13, 1836" (Cincinnati: James & Gazlay, 1838), 12–13.

7. A. Wylie, "An Address Delivered Before the Philomathean Society of the Wabash College, By A. Wylie, D.D., July 10, 1838" (Bloomington, IA: Philomathean Society, n.d.) (emphasis in original).

8. Drake, "Discourse," 244; P. P. Stewart to Levi Burnell, April 10, 1837, Roll 4, Frame 131, "Letters Received by Oberlin College, 1822–1866," Archives, Oberlin College, Oberlin Ohio (hereafter Oberlin Archives).

9. E. Anthony Rotundo, "Body and Soul: Changing Ideals of American Middle-Class Manhood, 1770–1920," *Journal of Social History* 16 (1983): 24–26.

10. Theodore D. Weld, *First Annual Report of the Society for Promoting Manual Labor in Literary Institutions* . . . (New York: S. W. Benedict, 1833). On New England, see Henry S. Wheaton to Asa Mahan, June 5, 1838, Roll

5, Frames 266–67, "Letters Received by Oberlin College, 1822–1866," Oberlin Archives, in which Wheaton writes that he hopes to enter Oberlin "for the reason that there is no Manual Labor College in New England," and Franklin Merrill to Asa Mahan, June 17, 1837, Roll 4, Frames 294–95, "Letters Received by Oberlin College, 1822–1866," Oberlin Archives. On the South, see James Insley Osborne and Theodore Gregory Gronert, *Wabash College: The First Hundred Years, 1832–1932* (Crawfordsville, IN: R. E. Banta, 1932), 33; Henry Morton Bullock, *A History of Emory University* (Nashville: Parthenon Press, 1936), 45, 53, 67, 81; and Allen P. Tenkersley, *College Life at Old Oglethorpe* (Athens: University of Georgia Press, 1951), 4–5.

11. George Washington Paschal, *History of Wake Forest College*, 3 vols. (Wake Forest, NC: Wake Forest College, 1935), 1:65–91; *Baptist Weekly Journal*, November 16, 1832, quoted in Carl B. Wilson, "The Baptist Manual Labor School Movement in the United States: Its Origin, Development, and Significance," *The Baylor Bulletin* 40 (1937): 101; Mary D. Beaty, *A History of Davidson College* (Davidson, NC: Briarpatch Press, 1988), 21–22; Robert S. Bailey, "Narrative of a Visit to the Right Rev. Philander Chase, Bishop of Illinois," *The Charleston Gospel Messenger, and Protestant Episcopal Register* 16 (1839): 276.

12. Horace Mann, "Demands of the Age on Colleges: Speech Delivered by the Hon. Horace Mann, President of Antioch College, Before the Christian Convention, at its Quadrennial Session, Held at Cincinnati, Ohio, October 5, 1854" (New York: Fowler & Wells, 1857), 22–23 (emphasis in original); Robert Samuel Fletcher, *A History of Oberlin College: From Its Foundations through the Civil War*, 2 vols. (Oberlin, OH: Oberlin College, 1943), 2:661–64; Henry Garst, *Otterbein University, 1847–1907* (Dayton, OH: W. R. Funk, 1907), 115–19; Henry W. Ward, *Western-Leander-Clark College, 1856–1911* (Dayton, OH: Otterbein Press, 1911), 50–51.

13. Philip Alexander Bruce, *History of the University of Virginia, 1819–1919*, 5 vols. (New York: Macmillan, 1920), 2:116–17; Rod Andrew Jr., *Long Gray Lines: The Southern Military School Tradition, 1839–1915* (Chapel Hill: University of North Carolina Press, 2001), 1–25; Bruce Allardice, "West Points of the Confederacy: Southern Military Schools and the Confederate Army," *Civil War History* 43 (1997): 310–31; Allen Kelton, "The University of Nashville, 1850–1875," PhD diss., George Peabody College for Teachers, 1969, 568.

14. New Hampshire's Darmouth College had a student military company, while Vermont's Norwich University included military science and military drill for all students. Wilder Dwight Quint, *The Story of Dartmouth* (Boston: Little, Brown, 1914), 136; William Arba Ellis, ed., *Norwich University, 1819–1911: Her History, Her Graduates, Her Roll of Honor*, 3 vols. (Montpelier, VT: Capital City Press, 1911), 1:2, 13, 72, 78, 119, 116–17; Bruce, *History*, 2:337–39, 3:153; James Edward Scanlon, *Randolph-Macon College: A Southern History, 1825–1967* (Charlottesville: University Press of Virginia,

1983), lithograph reproduced opposite the title page and located in the archives of the college; John M. Daley, *Georgetown University: Origin and Early Years* (Washington, DC Georgetown University Press, 1957), 245–46; Joseph T. Durkin, *Georgetown University: The Middle Years (1840–1900)* (Washington, DC: Georgetown University Press, 1963), 21–22; Robert Emmett Curran, *The Bicentennial History of Georgetown University: From Academy to University, 1789–1889* (Washington, DC: Georgetown University Press, 1993), 173–75; Thomas Jefferson Wertenbaker, *Princeton, 1746–1896* (Princeton, NJ: Princeton University Press, 1946), 278; Brooks Mather Kelley, *Yale: A History* (New Haven and London: Yale University Press, 1974), 213; Quint, *The Story of Dartmouth*, 247; David M. Stameshkin, *The Town's College: Middlebury College, 1800–1915* (Middlebury, VT: Middlebury College Press, 1985), 171; Louis C. Hatch, *The History of Bowdoin College* (Portland, ME: Loring, Short & Harmon, 1927), 344–45, William Gardiner Hammond, *Remembrance of Amherst: An Undergraduate's Diary, 1846–1848*, ed. George F. Whicher (New York: Columbia University Press, 1946), 25, 27, 36.

15. Lewis Clarke to Oliver Clarke, August 1, 1840, Folder 1840–1841, Correspondence, Stevens Mss II, Lilly Library, Indiana University, Bloomington, Indiana; John Meyer to Henry Wolf, July 8, 1848, Folder 6, Box 1, Series 2, Oberlin File, Oberlin Archives; William E. and Ophia D. Smith, eds., "The Diary of Charles Peabody," *Bulletin of the Historical and Philosophical Society of Ohio* 11 (1953): 286.

16. Henry Caswall, *America and the American Church* (1839; New York: Arno Press and The New York Times, 1969), 34. On college student ages, see Burke, *American Collegiate Populations*, especially 126–29. On deviations from the classical curriculum in the Old Northwest, see, for example, Fletcher, *A History of Oberlin College*, 1:434–36, and Timothy L. Smith, "Uncommon Schools: Christian Colleges and Social Idealism in Midwestern America, 1820–1950," in *Indiana Historical Society Lectures, 1976–1977: The History of Education in the Middle West* (Indianapolis: Indiana Historical Society, 1978), 11–13, 15–20, 32–36. On Farmers' College, begin with Carl M. Becker, "Freeman Cary and Farmers' College: An Ohio Educator and an Experiment in Nineteenth Century 'Practical' Education," *Cincinnati Historical Society Bulletin* 23 (1965): 104–18.

17. Some of the best works on coeducation are Ronald W. Hogeland, "Coeducation of the Sexes at Oberlin College: A Study of Social Ideas in Mid-nineteenth Century America," *Journal of Social History* 6 (1972): 160–71; Barbara Miller Solomon, *In the Company of Educated Women: A History of Women and Higher Education in America* (New Haven: Yale University Press, 1985); Carol Lasser, ed., *Educating Men and Women Together: Coeducation in a Changing World* (Urbana: University of Illinois Press, 1987); and Doris Jeanne Malkmus, "Capable Women and Refined Ladies: Two Visions of American Women's Higher Education, 1760–1861," PhD diss., University of Iowa, 2001. On women's single-sex education in New England and

the South, see, respectively, Malkmus, "Capable Women and Refined Ladies," and Christie Anne Farnham, *The Education of the Southern Belle: Higher Education and Student Socialization in the Antebellum South* (New York: New York University Press, 1994).

18. The anti-Oberlin effort is described in Clayton S. Ellsworth, "Ohio's Legislative Attack upon Abolition Schools," *Mississippi Valley Historical Review* 21 (1934): 379–86. Marginal denominations in the Old Northwest that adopted coeducation in the 1840s and 1850s included the Free Will Baptists (Hillsdale College), German Reformed (Heidelberg), Universalists (Lombard), Associate Reformed Presbyterian (Muskingum), Associate Presbyterian (Franklin), Disciples (Eureka), Brethren in Christ (Otterbein), Swedenborgian (Urbana), and Quakers (Earlham). Coeducational Methodist colleges included Baldwin, Lawrence, Mt. Union, Adrian, and others farther west in Iowa. On the religious groups that began coeducational colleges, see Malkmus, "Capable Women and Refined Ladies," a paper presented to the History of Education Society, Chicago, Illinois, October 30, 1998. On resistance elsewhere, while contemporary evidence is scant or nonexistent because coeducation was not even considered, see Amy Thompson McCandless, "Maintaining the Spirit and Tone of Robust Manliness: The Battle against Coeducation at Southern Colleges and Universities, 1890–1940," *NWSA Journal* 2 (1990): 199–216.

19. Charles Grandison Finney, *Lectures on Revivals of Religion* (Cambridge: Harvard University Press, 1960), 404–5 (emphasis in original); Aaron Sadner Lindsley to Rev. C. G. Finney, June 6, 1837, Folder "Cowles Papers—undated and 1835–1839," Box 4, Series 3, Robert S. Fletcher Papers, Oberlin Archives; Homer Wheeler to Maro Wheeler, July 22, August 20, 1846, Folder 2, Container 1, Thomas, Wheeler, and White Family Papers, MSS 3412, Western Reserve Historical Society (emphasis in original); Lori D. Ginzberg, "Women in an Evangelical Community: Oberlin, 1835–1850," *Ohio History* 89 (1980): 78–88, especially 85–86; Princess A. Miller Autograph Book (unpaginated), OHS.

20. Franklin Merrill to Asa Mahan, June 17, 1837, Roll 4, Frames 294–95, "Letters Received by Oberlin College, 1822–1866," Oberlin Archives; Charles Richard Williams, ed., *Diary and Letters of Rutherford Birchard Hayes: Nineteenth President of the United States,* 5 vols. (Columbus: Ohio State Archaeological and Historical Society, 1922), 1:36–37. On revivals at Ohio colleges, see, for example, Norman Rovick, "The Impact of Religious Revivalism upon Five Selected Colleges [Western Reserve, Marietta, Oberlin, Granville, and Ohio Wesleyan] of the Mid-nineteenth Century," MA thesis, Ohio State University, 1965; Samuel Williams to Stephen [Widney?], February 9, 1847, copied into "Memoirs of Samuel Williams," 5:869, Box 2, Samuel Williams and Samuel Wesley Williams Papers, MSS 148, OHS, in which Williams describes a religious revival at Ohio Wesleyan; and E. Thomson to Thomas A. Morris, March 3, 1850, Box 1, Morris Papers, Archives,

Ohio Wesleyan University, Delaware, Ohio, in which Thomson, then president of the college, reports that Ohio Wesleyan had "enjoyed a revival every year" since its founding in the early 1840s.

21. W. Le Conte Stevens, "University Education for Women," *North American Review* 136 (1883): 30. On manual labor's ongoing effects, see, for example, Earle D. Ross, "The Manual Labor Experiment in the Land Grant College," *Mississippi Valley Historical Review* 21 (1935): 513–28.

SIX

"My whole enjoyment & almost my existence depends upon my friends"

Family and Kinship in Early Ohio

TAMARA GASKELL MILLER

"I feel reconcile'd myself to any step that will promote the interest of my family," wrote Lucy Backus Woodbridge to her brother in 1788. Her hometown of Norwich, Connecticut, she feared, did not hold much promise for her young children. But word from the newly opened Ohio Country sounded promising. "In this place," she continued, "their is very little for any one to expect of course we do not hazard much in the attempt, and the descriptions of the western world are truly flattering. If the half of them are just I shall chearfully quit my prospects here. It would be painful parting with connections I must leave behind me, but the society of our friends but poorly compensates for the want of a subsistence. We have a large circle of little ones dependent on us, and I know of no persuit that would give me more pleasure than that of provideing an easy Liveing for them."[1]

In the decades following the American Revolution, thousands of men and women from New England and the mid-Atlantic states said "good-bye" to parents, siblings, and extended kin as they left what they perceived to be a land of shrinking opportunity and headed for what would become Ohio. Land shortages and commercial development led a growing number of American families to adopt new strategies for providing for children and maintaining the household during these years and, eventually, contributed to new ways of thinking about the family. Historians of New England, the mid-Atlantic, and even the southern states have described how during the early republican and antebellum years older forms of family organization characterized by strong kin networks, domestic patriarchy, fluid boundaries with the wider community, and a focus on production gave way to a new ideal embraced by an emerging middle class, an ideal characterized by affectionate ties between immediate family members, egalitarian relations, privacy, and a focus on consumption and the socialization of children. Migration, as Joan Cashin pointed out in her study of migrants from the South to the early Southwest, could contribute to this process.[2]

The men and women who moved to the Ohio Country, however, made different choices. Despite the apparent break with kin that migration entailed, early Ohioans put great stock in ties with extended kin. In fact, generational ties may have been even stronger in early Ohio than in regions farther east. These men and women were not so much beginning a new life in the West as trying to maintain an old life in a new setting. Like earlier generations of men and women who had moved from Europe to the British colonies and then from the eastern seaboard into interior communities, a significant number of the men and women who moved to early Ohio did so because they believed in the importance of the lineal family.[3] They moved west in hopes of preserving the life they knew. Thus, as middle-class northeasterners, and even some southerners, began to adopt a more domestic, nuclear ideal of family life in the early decades of the nineteenth century, the men and women of southeastern Ohio set to work weaving together strong extended kin networks, both locally and with family in the East. In time Ohioans, too, came to place greater value on more intimate ties as Ohio developed to look more like the Northeast, but the shift in orientation was slow and uneven, and strong extended kin bonds remained an important component of family and community life well into the nineteenth century. The experiences of early Ohio families remind us, though, that the choices made by individual men and women, as well as larger societal changes, have shaped the history of family life.

Lucy and Dudley Woodbridge moved their family to Marietta, the first permanent Anglo-American settlement in what is now Ohio, in 1789, just one year after the initial settlement of this community. Though both the Backus and Woodbridge families were prominent in Norwich—Dudley was a lawyer and merchant, involved with his brother in the West Indies trade—Lucy and Dudley looked to the future with trepidation. Lucy's brother James Backus, who had gone to the Ohio Country as a surveyor in 1788, had reported back favorably about conditions, while Dudley told James that prospects in Connecticut were "gloomy and dull."[4]

Situated where the Muskingum River flows into the Ohio, Marietta was from the beginning a market town, located on navigable steams and serving an agricultural hinterland. It also became the county seat of Washington County. Though initially founded and settled by New Englanders, its location soon attracted migrants from the mid-Atlantic and southern states. Yet its hilly terrain led many immigrants to pass it by, and Washington County grew more slowly than did many counties farther west. In 1850 the commercial center of Marietta had a population of just over three thousand. Washington County's population was less than six thousand.[5] While atypical of Ohio Valley communities in its high proportion of middle-class New England families, Washington County in many ways represents the whole of Ohio. Here families from New England, the mid-Atlantic, and the South came together and mostly stayed apart. Here high hopes and expectations were followed by modest growth and provincial development. And here families were the mainstay of community life.

As Lucy Woodbridge told her brother in 1792, "My whole enjoyment & almost my existence depends upon my friends."[6] When Lucy moved to Marietta, her sister Clarina accompanied her. Clarina did not make her permanent home in Marietta but traveled frequently between the various branches of her family, helping to maintain ties between East and West. Four of the six Woodbridge children moved to the Ohio Country with their mother, daughters Lucy and Sarah and sons David and John. But Lucy's two oldest sons remained in Connecticut under the care of relatives to continue their education. Dudley Woodbridge quickly established himself as the new community's leading merchant, building on kinship ties both in the West and in the East. Dudley went into partnership with his brother-in-law James Backus when he opened his store in 1789. Later, when James returned to Connecticut, Dudley depended upon James to supply him with goods from the East. With the help of kin, the family prospered in Marietta.[7]

But, as Lucy made clear, a move across the mountains was not undertaken lightly. And the hardship fell on those who stayed as well as on those who left. Though a move west might benefit her children, Lucy knew that her leaving would be hard on her parents. Although they did not depend upon Lucy for economic support, they valued the emotional bonds they shared with their daughter. "Were I determined on going," Lucy confessed to her brother as she contemplated a move, "I should wish to conceal it from our good Parents; It would be an affliction to them tho they can well spare me." Lucy and Elijah Backus were not the only parents reluctant to see their children move to the Ohio Country. When Hannah Gilman of Plymouth, Massachusetts, moved to Marietta, her mother wrote to Hannah's new mother-in-law, "I once pleas'd myself with the fond expectation that my Children (particularly my daughters) would live near me and be the solace of my declining years." To Hannah she wrote, "If any persons are to be envied tis those parents, that have their Children settl'd where there is a possibility of seeing them."[8]

Yet fewer and fewer New England families could hope to have all their children nearby. In fact, it was precisely this desire to keep families together that prompted so many to move west. While for the Woodbridges it was the commercial opportunities of the West that beckoned, for most it was the land. Zara Howe, searching for land in Pennsylvania and the Ohio Country, expressed the motivation of many in a letter to his brother: "I want to git on some Land were I can have my children around me," he wrote.[9]

And it was the Ohio families that seem to have felt the separation most keenly. For these families, sentimental attachment coupled with economic realities heightened the significance of bonds with extended kin. While few collections of personal papers from the initial years of Washington County's settlement survive, quantitative as well as qualitative sources suggest that the experiences of and feelings expressed by Lucy Woodbridge and Zara Howe were not uncommon. Migration and residence patterns, choice of spouse, fertility rates, naming practices, and even divorce rates all suggest that early Ohio families may have placed even greater value upon extended kin ties than did the families that stayed behind.

As in other midwestern communities, the presence of kin was an important factor in determining whether or not a family stayed, especially in the earliest years of settlement.[10] Many families moved west either with or to join kin. By 1800 over one-third of household heads in Marietta shared a surname with at least one other household head, and that percentage increased over time as children set up new households near their parents. Half of these household heads remained in Marietta at least ten years, while just over one-quarter of those without a shared surname remained that long. Thus having relatives nearby greatly increased the chances that a family would stay. Over time, the importance of nearby kin as a factor in persistence declined as the economic significance of kin ties decreased and other institutions, such as churches and voluntary societies, helped bind individuals to the community. But in every decade those with family in town were more likely to stay than those without relatives close at hand.[11] Persistence rates based on surname, of course, tell only half the story. Could female kinship ties be easily identified, the relationship between the presence of kin and persistence would undoubtedly be even more striking.

While migration patterns established many extended kin networks in the West, marriage expanded them. Washington County's marriage records attest to the growing density of kin networks over the antebellum period. Throughout the early nineteenth century, the vast majority of Marietta men and women marrying in the county married someone from the same town. Eighty-nine percent of Marietta residents who married in the county before 1801 wed a fellow Mariettan. As the county grew and new towns were established, the percentage of intra-Marietta marriages declined somewhat. But it was the proportion of marriages to other county residents outside of Marietta that increased rather than marriages to partners farther away. As late as the 1840s, 71 percent of Marietta men and women marrying in the county married a fellow Mariettan, while only 12 percent married someone from outside the county.[12] Over time, therefore, local extended kin networks expanded.

The relationships between the Jennings, Reckard, and Fuller families are just one particularly vivid example of how kinship served to structure community life. Jonathan and Elizabeth Jennings and their five young children moved to Marietta Township from Pennsylvania in 1801 and settled near the mouth of the Little Muskingum. Elizabeth gave birth to four more children before Jonathan's death in 1808. Five years after the Jenningses settled in Marietta, in 1806, Calvin and Huldah Reckard moved their family of twelve children from Ashfield, Massachusetts, and settled near the Jenningses' farm. In 1808 Solomon and Ziporah Fuller left Ashfield with their nine children and settled near their old neighbors. The men of these families were mostly farmers and artisans, in such trades as shoemaking, blacksmithing, and tanning, and their sons would be the same. These families were also active in the Methodist church.

Within a few short years these families were extensively inter-married. In 1809 Mary Reckard married Stephen Fuller. Four years later Huldah Reckard married Samuel Fuller. In that same year the first of five Reckard-Jennings sibling marriages took place when Otis Reckard married Nancy Jennings. To further complicate the kinship ties of these families, Elizabeth Jennings, widowed in 1808, married a neighbor, William Nixon, in 1810. A native of Pennsylvania, William was a tanner and a widower with several children of his own. In 1811 Elizabeth's daughter Margaret married her step-brother George Nixon. These families that settled at the mouth of the Little Mus-kingum at the beginning of the nineteenth century were bound to-gether in countless ways. Sibling exchange served to help these fami-lies remain together in this corner of Ohio.[13]

While the Jennings, Reckard, and Fuller network was particu-larly dense, it was not unique. But though marriages both widened and deepened the bonds of kinship, marriage did not bring all the residents of Washington County into one big happy family. Young men and women tended to marry into families very much like their own. Like the Jennings, Reckard, and Fuller children, they chose their spouses from their parents' circle of friends. Young wives and husbands generally came from similar economic backgrounds and usually attended the same church. In many cases, their parents moved to Ohio at about the same time and were from the same re-gion. Marriage united families, but it did so within limits.[14]

The Barker, Dana, and Stone families provide an example of how kinship also bound more prominent families. All three of these families moved to Washington County from New England before 1795 and became prosperous farming families, among the most suc-cessful in the county. The marriages between these families served both to consolidate wealth and to confirm their status. These fami-lies were first joined when Elizabeth Dana and Joseph Barker, both of Massachusetts, married in 1789, just prior to moving to Marietta to join Elizabeth's family. The Dana and Stone families were united ten years later when Elizabeth's brother Luther married Grace Stone, the daughter of Jonathan and Susanna Stone. The Barkers, Danas, and Stones all shortly moved down the Ohio to Belpre. Even-tually Joseph and Elizabeth Barker moved up the Muskingum to

Union and Luther and Grace Dana moved back up the Ohio to Newport. But the families kept in touch and in 1814 family ties were strengthened when Elizabeth and Joseph Barker's oldest daughter married Rufus Stone, the brother of Grace Stone. Three years later Melissa Stone married Joseph Barker Jr. Thus, through sibling exchange and other relationships, these families that were now scattered throughout the county maintained their ties and demonstrated the importance of kinship.[15]

High birth rates also contributed to dense kin networks, and Ohio women had more children on average than did women in the East. Historians have long pointed to the steady fall in birth rates over the course of the nineteenth century as evidence of both declining access to land and an increased emphasis on the nuclear family. Families who moved west for more fertile and larger farms could better afford to have large families. They may also have been more interested in doing so. Throughout the antebellum years fertility rates were higher in Ohio than in the country as a whole, and birth rates in Washington County were similar to those for the rest of the state—a bit lower during the first forty years of the century but then leveling off at a rate a bit higher than the state average by the middle of the century. In 1810 Washington County had 2.25 children under the age of ten for every white woman between the ages of sixteen and forty-four, while the ratio for the country as a whole was only 1.82. By 1830 Washington County's fertility rate had declined considerably, to 1.72, but was still higher than the national average of 1.59.[16]

Naming patterns suggest that more than economics was involved. Not only did Washington County men and women tend to have large families, they chose to name their many children for extended kin. For the most part, Washington County's early settlers followed traditional New England naming practices, more often naming first-born daughters and sons for parents than for grandparents. But as new families formed in the West, parents began to name children for grandparents more often. On the other hand, Washington County parents were less likely to name a child for themselves than were their New England counterparts (see tables 1–3). These Ohio families were less likely than New England families to emphasize the importance of the nuclear family at the expense of lineal ties.[17]

Hannah Robbins Gilman was three months' pregnant when she left her mother in Plymouth, Massachusetts, to join her husband's family in Marietta. In November 1790 Hannah gave birth to a baby girl and named her Jane for the mother she had left. Hannah and Benjamin Gilman named their second child, a boy, for his paternal grandfather, thereby recognizing both sides of the family. They named their second daughter for Benjamin's mother and a later son for Hannah's father. One son was named Benjamin, for his father, but Hannah never did name a daughter after herself. They named two other children for ancestors of Benjamin on his mother's side. Hannah and Benjamin Gilman, in naming their children, emphasized generational ties.[18]

Not all families named children for grandparents first. Lateral ties also appear to have increased in importance, and parents frequently named children for the parents' own siblings. No one naming pattern stands out as clearly dominant in early Washington County. Some families placed more emphasis on generational ties, others on bonds with siblings. Most families chose names from both sides of the family about equally, suggesting that male and female ties were equally important. When parents honored one side of the family more often, it was generally because those relatives lived in Ohio while the others did not. While some parents, like Hannah and Benjamin Gilman, did name children for relatives left behind, it was the family that was part of everyday life that was most often recognized in naming.

Elizabeth Dana and Joseph Barker had ten children. Following traditional New England naming practices, they named their first-born son and daughter for themselves. One daughter they named Mary for both their mothers. They named one son William for Elizabeth's father but they did not name a son for Joseph's father. And they named three children for Elizabeth's siblings but none for Joseph's. Ties to Elizabeth's family were especially important, as it was her family, not Joseph's, that was in Ohio, and the couple recognized those ties in the names they chose for their children.[19]

Several of the Jennings daughters adopted a similar naming pattern. Margaret, the oldest Jennings daughter, had three children, all boys, with her husband George Nixon. Following the more lineal naming practices common in western Pennsylvania, Margaret and George named their first son Jonathan Jennings for Margaret's father. They named their second son William, for George's father, and the youngest, finally, they named George. Nancy and Otis Reckard, however, honored neither of their fathers in naming their children, though they had five sons. They named their oldest daughter Eliza-beth after Nancy's mother but named all the rest of their children for siblings—not surprising given the numerous sibling ties between their families. Delilah and Joseph Leonard Reckard chose names in a similar fashion. They had eleven children. They named none for grandparents and only the youngest son for his father. They named six children, however, for siblings.[20] In their choice of names, all of these Ohio families both honored and cemented their bonds with extended kin.

Of course tensions could and did arise within families, and di-vorce and desertion were also a part of life in early Ohio. Yet even evidence from divorces is revealing of the importance of extended kin, especially for women who found themselves both legally and economically subordinate to sometimes abusive or negligent men.

Lucy Woodbridge Petit, the oldest daughter of Lucy and Dudley Woodbridge, was granted the first divorce by the legislature of the Northwest Territory in 1800. Lucy had married Jean Petit, a doctor who resided in the French settlement of Gallipolis, in 1795. It was not long, however, before Lucy's matrimonial bonds became "matri-monial shackles." Lucy obtained a separation agreement in October 1798, and she and her young son returned to her parents' home.

In the divorce proceedings Dudley Woodbridge noted that, "Doc^r Petit treatment To his Wife was from time to time such that her Life was a Life of trouble fear and anxiety." Lucy also testified to Petit's cruelty, recounting the time he pulled a knife on her when she once pointed out that he was contradicting himself and the times in which he neglected her and deprived her of the aid of her family when she was pregnant. Lucy reported that "during a con-finement to her bed in a house near her father's he forbid any of her friends to enter his house & actually turned her mother out of it at midnight at a time when she was in great want of her assistance locked his doors against her sister when she the next morning called to see her." For Jean Petit, these women posed a threat to his au-thority over his wife. After this incident "he threatened to take her out of the reach of her friends so that he might treat her as he pleased . . . which was a threat he had often before repeated." From Jean Petit's perspective, the interference of Lucy's family weakened his control over his wife and undermined the nuclear family. Lucy's perspective was quite different. She clearly recognized the impor-tance of having her relatives nearby. As her deposition to the legislature declared, "she could not have considered her life as safe in his power, had he removed her out of the country as he intended to do—she firmly believes that the fear of her friends alone restrained him often from treating her with the most cruel personal abuse."[21]

While many women could count on similar family support, few had the financial resources of Lucy Petit. Elizabeth Jennings Nixon faced abuse by her husband, too, but like many other women, rather than file for divorce she just moved out. In October 1831 William Nixon advertised in the *American Friend and Marietta Gazette* that Elizabeth had left his bed and board about a year before and refused to return. He warned readers not to trust her on his account. Though he did not say why she left, evidently religious differences and alcohol had persuaded Elizabeth to leave. While both Elizabeth and William had been Methodists when they married, in later years William became a Unitarian. He also became an alcoholic and was known to be a tyrant at home. Elizabeth never returned to William Nixon's bed. Aged fifty-five and with several grown children nearby, Elizabeth was able to live by herself in Marietta until her death in 1852.[22]

Divorce was relatively rare in early Ohio. Although laws were liberal by nineteenth-century standards, throughout most of the antebellum period divorce rates in Ohio were lower than those in New England and Pennsylvania, though higher than those in the South. Washington County's divorce records are incomplete, but those that do survive suggest that divorce patterns were in keeping with those for the rest of the state. Women made up the majority of petitioners, and the number of spouses seeking legal separations increased over time. Both men and women most often listed desertion as the grounds for divorce. Adultery was the second most common reason given by men. Women were more likely to list abuse, cruelty, or drunkenness.[23]

Though both legal and, evidently, cultural constraints kept divorce rates low in early Ohio, more women, and some men, followed the lead of Elizabeth Nixon and simply left untenable marriages. Desertion rates, of course, are harder to quantify. In many cases, if not most, no public record was made. Yet we do know that women, at least, deserted their husbands in significant numbers because many men, like William Nixon, published notices of their wives' leaving their "bed and board" and thus absolved themselves of responsibility for debts their wives might contract. The number of men who abandoned their wives is much more difficult to estimate as few wives had a legal reason to publicize the desertion.[24] Divorce records, though, suggest that men also abandoned their wives in significant numbers. Men's greater mobility, in fact, made it easier to pick up and move. John Walker, for example, was just one of many men who traveled down the Ohio and Mississippi to New Orleans every year. In 1809 his wife, Mary, filed for divorce, claiming John had been "unmindful of his marriage vows" for several years past and had "left her to penury and want with the charge of a helpless infant." John had, according to Mary, also committed adultery with a number of women in New Orleans. The court granted Mary a divorce and guardianship of her child.[25]

The majority of deserted men, and probably of women as well, did not seek a divorce. Elizabeth and William Nixon were more typical, in that respect, than Mary and John Walker. Divorce was a last resort. Even Mary did not petition for a divorce until she wanted to remarry. Mary Walker married Elizur Carver less than a month after receiving her divorce decree.[26] Families were not always harmonious, but family values were such that conflict only rarely led to divorce—despite its availability.

By the time Mary Walker petitioned the court for a divorce from her roving husband, however, economic changes had already begun to alter the nature of family life and undermine the importance of extended kin networks. John Walker's trips to New Orleans were just one early sign of the growing commercial orientation of Ohio's farming families. By the second quarter of the nineteenth century Washington County's farmers had become even more extensively involved in commercial agriculture, and cash began to permeate the local economy. Household production declined, and both men and women spent more time preparing marketable commodities such as fruit and wool, which were sold in distant markets. A growing number of men, and some women, began to work for wages. Women from more affluent families found time to pursue their own educations and charitable activities. Women also began to allocate more time to such tasks as cooking, cleaning, sewing, and shopping as they strove to meet new standards of domesticity. Changes in religion, too, had an impact on family life. Evangelical religion de-emphasized the significance of ancestral lines and elevated the importance of close family ties.[27] All of these developments served to further link East and West, as Ohio came to look more and more like New England and the mid-Atlantic states rather than like the gateway to a distinctive region. As Ohioans developed strong local ties, they also strengthened bonds with the East. And as Ohioans became more firmly tied together by blood and marriage, they began to idealize the conjugal unit and the nuclear family more.

Yet the shift in emphasis away from the lineal family and toward the nuclear family was gradual and uneven. Only slowly did these Ohioans come to view the family as private, nuclear, and based in marriage. For many families, extended kin continued to be an important part of everyday life. By the 1840s, however, changing ideals were clearly evident.

Both fertility rates and naming patterns are suggestive of the new emphasis. As in the rest of the country, fertility rates declined as Washington County shifted away from household production and became more enmeshed in the market economy. Rates fell most dramatically in the commercial center of Marietta. Agrarian values persisted, though, and after 1830, while fertility rates in other parts of Ohio and the nation continued to fall, rates in Marietta and Washington County leveled off, at about 1.3 and 1.7, respectively. Initially settled by New Englanders, by the 1830s the county had significant numbers of emigrants from non–New England states. Gravitating to the towns known as the Seven Ranges, these families had more children on average than did families in towns dominated by those of New England origin. Demographic changes thus slowed the rate of decline. But even in decidedly commercial Marietta and in towns preferred by those of New England origin, fertility rates stabilized between 1830 and 1850 at rates higher than those of other regions. For many Ohio Valley men and women, lineal family values remained strong.[28]

Naming patterns too reflected these economic and cultural changes. The percentage of families naming children for grandparents rose steadily from 1788 through 1840, while the trend was exactly the reverse in Massachusetts. During these same years, fewer Washington County parents named first and second children for themselves than did New England parents. These patterns were in part a reflection of the growing numbers of migrants from the southern and mid-Atlantic states. The gradual shift from a generational to a nuclear naming system provides further evidence of the tenacity of lineal ties in spite of the growing significance of the nuclear family. By the 1840s, however, a change in naming practices was clearly evident as parents recognized their own parents in naming less often and instead named first and second children for themselves. And an increasing number of children received names that were uniquely their own (tables 1–3).[29]

TABLE 1

Naming Patterns by Marriage Cohort—Parents and Grandparents

cohort*	n**	1ST DAU. NAMED FOR			1ST SON NAMED FOR			2ND DAU. NAMED FOR			2ND SON NAMED FOR		
		Mo***	FaMo	MoMo	Fa***	FaFa	MoFa	Mo***	FaMo	MoMo	Fa***	FaFa	MoFa
pre-1781	10	10%	20%	10%	30%	10%	0%	44%	11%	0%	33%	0%	11%
1781–1800	19	17%	11%	11%	21%	11%	11%	22%	11%	11%	13%	0%	6%
1801–20	30	24%	3%	14%	18%	4%	25%	4%	12%	4%	9%	13%	17%
1821–40	45	8%	10%	23%	14%	11%	23%	7%	6%	9%	29%	7%	10%
1841–60	41	14%	3%	16%	20%	14%	14%	17%	0%	0%	21%	7%	7%

*Cohorts are based upon date of parents' marriage.

**Number; includes all those first marriages—or second marriages in which neither partner had children from a first marriage—for which the names of all children were known as well as order of birth, and for which the names of all four grandparents were known.

***In cases where a parent and grandparent shared a name, the child was considered to have been named for the parent.

TABLE 2

Naming Patterns: Percentage of Families in Which a Child Was Named for the Father or the Mother by Number of Children of Each Sex in the Family

	DAUGHTERS		SONS	
cohort	*1 or 2*	*3 or more*	*1 or 2*	*3 or more*
pre-1781	60%	83%	80%	78%
1781–1800	83%	93%	68%	86%
1801–20	45%	48%	46%	65%
1821–40	31%	45%	52%	61%
1841–60	38%	46%	50%	62%

TABLE 3

Naming Patterns: Percentage of Families with at Least Three Children in Which at Least One of Those Children Was Named for a Grandparent*

cohort	MoMo	MoFa	FaMo	FaFa
pre-1781	33%	33%	17%	11%
1781–1800	40%	57%	26%	14%
1801–20	33%	41%	29%	35%
1821–40	50%	56%	40%	40%
1841–60	21%	23%	13%	23%

*In cases where a parent and grandparent shared a name, the child was considered to have been named for the parent and was not included here.

Ironically, changing divorce rates, too, suggest the development of a new, more intimate family ideal. By 1830 divorce rates in Ohio and Washington County had begun a steady rise. In 1833 the Supreme Court of Ohio heard about 200 divorce cases. By 1842 the number had more than doubled to 444, during a period when the population of Ohio grew by just over 60 percent.[30] Part of the rise can be attributed to more liberalized laws as the Ohio legislature expanded the grounds for divorce.[31] But the higher divorce rates also reflected ideological changes. Despite relatively liberal divorce laws in the early years of the century, Ohio divorce rates were lower than those in the Northeast. Only once men and women began to accept the primacy of the nuclear family and the ideology of romantic love did divorce rates begin to rise.

The most compelling evidence of a change in family orientation, however, is found in personal papers. Letters between husbands and wives reveal that despite the endurance of strong kinship networks, by the mid-nineteenth century Washington County's women and men did begin to turn more often to their nuclear families for emotional fulfillment. As early as 1827, Nahum Ward, one of Marietta's wealthiest landowners, wrote from Washington to his wife of ten years, "I do really wish it may be so ordered that I may never cross the Mountains again without your blessed company. I was made a happy man when you consented to be mine . . . may nothing rise to mare the happiness we enjoy in the society of each other and of our lovely children." He echoed these thoughts in a letter to his brother in Massachusetts. "Although I am much from home, yet I am more attached to home than most men—I like to be in my family which is now becoming quite interesting . . . I like the play—and enter into all the little amusements of these little fellows."[32] Sala Bosworth expressed similar sentiments in 1840, one year after his marriage. "This year has been the happiest of my life," he wrote his wife, Joanna, shortly after the birth of their first child. "I have anxiously looked forward to the time when I could have a home and family of my own."[33] And when Frances Dana gave birth to her first child in 1846, her friend Mary remarked, "The girl of sober thoughts is a wife . . . is that not happiness, and now a mother, have you not arrived at the height of all imaginery earthly happiness."[34]

A focus on the intimate domestic circle, however, did not preclude strong bonds with extended kin. While Nahum Ward appears to have had little contact with his parents in Massachusetts, the Wards socialized frequently with Sarah Skinner's family in Marietta. Sala Bosworth and his wife, Joanna Shipman, had close relationships with both their families. Frances Dana's childhood in Belpre had been one of constant visits with relatives. Marriage and a move to Cincinnati removed her physically from her family circle, but through letters, visits, and news from friends she maintained her ties to her extended kin. But it is the letters of Ann and Dexter Cotton of Marietta that most beautifully illustrate the coexistence of intimate bonds between husbands and wives and parents and children with lasting ties with extended kin.

Ann Steece of Mount Vernon Furnace, Ohio, and Josiah Dexter Cotton of Marietta married in 1848, and Ann moved to Marietta, eighty miles from her parents' home. "There's something strange about the <u>love</u> of woman for man," Ann wrote Dexter three months after they were married. "She is so ready to relinquish all for his sake, go forth from home & friends depending entirely on him for happiness."[35]

Ann and Dexter's relationship was an intimate one and perhaps even a passionate one. When Ann was on a three-month visit to her parents' house, Dexter assured Ann, "I miss that smile & kiss <u>very very much.</u> I used to tell you that you kept me awake, but I believe I do not sleep as well alone as I did with you, even if you did keep me awake an hour or so after we went to bed."[36] Ann, too, missed Dexter's company at night. As she told Dexter, "There's no need in having a <u>husband</u> or <u>wife</u> if we do not live with them, <u>particularly</u> in the winter for its so very cold of <u>nights</u>—I almost <u>freeze</u> to death these cold nights, for when the clothes get off—as <u>you</u> know they will—there's no one to put them on again—there are a thousand <u>little</u> ways—as well as great ones—in which I miss you."[37]

Ann and Dexter Cotton were intimate friends, and they were also lovers. Dexter acknowledged the importance of sexuality to their relationship when he discussed the upcoming birth of their first child. Ann looked forward to childbirth with apprehension, fearing the worst. But Dexter assured her that there was little to fear by pointing to all the women who had gone through it numerous times. As he pointed out to Ann, "It is true there is some danger and suffering, but when you look around and see the thousand women that have passed through the trial and are willing to go through the same again and again for the sake of having their passions gratified, I do not think you have <u>much reason</u> to fear."[38] Of course Dexter did not know how many of these women actually had much say in the matter, but he does suggest that at least he and Ann found their sexual relationship mutually satisfying.

As Dexter pointed out, the love between wife and husband was naturally supposed to lead to the birth of children, and the relationship between parent and child was as sacred as that between husband and wife. Ann Cotton gave birth to her first child, Ella, within a year of her marriage. During her pregnancy Ann had worried that a child would take away from the love she and Dexter felt for each other. But Dexter thought the child would only strengthen their love. He believed that a child "is one of the links that binds husband and wife closer together. They then have a new interest to live for, which I should think would make them love each other more than ever." Dexter turned out to be right. By the time Ella was six months old Ann could not imagine life without her. "She is so much company, I do not know how I could live without her," she confessed. Dexter, too, was happy as a husband and father. "You used to be afraid, if we had a child, our love for each other would diminish in proportion as our love for the child increased," he reminded Ann. "Are you not satisfied that you was mistaken. . . . I believe Ella has been the means of increasing my [love] for you. Although I love her a great deal I love you none the less. I think I have love enough left for two more!! What do you say to that?" In fact Dexter and Ann had six more children, though three died in infancy.[39]

In many ways the Cottons were representative of other Marietta men and women of their generation and status. Their most intense emotional ties were to each other and to their children. Ann and Dexter expressed their love in romantic terms. They demonstrated their belief in the primacy of nuclear over lineal ties in the names they chose for their children—none of the Cotton children was named for a grandparent, though Ann and Dexter each named one child for themselves. The Cottons clearly had adopted much of the new domestic ideal.

But the Cottons were typical of Marietta couples in other ways as well. Despite their commitment to their own small nuclear family, Ann and Dexter still placed great value on their network of extended kin. When Ann moved to Marietta with her new husband she did not move into a home of her own but into the household of her mother-in-law. Ann and Dexter lived with Susan Cotton, Dexter's younger brother and sister, and several other boarders for a number of years before establishing a household of their own. Ann's two sisters, Mary Jane and Eliza, also boarded with Susan Cotton for a time. Ann also had frequent contact with her mother. She visited her family only three months after her marriage. Six months later she was back again. After Ella was born Ann spent three months with her mother while her sisters were away at school. In 1850 she made two more trips to Mount Vernon Furnace and another to Charleston to visit the family of Dexter's brother John. Though Ann once wrote to Dexter, "I'd much rather see you than any one els, or a thousand relatives," she traveled often and admitted that she would like to visit friends and family more if only Dexter were with her.[40]

Dexter, too, relied upon extended kin. His close bonds with his mother and sister did not weaken with his marriage to Ann. In fact,

Ann often felt that Dexter was more influenced by his mother and sister than he was by her, though Dexter denied that such was the case. Dexter was in no hurry to leave his mother's house, however. Two and a half years after their marriage, Dexter began to talk about building a house, "not because I care much about it but because I know you are anxious to have me build."

Dexter also relied upon extended kin economically and professionally. He studied medicine with his father and then at the University of Louisville. After practicing in Mount Vernon Furnace, where he met Ann, for a year, he returned to Marietta when his father died to take over his medical practice and drug store. In 1849 Dexter borrowed money from his new father-in-law for his store. Dexter also considered going into partnership with his friend Bill Thomas, the fiancé of Ann's cousin and closest friend, Mary Jane Cole. Extended family ties clearly continued to play an important role in the lives of both Ann and Dexter Cotton.[41]

Thus while Ann and Dexter adopted the ideals of the nuclear family, they realized that the nuclear unit was not and could not be self-sufficient. Extended kin continued to provide both emotional and economic support to individuals and families well into the nineteenth century. The sense of the family as part of a long chain stretching back over generations had certainly diminished. Washington County's men and women increasingly turned to the intimate domestic circle of parents and children for their sense of identity and for emotional fulfillment. But they did not view the nuclear family as independent or isolated. Rather, each family remained part of a larger fabric woven together by bonds of marriage and blood. Only once that fabric had been woven and was secure were Ohio's men and women free to invest so much emotional energy into their nuclear relationships.

Notes

1. Louise Rau, "Lucy Backus Woodbridge, Pioneer Mother," *Ohio State Archaeological and Historical Quarterly* 44 (1935): 405–13; Dudley Woodbridge (Norwich) to James Backus (Marietta), December 9, 1788, Backus-Woodbridge Collection, Box 1, Folder 1, Microfilm 120, Ohio Historical Society (hereafter OHS); Donald Grant and Alfred Mitchell, *The Woodbridge Record, being an Account of the Descendants of Rev. John Woodbridge of Newbury, Mass.* (New Haven: privately printed, 1883).

2. See, for example, Nancy F. Cott, *The Bonds of Womanhood: "Woman's Sphere" in New England, 1780–1835* (New Haven: Yale University Press, 1977); Carl N. Degler, *At Odds: Women and the Family in America from the Revolution to the Present* (New York: Oxford University Press, 1980); Mary P. Ryan, *Cradle of the Middle Class: The Family in Oneida County, New York, 1790–1865* (New York: Cambridge University Press, 1981); Jan Lewis, *The Pursuit of Happiness: Family and Values in Jefferson's Virginia* (New York: Cambridge University Press, 1983); Anya Jabour, *Marriage in the Early Republic: Elizabeth and William Wirt and the Companionate Ideal* (Baltimore: Johns Hopkins University Press, 1998); Joan E. Cashin, *A Family Venture: Men and Women on the Southern Frontier* (New York: Oxford University Press, 1991).

3. For works that look at the importance of kin ties in the settlement of Kentucky, see Ellen Eslinger, "Migration and Kinship on the Trans-Appalachian Frontier: Strode's Station, Kentucky," *Filson Club History Quarterly* 62 (1988): 52–66; Marion Nelson Winship, "The Land of Connected Men: A New Migration Story from the Early American Republic," *Pennsylvania History* 64, special issue (1977): 88–104; Hazel Dicken-Garcia, *To Western Woods: The Breckenridge Family Moves to Kentucky in 1793* (Rutherford, NJ: Fairleigh Dickinson University Press, 1991); Gail S. Terry, "Sustaining the Bonds of Kinship in a Trans-Appalachian Migration, 1790–1811," *Virginia Magazine of History and Biography* 102 (1994): 455–75.

4. For two works that discuss in detail the ways in which social and economic conditions in New England contributed to the formation of the Ohio Company and the settlement of Washington County, Ohio, see Andrew R. L. Cayton, "'A Quiet Independence': The Western Vision of the Ohio Company," *Ohio History* 90 (1981): 5–32, and Timothy J. Shannon, "The Ohio Company and the Meaning of Opportunity in the American West, 1786–1795," *New England Quarterly* 64 (1991): 393–401.

5. U.S. Federal Census, 1850.

6. Lucy Woodbridge (Marietta) to James Backus (Norwich), July 12, 1792, Backus-Woodbridge Collection, Box 1 Folder 2, OHS.

7. Rau, "Lucy Backus Woodbridge"; Washington County Tax Lists, 1801, 1810, 1813, 1821, Ohio University Special Collections (microfilm edition available from the Church of Latter-Day Saints); Dudley Woodbridge was always among the top 5 percent of Marietta property owners and was listed as the town's wealthiest taxpayer as early as 1801 and was still in that position when he died in 1823.

8. Jane Robbins (Plymouth, MA) to Rebecca Gilman (Marietta), June 6, 1790 and Jane Robbins (Plymouth) to Hannah Gilman (Marietta), October 5, 1792–January 26, 1793, in *A Family History in Letters and Documents, 1667–1837*, ed. Mrs. Charles Noyes (St. Paul, MN: privately printed, 1919), 168–69, 182–82.

9. Zara D. Howe (Erie, Pennsylvania) to Perley Howe, June 30, 1817, Perley Howe Papers, Campus Martius Museum, Marietta, Ohio.

10. For persistence rates in other midwestern communities see, John Mack Faragher, *Sugar Creek: Life on the Illinois Prairie* (New Haven: Yale University Press, 1986), 56; Don H. Doyle, *The Social Order of a Frontier Community: Jacksonville, Illinois, 1825–70* (Urbana: University of Illinois Press), 118, 267; and Robert E. Bieder, "Kinship as a Factor in Migration," *Journal of Marriage and the Family* 35 (1973): 435–38. Faragher found that in the Sangamo region of Illinois between 1830 and 1840, 80 percent of persistent households lived near kin, while only 30 percent of nonpersistent households did. Overall persistence rates were higher than for Marietta during its earliest years. Persistence rates were lower in Jacksonville, Illinois. Doyle reports rates of between 25 percent and 31 percent in the 1850s and 1860s. Rates were higher among those with kin in town than for those without kin. Bieder goes beyond census reports to reconstruct family networks in Benzonia, Michigan. He reports persistence rates of 68 percent between 1864 and 1875 for those with local kin, and rates of only 25 percent for those without relatives nearby, figures similar to those in Marietta during the earliest decades of settlement.

11. U.S. Federal Census, 1800–1850. By 1840, 55 percent of household heads in Marietta shared a surname with at least one other household head. Half of these heads of household are listed on the 1850 Marietta census, while only 35 percent of those without a shared surname appear. Overall persistence was not as high in every decade, but even in the least stable decade, 1820–30, 39 percent of household heads with a shared surname persisted, while only 28 percent of those without a shared surname did so.

12. Bernice Graham and Elizabeth S. Cottle, comps., *Washington County, Ohio Marriages (1789–1840)* (Marietta, OH: privately printed, 1976) and Washington County Marriage Records, 1789–1850, Washington County Courthouse, Marietta, Ohio (microfilm edition, Church of Latter-Day Saints).

13. William Henry Jennings, *A Genealogical History of the Jennings Families in England and America*, vol. 2: *The American Families* (Columbus, OH: privately printed, 1899), 18–42, 605–6, 631–40. On the role of kinship marriage and sibling exchanges in Massachusetts see Peter Dobkin Hall, "Marital Selection and Business in Massachusetts Merchant Families, 1700–1900," in *The Family: Its Structure and Functions*, 2nd ed., ed. Rose Laub Coser (New York: St. Martin's Press, 1974), 226–40, and Bernard Farber, *Guardians of Virtue: Salem Families in 1800* (New York: Basic Books, 1972), 115–55.

14. On the clannishness of Ohio settlers, see Andrew R. L. Cayton, *Ohio: The History of a People* (Columbus: Ohio State University Press, 2002), 13–43.

15. Elizabeth Frye Barker, *Barker Genealogy* (New York: Frye Publishing Co., 1927), 400–401, 409–10; J. Gardner Bartlett, *Gregory Stone Genealogy* (Boston: New England Historic Genealogical Society, 1918), 240–42, 399; Elizabeth Ellery Dana, *The Dana Family in America* (Cambridge, MA: Wright & Polter, 1956), 261–64, 314–15, 320.

16. U.S. Federal Census, 1810–1850; Yasukichi Yasuba, *Birth Rates of the White Population in the United States, 1800–1860: An Economic Study* (Baltimore: Johns Hopkins University Press, 1962), 32–33, 50–55, 60–65; Don R. Leet, *Population Pressure and Human Fertility Response: Ohio, 1810–1860* (New York: Arno Press, 1978), 22–23, 30–33, 40–63, 127–29, 150, 156–58, 179, 186, 191–93, 251.

17. For comparisons with Hingham, Massachusetts, see Daniel Scott Smith, "Child-Naming Practices, Kinship Ties, and Change in Family Attitudes in Hingham, Massachusetts, 1641 to 1880," *Journal of Social History* 18 (1985): 541–66. Smith found that over 50 percent of Hingham, Massachusetts, parents married between 1761 and 1800 named their first daughter for her mother and nearly 60 percent named their first son for his father. The same cohort in Washington County named only 14 percent of their first-born daughters and 25 percent of their first-born sons for themselves. David Hackett Fischer has also examined naming patterns in New England for the same period in "Forenames and Family in New England: An Exercise in Historical Onomastics," in *Generations and Change: Genealogical Perspectives in Social History,* ed. Robert M. Taylor Jr. and Ralph J. Crandall (Macon, GA: Mercer University Press, 1986), 215–41. Fischer found that the percentage of Concord, Massachusetts, parents married before 1780 who named children for themselves was lower than in Hingham, though still quite high. Washington County's figures match Concord's more closely than they do Hingham's in this respect. Fischer describes a revolution in naming patterns in New England between 1770 and 1820 in which there was a sharp decline in the naming of children for parents and grandparents. The decline in southeastern Ohio was not as marked, especially with regard to naming children for grandparents between 1800 and 1840. A significant decline is not clear until after 1840. For other studies of naming patterns, see David W. Dumas, "The Naming of Children in New England, 1780–1850," *New England Historic Genealogical Register* 132 (1978): 196–210; John J. Waters, "Naming and Kinship in New England: Guilford Patterns and Usage, 1693–1759," *New England Historic Genealogical Register* 138 (1984): 161–81; Edward Tebbenhoff, "Tacit Rules and Hidden Family Structures: Naming Practices and Godparentage in Schenectady, New York, 1680–1800," *Journal of Social History* 18 (1985): 567–85; and Darret B. Rutman and Anita H. Rutman, "'In Nomine Avi': Childnaming Patterns in a Chesapeake County, 1650–1750," in *Generations and Change,* ed. Taylor and Crandall, 243–65.

18. Charles P. Noyes, *Noyes-Gilman Ancestry* (St. Paul, MN: privately printed, 1907), 198–99, 210–11, 288–89.

19. Dana, *Dana Family in America,* 261–64; Barker, *Barker Genealogy,* 395, 400–401.

20. Jennings, *Genealogical History of the Jennings Families,* 2:18, 30, 32–33, 631–32.

21. Dudley Woodbridge Jr. (Marietta) to James Backus (Norwich), February 15, 1799, Clarina Backus (Marietta) to James Backus (Norwich),

December 9, 1800, and Papers pertaining to the Petit Divorce, Backus-Woodbridge Collection, Box 2, Folder 1 and Box 5, Folder 3, OHS.

22. *American Friend and Marietta Gazette,* October 22, 1831; Jennings, *Genealogical History of the Jennings Families,* 2:605–6; U.S. Federal Census, 1840 and 1850.

23. Martin Schultz has done more to estimate divorce rates in the early nineteenth century than anyone else. See Schultz, "Divorce in Early America: Origins and Patterns in Three North Central States," *Sociological Quarterly* 25 (1984): 511–26; Schultz, "Divorce in the South Atlantic States: Origins, Historical Patterns, and Recent Trends," *International Journal of Sociology of the Family* 16 (1986): 225–50; Schultz, "Divorce Patterns in Nineteenth-Century New England," *Journal of Family History* 15 (1990): 101–15; and Schultz, "Two Hundred Years of Divorce in Pennsylvania: Past Trends and Implications for the Future," in *Sociology toward the Year 2000: The Sociological Galaxy,* ed. Charles E. Babbitt (Harrisburg: Pennsylvania Sociological Society, 1983), 309–18. On divorce in Ohio and Washington County see David G. Null, "Ohio Divorces, 1803–1852," *National Genealogical Society Quarterly* 69 (1981): 109–14; Elizabeth S. Cottle, "Some Early Divorces in Washington County," *Tallow Light* 18 (1987): 33–35; and Henry Folsom Page, *A View of the Law Relative to the Subject of Divorce in Ohio, Indiana and Michigan* (Columbus: J. H. Riley & Co., 1850). Ohio's early divorce laws were modeled on those of Massachusetts and were thus more liberal than those of most southern and mid-Atlantic states. Records of Washington County divorce petitions can be found in the records of the Washington County Court of Common Pleas and in the Ohio Supreme Court Records, both available in Special Collections at Ohio University and on microfilm from the Church of Latter-Day Saints. Marietta's various newspapers also published notices of divorce petitions filed. In addition, a few legislative divorces were granted.

24. In fact, between 1806 and 1850 only one wife advertised the desertion of her husband in local papers. In October 1829 Abigail Robertson published a notice that her husband Henry had deserted her and contracted debts which she had been obliged to pay. She warned that she would pay no more of Henry's debts (*Marietta and Washington County Pilot,* October 31, 1829). Eighty-four husbands published such notices during the same period.

25. *Marietta Commentator,* July 1, 1809; Records of the Washington County, Ohio, Court of Common Pleas, 1804–1811, 359–60, and Ohio Supreme Court Docket and Journal, Washington County, 1808–1841 (October 1809), 6, 34, Special Collections, Ohio University (microfilm available from Church of Latter-Day Saints).

26. Graham and Cottle, *Washington County, Ohio Marriages,* 22.

27. See Tamara G. Miller, "'Seeking to Strengthen the Ties of Friendship': Women and Community in Southeastern Ohio, 1788–1850," PhD diss., Brandeis University, 1994, 67–153; Tamara G. Miller, "'Many Kinds of

Busyness': Women's Household Labor in Early Ohio," paper presented at the SHEAR Conference, Lexington, Kentucky, July 1999.

28. U.S. Federal Census, 1810–1850; Yasuba, *Birth Rates*, 32–33, 50–55, 60–65; Leet, *Population Pressure*, 22–23, 30–33, 40–63, 127–29, 150, 156–58, 179, 186, 191–93, 251.

29. Smith, "Child-Naming Practices," 549. During these same years, fewer Washington County parents named first and second children for themselves than did New England parents. These changes were in part a reflection of the growing number of emigrants from outside New England settling in the county.

30. The 1833 figure was reported by the *Cleveland Herald* and is cited in Nelson Manfield Blake, *The Road to Reno: A History of Divorce in the United States* (New York: Macmillan, 1962), 62. The *Marietta Gazette*, January 7, 1843, reported the figure for 1842. Population growth determined from the U.S. Federal Census, 1830 and 1840. This rise occurred without an accompanying decline in rates of desertion.

31. Null, "Ohio Divorces," 109; Maskell E. Curwen, ed., *The Public Statutes at Large of the State of Ohio . . .* vol. 1 (Cincinnati: Maskell E. Curwen, 1853), 602–3. In 1804 the acceptable grounds were bigamy, willful absence for five years, adultery, and extreme cruelty. By 1840 habitual drunkenness, fraudulent contract, gross neglect of duty, impotency, and imprisonment had been added, and the necessary period of desertion had been lowered to three years.

32. Nahum Ward (Washington) to Sarah Catharine Ward (Marietta), January 17 1827, DLMC.

33. Sala Bosworth to Joanna Shipman Bosworth, September 4, 1840, DLMC.

34. Mary to Frances Price, February 20, 1846, Dana Family Papers, Box 1, Folder 2, MSS 181, OHS.

35. Ann Cotton (Mount Vernon Furnace) to J. Dexter Cotton (Marietta), October 7, 1848, DLMC.

36. J. Dexter Cotton (Marietta) to Ann Cotton (Mount Vernon Furnace), November 26, 1849, DLMC.

37. Ann Cotton (Mount Vernon Furnace) to J. Dexter Cotton (Marietta), January 6, 1850, DLMC.

38. J. Dexter Cotton (Marietta) to Ann Cotton (Mount Vernon Furnace), March 12, 1849, DLMC.

39. J. Dexter Cotton (Marietta) to Ann Cotton (Mount Vernon Furnace), March 12, 1849, Ann Cotton to J. Dexter Cotton, November 11, 1849, and J. Dexter Cotton to Ann Cotton, December 16, 1849, DLMC; LaVerne C. Cooley, comp., *A Short Biography of the Rev. John Cotton of Boston and a Cotton Genealogy of His Descendants* (Batavia, NY: privately printed, 1945), 69.

40. Ann Cotton (Mount Vernon Furnace) to J. Dexter Cotton (Marietta), March 11, 1849, and October 7, 1848, and J. Dexter Cotton (Mari-

etta) to Ann Cotton (Mount Vernon Furnace), December 9, 1849, and November 25, 1850, DLMC.

41. Andrews, *History of Marietta,* 472; Mathews, *History of Washington County,* 367, 411–12; J. Dexter Cotton (Marietta) to Ann Cotton (Mount Vernon Furnace), November 26, December 9, 30, 1849, and November 25, 1850, DLMC.

SEVEN

The Ohio Country in the Political Economy of Nation Building

CHRISTOPHER CLARK

Writing about the historiography of Ohio and the Midwest, Andrew Cayton and Stuart Hobbs have each noted the need for cultural, social, and economic histories of the region to be more thoroughly integrated with those of other parts of the nation, in a manner that historians of politics are already undertaking. The most important frameworks for doing this, and probably the most obvious, are those provided by frontier history and the history of the American West. Ohio and the Ohio Valley were, after all, key regions in the early republic's initial expansion beyond the original boundaries of the United States and helped set patterns that would mark the occupation and settlement of much of the rest of the continent. They were, wrote Malcolm J. Rohrbough in 1978, part of "the first frontier of the new American nation."[1] Recently, as Hobbs has remarked, "the revival of interest in frontier history, along with the new western history," has offered renewed intellectual thrust to studies of Ohio and the Ohio Valley conceived in these traditions. R. Douglas Hurt, for instance, places his 1996 study of early Ohio firmly in the vein of frontier history, and the book's series editors refer to it as a history of "the first American West." Andrew Cayton and Susan E. Gray, among others, have also explored Ohio and Ohio Valley history as part of the formation of a broader American Midwest, whose part in national history was shaped by the emergence of distinctive regional patterns of institutional development and identity. Though it varies the tradition, this perspective is nevertheless rooted west of the Appalachians.[2]

My purpose in this essay, however, is to suggest what the Ohio region might reveal when looked at from the perspective of the East and in light of the historiography of places from which the area was settled. Early Ohio need not be seen only as part of the frontier West. As Donald Ratcliffe has noted in respect to the state's political culture, early Ohioans were at times uncertain whether they were westerners or northerners and frequently determined that they were both.[3] Ohio's political economy, like that of other parts of the trans-Appalachian zone, was forged from the conditions, constraints, and aspirations of older European settlement regions in North America; it was one area in which American settlers worked out the implications of those conditions in a new environment. To a social historian of the Northeast like myself, the parallels between early Ohio and older regions can be as striking as the contrasts. If it was a new frontier, it was one on which older patterns were projected. Like Kentucky to the south, early Ohio represented an extension of eastern social structures and objectives. Though there were many respects in which Ohio was successful and not—like the Kentucky of Stephen Aron's 1996 study—"a broken promised land," it was nevertheless powerfully shaped by characteristics imported from the East. And just as much as Aron's Kentucky, Ohio would become a place where "the West was lost."[4]

To consider how the early social history of Ohio might fit into the broader picture of American social history, this essay briefly explores six interconnected themes. First, the Ohio Valley and the Ohio Country were stark witnesses to the clearance of Native American inhabitants between the American Revolution and the War of 1812, a process that set up important conditions for the settler societies that replaced them on the land. Second, white settlers evinced a range of conceptions about the land they were occupying, conceptions that were rooted in the social distinctions among them. Third, the occupation and cultivation of Ohio was part of a wider pattern of household production and family-based farming adapted from older regions. Just as in the East, processes of land settlement and farm creation in a household-based economy involved social networks and patterns of exchange that shaped the area's integration into wider national markets in the first half of the nineteenth century. Fourth, a combination of geography, family aspirations, and market developments fostered patterns of diversified production in Ohio that also gave it much in common with older regions of the Northeast. Fifth, the Ohio River marked an increasingly sharp distinction between Ohio's non-slave-based, freehold farming system and the slave-based plantation economies that lay to its south. Finally, this distinction was evident in the structures of wealth and power in the respective zones. In Ohio there evolved relationships between rural and urban areas and between elite and non-elite groups that bore closer comparison with those of the Northeast than with those of the South.

For the first half of the eighteenth century, the Ohio Country had been a zone of Native American migration and resettlement and of intercultural trade, both among native groups and with early European venturers. Only after 1763 did divisions harden into race-based categories of "native" and "settler." During and after the American Revolution conflict flared on both sides of the Ohio River over who would control the land that lay south of the Great Lakes and east of the Mississippi. As a recent historian has noted, "the Revolution . . . justified and accelerated the process by which Euro-Americans drove Indians off the land and claimed it for themselves."[5] The fierce opposition of the Shawnee Confederacy and other native groups north of the Ohio delayed and shaped the process of conquest, constituting one of the strongest phases of Indian resistance to white encroachment anywhere on the continent. Even so, the outcome was what we could call the Great Clearance of Native American inhabitants, a process that would continue until the removal under an 1842 treaty of the Wyandots from northwest Ohio to what later became Kansas. Massacre, disease, forced migration, and the transformation of landscapes left those Indians who were not killed or expelled in positions of poverty, marginality, and virtual invisibility in the new settler societies that grew up. The fate of Native Americans in Ohio was comparable to that of their counterparts in New York and New England.[6]

Among the important implications of this conflict for white settlers were the social and political dynamics that it helped to create. Government ("the State") was profoundly engaged in the process of conquest and settlement from the start. This fact in itself forged a framework in which white migration and settlement formation were linked to nation building. The agents of clearance included military power, the instruments of law and political authority, and assertions of cultural superiority based on those very instruments, assertions that both physically and discursively claimed and controlled the land on behalf of its new owners. During the 1780s, as white settlers were intruding into the Ohio Country but before they arrived in substantial numbers, representatives of national government hammered out terms for its settlement, incorporation, and governance. Provisions for the region included both specific measures, such as the land ordinances of the middle of the decade, and general principles, such as those for new territories and states laid out in the U.S. Constitution. Military action to overcome Indian resistance helped to fulfill the demands of white emigrants for secure access to land and helped to align the new national government with the demands of its western citizens.[7] Government held the ring not only for proponents of national development by expansion but also for particular groups with interests in the region. Those seeking to make large-scale land purchases were hoping to secure either domains over which they could exercise paternalistic control or, more commonly, tracts which they could sell to settlers for a profit. Ordinary settlers looking for modest-scale parcels of land to farm were driven by long-term aspirations for landholding and by the constraints of societies farther east.[8] Settlers and speculators both combined (indeed they were sometimes the same people) and conflicted with one another, setting up a dialectic of tension that would shape Ohio as it developed.

The Ohio Valley and the Ohio Country above all offered land, but different groups had different conceptions of its uses. A key theme in settlers' concerns was the hope of establishing themselves as "independent" farmers. Pressure for settlement north of the Ohio River in the 1780s came from yeoman farmers and squatters in what became Kentucky. These farmers were keen to avoid the control of large landowners there; in the words of some 1779 petitioners, Kentucky land had been "Engrossed into the hands of a few Interested men," and they felt in danger of becoming "Slaves to those Engrossers of Lands and to the Court of Virginia."[9] As the historian Lee Soltow demonstrated, though, early Ohio was not egalitarian either. In 1810 only 45 percent of household heads owned land, a figure no greater than could be found in parts of western Pennsylvania and New York. Speculators held some large pockets of land; tenancy was rising.[10] In towns across the settled areas of the state, members of a wealthy commercial elite were seeking to exercise political power on the basis of their economic standing and influence.

Yet ordinary farmers and settlers, sometimes consciously and directly, often silently and unintentionally, challenged the position of these elites. Donald Ratcliffe has pointed out that the tax records on which Soltow based his calculations of wealth distribution may have underrecorded the extent to which land was widely owned. By the standard of most national or international comparisons, landownership in Ohio was broadly distributed, and changes to the rules for acquiring federal land tended to widen access to property in the early nineteenth century. Outside towns, a high proportion of adult white men owned land.[11] As had already occurred in upstate New York, the availability of land, the rate at which it changed hands, and the extent to which ordinary settlers had a degree of choice as to where to establish themselves and under what terms limited the power of large landholders and speculators to exercise influence. Those with hopes of patriarchal or paternalistic grandeur found their illusions punctured by the unwillingness of settlers to accept their authority.[12] Early Ohio's political leaders often had to temper their actions to democratic pressure. In the same way, popular aspirations and ideas about landholding curbed the ability of elites to exercise direct control over the land and its new inhabitants.[13]

One result was that Ohio expanded rapidly. Between 1800 and 1810, the state's population grew by 413 percent, and between 1810 and 1820 it rose another 152 percent. Kentucky's population grew more slowly decade by decade from 1790 to 1820, despite the importation of slaves to augment it. Contemporaries and historians alike have attributed Ohio's faster growth to the availability there of relatively small parcels of land for farming and of comparatively secure titles to them. The Louisville lawyer and politician Richard Clough Anderson Jr. observed while traversing south-central Ohio in 1817 that "the rapid improvement of this Country shews the good policy of excluding slaves & of the high benefit of dividing land into small parcels in the congress manner." Lancaster in the Hocking Valley was "thriving and busy," while even the poorer land near Chillicothe he found "thickly settled . . . and the towns populous and populating beyond my expectations."[14]

The desire for "independence" on the land was strongly shaped by family aspirations. The interest of the "lineal family," whose pursuit historian James A. Henretta identified as a common hallmark of early American rural society, gave a powerful thrust to western settlement. Many families hoped to be able to settle their offspring on the land.[15] Soil exhaustion, increasing crowdedness of settlement, and economic disruptions farther east had threatened many farm households' ability to do so. "My wishes . . . and my exertions," wrote the Maryland Quaker Isaac Briggs, "have in view . . . a place where my whole family, for a generation or two to come, may sit down, in *one* neighborhood, in peace, competence, and humble virtue." When Briggs's daughter at length reached her family's new land in Ohio, she would write that "a feeling of thankfulness arose in my heart as I thought, here *is* my home, here *is* an inheritance for my children where they *may* earn their bread [even] if it *is* by the sweat of their brow."[16]

These connections between family and land drove both the speed of settlement and families' conceptions of the land itself. Settlement in Ohio, after all, was in many ways merely an extension of patterns of migration and occupation of land that had begun in the colonial period.[17] New Englanders faced with increasing population density and unequal access to adequate land had started to regard their land not simply as a possession to be treasured for itself but as a commodity that could be traded in pursuit of the family's interests. In late-eighteenth-century Connecticut, for example, increasing numbers of families altered their bequest strategies to try to help out their offspring equally and in doing so came to regard land not as an heirloom to be attached to but as a resource to be made use of.[18] Emigrants like Jeremiah Root of western Massachusetts swapped farms in the East for title to new land in Ohio, and the practice became common enough that farmers had to be cautioned against the frauds that could be perpetrated against them in the process.[19] The bargain they sought, of course, was that with land prices much lower in the West than back home, they could gain large acreages on which to settle themselves and their offspring. This precisely fitted their purpose; by choosing areas with relatively low population densities in which to set up farms, many hoped to preserve a generation or two's future on their new land.[20]

In due course, as families who had settled in older regions of Ohio also found populations growing around them, they adopted similar strategies to advance their own children's interests. Butler County bequests by the middle of the century increasingly reflected both equality of treatment and a willingness to trade land for greater opportunities elsewhere.[21] In Harrison County in 1825 the parents of William Cooper Howells opted to buy a 160-acre farm at $3.75 per acre; Howells later considered that they had been mistaken not to move farther west to obtain more land at a lower unit price.[22] Many families did just that. The desire for independence and families' pursuit of it for their children had populated Ohio rapidly after 1795. From the late 1810s onward, this desire also became a source of considerable out-migration from the state as land in Indiana and Illinois was opened up. Even as its population expanded more than threefold between 1810 and 1830, emigration to newer regions was turning Ohio into an "eastern" state.

Despite some efforts to circumvent the Northwest Ordinance's prohibition of slavery, Ohio became a center of freehold farming, which took it on a trajectory and created social relationships distinct from those of plantation-based regions and more similar to those of New York and New England. Traveling the Ohio River in 1807, Fortescue Cuming had contrasted the "reasonable rate" at which Ohio's small farms could be purchased with the Kentucky "lands belonging mostly to wealthy and great landowners . . . held at four or five times the Ohio price."[23] In common with other rural areas of early America, Ohio was a region rooted in household production. Unlike slave-worked farms and plantations in the South, however, its farm families had to depend on their own labor, on the gendered division of labor in the household, on what they could hire in, and on often complex patterns of exchange with neighbors and kin. This tied them to practices and attitudes that had already been common in nonslave rural areas farther east.[24]

As Susan Gray emphasized in her study of early Michigan settlement, many decisions and activities were shaped by familial or collective concerns, not by individual actions or aspirations. Families frequently migrated in groups. Kin groups from Granville, Massachusetts, and adjacent Granby, Connecticut, were at the core of a migration to Granville, Ohio, in the Licking Valley. From Virginia in 1805, Benjamin Adair and his family moved to the Paint Valley in south-central Ohio; over the next ten years several cousins followed them, so that there were fifty or more Adair relatives settled in the area. Jeremiah Root migrated in 1807 in a party of thirty-two, all friends and neighbors from western Massachusetts.[25] Families' previous migrations helped shape subsequent ones. Joseph Bentley moved his family to Columbiana County in 1826, to a region where an uncle had bought land twenty years previously; moreover, Bentley noted, the prospect that his brother might also settle nearby with some of his relatives was "a great comfort."[26] Most settlers came from literate populations, and many maintained contacts with the relatives and friends left behind. Letters exchanged and newspapers sent and returned marked patterns of kinship and friendship that not only breached the isolation of farm life but wove webs of continuing connection. These personal connections were often more important than broader cultural identities based on region or ethnicity. The Briggs family of Columbiana County sustained most of its links to family and fellow members of the Society of Friends back in Maryland, though those links did come under stress when the Ohio Briggses took the side of Elias Hicks in the great Quaker schism of the late 1820s. In a study of the settlement of Claridon in Geauga County, Robert Wheeler noted that applying the designation "Yankee" to each of two separate waves of New England migrants to the town disguised a set of quite distinct social and religious characteristics that kept the groups separate even to the extent of limiting intermarriage. Tamara G. Miller's work on family and kin in Marietta and Washington County notes both the consistency of distinct patterns between different networks of connections and the greater significance of these networks for those who had moved to Ohio than for those who remained in older regions.[27]

As had occurred in New England and parts of New York, household production and the reliance on family labor created particular conditions for the emergence of a rural labor market in Ohio.[28] Newly established farm families required extra labor to help clear and cultivate land and establish domestic life; hiring labor was common for these purposes. But in many areas labor for hire was scarce. It was necessary to make arrangements with other local families to exchange goods and work. Anna Briggs Bentley described a neighbor at her new home in Columbiana County who offered to "supply [her] with beans, potatoes, and roasting ears," and said that Anna "must not be any ways backward with us. . . . New begginers have all to buy till they can make for themselves."[29] Even as farms became more established, neighborhood cooperation and "'changing works" remained essential to sustaining them, just as in New England and elsewhere. William Cooper Howells noted the importance of sending a family representative to neighborhood logrollings and other collective work events so as to have a call on others' labor in exchange when it became necessary.[30] "Spare" children were sent to live and work with neighbors or relatives who needed help. Crop mixes and output were determined as much by a household's labor supply and ability to obtain assistance as by soil conditions or market prices.

Family and exchange labor also influenced the means by which farm households established connections with the wider market. Middling and poorer families often had restricted access to cash, and what cash they did obtain was reserved for specific uses, such as paying taxes, servicing mortgage debt, or buying goods that were not obtainable by other means. Local exchange was often contrived to conserve it.[31] But there were also constraints that drew farmers toward production for sale. Indebtedness for land was the most common, the principal factor that instilled what the historical sociologist Charles Post has called "market discipline" in a wide variety of instances.[32] Early settlements often went through a cycle of stages of dependence: first a period of reliance on merchants and outsiders for many provisions and needs, and then a period of austerity and comparative self-sufficiency, when resources were dedicated to family needs and to the paying off of incurred debts. In these phases, kin connections often provided an important vector for trade. In Columbiana County, the Bentley family at first relied substantially for some supplies on shipments from kin in Maryland. When one package arrived without some items they had hoped for, Anna Briggs Bentley wrote to her relatives, "We were all disappointed. I cried a little, and then joined the rest in abusing you." Later, by 1829, Bentley was sending butter, maple sugar, and other items to sell at the local store: "If we can make more than with great economy is enough for our own use . . . it will help to extricate us from debt." Strategies for doing so included intensifying home production (to reduce the need for outlays) and producing goods for sale. With the first $2.50 "I can *come honestly* by," Bentley wrote, "I intend getting a wheel to learn to spin on. It is high time Maria [her thirteen-year-old daughter] was put to it."[33] As on New England farms, market and household production were closely intertwined for Ohio farm families. Their needs also underpinned the high value placed on practicality, on manual-labor skills, and on the roles of both in the development of educational traditions that Kenneth Wheeler notes in his essay in this volume.[34]

Just as had been occurring in longer-settled regions, market discipline and the passage of time produced two somewhat distinct effects in Ohio farm communities. One, as we have already noted, was out-migration. As settlement progressed, population density rose, and land was improved, land prices had risen, sometimes markedly. Pursuing the lineal family ideal of settling their children on farms of their own, many settlers opted to sell their Ohio land and seek out larger acreages farther west, and at times in the mid-nineteenth century out-migration exceeded in-migration. After the death of Benjamin Adair in the Paint Valley in 1829, seven of nine sons who lived in the region moved away, five of them to one township in Indiana's Wabash Valley.[35] A group of German families who settled in southwestern Ohio in the early 1830s moved on again to land in Dubuque County, Iowa, in 1843, subsequently persuading friends from both Ohio and their German home region to join them there.[36]

An alternative approach was for families to diversify their activities to secure their livelihoods where they were already settled. As settlement became denser and families progressed through their life cycles, there were both opportunities and means of achieving diversity. Women and their daughters adopted dairying or household manufactures. Some men, including William Cooper Howells's Welsh-immigrant father, worked at manufacturing trades along with farming, in a pattern of "by-employment" that was increasingly common.[37] Sons grew up to learn different trades. By the mid-1840s the two Bentley sons were working at manual trades in towns near their family's home. The elder, Granville S. Bentley, combined wagonmaking with working on the farm so that—as he dryly noted to a cousin—"when one missed, 'tother is sure to fail." Subsequently he or his wife began operating a small store, and he obtained a postmastership to add to these activities.[38] While individual families took different paths, the aggregate effect was indeed to diversify the Ohio economy to a significant degree. Occupational data in U.S. censuses before 1850 is crude and hard to rely on but nevertheless can indicate some broad tendencies. Already by 1820, 14.4 percent of occupations reported in the census were given under the category "manufactures," and out of twenty-four states Ohio ranked ninth in the ratio of people listed in manufacturing to those

in agricultural occupations. Twenty years later, although its population had grown by more than two-and-a-half times and its agricultural population somewhat faster, the proportion of all occupations
given under "manufacture and trades" had increased to 19 percent.[39] Diversification and manufacturing developments were drawing Ohio into a broad belt of mixed agriculture and industry that
stretched from southern New England to the northern Chesapeake
and west to Cincinnati. This was, of course, the basis for the later
northeastern/midwestern industrial belt that was to become the
great dynamo of American economic power in the later nineteenth
century.[40]

The relative merits of emigration and diversification were a theme
in economic commentary from the 1820s onward. Mathew Carey,
writing in 1822, criticized the tendency that he ascribed to many
Ohio farmers, of acquiring more land than they needed: "Men are
everywhere . . . half-cultivating large farms, when they might treble
the result from half the surface." He urged instead the improvement
of farm produce "and the encouragement of a market at home, by
fostering and protecting domestic manufactures." A quarter-century
later, Carey's son Henry turned this observation into an extended series of writings on the advantages of intensive over extensive development. Urging the investment of labor in the land and in other
production that could keep economic activities close to one another,
the younger Carey sought to discourage the hunger for dispersed
settlement and land acquisition that had characterized expansion
across the continent.[41]

By the time Henry C. Carey was writing in the late 1840s and 1850s,
diversified farming and manufacturing developments were becoming strongly associated with the North, and they contrasted with the
seemingly different patterns of the South's slave-based plantation
economies. Since early in the century, travelers on the Ohio River
had claimed to notice the effects of different patterns of rural economy on the societies that grew up on either bank. In 1807 Fortescue
Cuming compared the small Ohio farms with the large "Virginian"
estates to be seen opposite in Kentucky. When he drew his famous
contrast in the 1830s between the buzz of activity on the river's right
bank with the lassitude of slave-based Kentucky on the left, Alexis de
Tocqueville was voicing what was becoming quite a commonplace
observation.[42] Such comparisons had not been limited to travel ac-

counts or political commentary; at various levels they had shaped hardheaded calculations too. Looking for speculative opportunities in the land boom of 1815–18, Louisville's Richard Clough Anderson noted the greater likelihood of profits from investing in Indiana, where small-scale farming and rapid settlement would drive up land prices and generate commercial demand, than in the slave-based economy of his own state. Anderson's evaluation is the more note-worthy for the fact that he was himself from a Virginia slaveholding family.[43] East Coast emigrants coming from everywhere from Maine to Virginia opted for Ohio and other nonslave states more frequently than they did the South, as would European immigrants heading for the American interior. Ohio would share in the Northeast's experi-ence of receiving growing numbers of European migrants in the decades after 1840.

But of course Ohio's growth and diversification had not come about solely from the activities of farm families and their offspring. Merchants had always been an essential part of the process of settle-ment. They often intermarried with farm families and often adopted business practices similar to those of farmers, but their functions and, to some degree, their wealth marked a pattern of social diver-sification.[44] The towns and village centers that they founded and populated became distinctive elements of the Ohio landscape. Most of these towns had originated as speculative developments that helped spearhead the settlement of land, and many fell into decline as the initial stages of settlement were completed. Nevertheless, the frequency and importance of urban centers became a parallel be-tween Ohio and older regions of New England, the mid-Atlantic, and western New York.[45] This was bolstered by the practices of rural exchange that we have discussed. The operation of rural, cash-poor, quasi-barter economies depended to a great extent on the presence of merchants and storekeepers to provide credit, goods, and means of executing complicated third-party arrangements. Merchants in-serted themselves into the local economies of the rural districts sur-rounding them. By supplying goods and, often, by selling, renting, or mortgaging land as well, they created the structures of "market discipline" that drew farmers increasingly into participation in na-tional and international trade. As farmers became engaged in wider markets, they also made their regions markets for manufactured and other goods from elsewhere. Merchants and storekeepers were the conduits for these goods and profited from them. As Richard Clough

Anderson reflected in 1815, "I am impressed that I could make money into Merchandizing . . . [;] if I can get a partner perfectly safe I will convert a part of my property into a mercantile capital."[46]

Towns, with the merchants and lawyers who formed their elites, became the leading foci of social and political power in Ohio and other nonplantation, nonslave regions. In plantation-based societies, wealth tended to lie with slaveholders, and slaves were a significant component of wealth. Planters were the chief group in North America to earn profits and wealth substantially from the land through the labor of others. In the family-labor systems of the freehold, nonslave North, the ability to earn profits directly from others' labor on the land was strictly limited to the relatively few people who owned large estates and employed wage laborers in quantity to work their land. In Ohio, as in most other parts of the Midwest and most of the Northeast, large farms were relatively rare. Wealth and power derived not directly from the ability to grow crops but from the commercial transactions connected with buying, selling, financing, and provisioning for them.

The structure of nonslave society emphasized instead the local influence of town founders such as David Hudson, who moved from Connecticut to northeastern Ohio at the end of the eighteenth century.[47] Along with mixed farming, diversified production, and the trading relationships that they generated, small towns would help foster the emergence of large, urban commercial and industrial centers and, eventually, the accumulation of great urban fortunes, such as that of John D. Rockefeller in Cleveland during and after the Civil War. The ubiquity of urban commercial activity and the growing hegemony of urban centers over rural economic life secured the expansion of a new middle class in the mid-nineteenth century and shaped whole generations' concepts of the career possibilities open to young men from this class.[48] As Rutherford B. Hayes advised his former aide-de-camp William McKinley in 1866, while the younger man was considering his postwar prospects, "My notion of the place for a young man is a fine large growing town anywhere, but would prefer a new town in the West. St. Louis, Kansas City, Leavenworth, Omaha, Chicago, etc., etc., are my favorites. With your business capacity and experience I would have preferred railroading or some commercial business. A man in any of our Western towns with half your wit ought to be independent at forty in business."[49]

George F. Babbitt and his predecessors were created in the commercial town and city networks of the nation's freehold farming regions. The Northeast and Ohio provided the prototypes for these networks.

Placing Ohio and the Ohio Valley in the context of wider social and economic developments in the early republic requires attention to the structures and practices that forged rural societies across the American North and that also built the urban societies that complemented and to some extent came to dominate them. Though it received migrant settlers from Virginia, Maryland, and Kentucky, as well as from the mid-Atlantic and New England states, Ohio's mixed farming, diversifying rural economy, emergent manufacturing, and urban development made it increasingly an integral part of the North-East. Its identity as a "western" state rapidly diminished in significance. In the minds of many farther west, Ohio by the 1850s already lay firmly in the "East." "Let them come," declared an Iowa newspaper editor early in that decade, anxious (like so many) to promote settlement in his vicinity: "Let them flee from their tax-ridden and miserably governed Egypts of Ohio and Pennsylvania to the Land of Promise."[50] Ohio's role in the antislavery movement, its contribution to the Civil War, and its prominent share in the exercise of national economic and political power after the war marked its convergence with the northeastern sources of that power. The fact that Ohio provided no fewer than seven of the eleven presidents who served between 1865 and 1923 was a symbol, and to some extent a measure, of its consolidation with the regions that had founded and settled it.

In a 1996 article, Kim M. Gruenwald argued that trade and the extension of commercial systems provided the sinews of national development and identity. Without commerce, she suggested, the United States would simply have been a collection of kin groups. Commerce, this implies, was what tied otherwise local concerns together.[51] But the early history of regions like Ohio, which received and then in its turn fed migrants to and from other parts of the continent, suggests an alternative, or at least a more refined formulation. Commerce alone was not what made national identity. Kinship ties also assisted in the maintenance of long-distance connections among and between families, which in turn sustained concepts of nationhood. The "political economy of nation building," in other words, involved both commerce *and* kinship. Indeed, there was a good deal of symmetry between them: commerce and kinship each had both local and long-distance permutations. Trying desperately to hold the nation together at the end of the 1850s, President James Buchanan would appeal as a basis for national unity to the ties of kinship and consanguinity that now stretched from coast to coast. Yet those connections, just like the ties of trade, had not run evenly or in all directions. Because of the patterns of the preceding few decades, trading and kinship connections that ran from east to west proved more durable and significant than those that ran from north to south across the Ohio River.[52]

An emphasis on trade and kinship, in turn, reinforces the significance of Susan E. Gray's argument that "western" development—hence national development—was at least as much a collective process as it was an individualistic one. Patterns of family, kinship, chain migration, local exchange, and 'changing works shaped the character of settlement, farm building, and the social and economic processes that grew out of them. Even the elements of western expansion that seem so often to be regarded as aspects of "restless individualism"—such as the tendency to push settlement forward into new and hence cheaper zones—derived as much from the collective aspirations of families and kin groups as from the ambitions of individuals. Even though they also gave rise to conflicts and constraints, in the "political economy of nation building" the importance of cooperation, coordination, and collaboration can scarcely be exaggerated.

Notes

Preparation of this essay was assisted by a Residential Fellowship at the University of Connecticut Humanities Institute, Storrs, Connecticut, and by a research leave award from the UK Arts and Humanities Research Board; I gratefully acknowledge these, and the comments of fellow participants in the SHEAR conference panels on the Ohio Valley in the Early American Republic. Original spellings have been retained in quotations.
1. Andrew R. L. Cayton, "The State of Ohio's History: A Review Article," *Ohio History* 106 (1997): 192–99. Malcolm J. Rohrbough, *The Trans-Appalachian Frontier: Peoples, Societies, and Institutions, 1775–1850* (New York: Oxford University Press, 1978), 7; while also noting the importance of con-

tinuity with the past, Rohrbough's book stresses the common characteristics of frontier regions and processes.

2. Stuart D. Hobbs, review of Donald Ratcliffe, *Party Spirit in a Frontier Republic* [1998] published on H-Ohio (March 1999), http://www2.h-net .msu.edu/reviews/showlist.cgi?lists=h-ohio (consulted June 21, 2003); R. Douglas Hurt, *The Ohio Frontier: Crucible of the Old Northwest, 1720–1830* (Bloomington: Indiana University Press, 1996), author's preface and fore-word by Walter Nugent and Malcolm J. Rohrbough; Andrew R. L. Cayton and Susan E. Gray, eds., *The American Midwest: Essays on Regional History* (Bloomington: Indiana University Press, 2001), especially 8–9.

3. Donald J. Ratcliffe, *The Politics of Long Division: The Birth of the Second Party System in Ohio, 1818–1828* (Columbus: Ohio State University Press, 2000), 86–92, 135.

4. Stephen Aron, *How the West Was Lost: The Transformation of Kentucky from Daniel Boone to Henry Clay* (Baltimore: Johns Hopkins University Press, 1996), 4.

5. See Michael N. McConnell, *A Country Between: The Upper Ohio Valley and Its Peoples, 1724–1774* (Lincoln: University of Nebraska Press, 1992), es-pecially 233–54; the quotation is from Eric Hinderaker, *Elusive Empires: Con-structing Colonialism in the Ohio Valley, 1673–1800* (New York: Cambridge University Press, 1997), xii.

6. Gregory Evans Dowd, *A Spirited Resistance: The North American Indian Struggle for Unity, 1745–1815* (Baltimore: Johns Hopkins University Press, 1992); R. Douglas Hurt, *The Indian Frontier, 1763–1846* (Albuquerque: Uni-versity of New Mexico Press, 2002), chapter 5; Alan Taylor, "Land and Lib-erty on the Post-revolutionary Frontier," in *Devising Liberty: Preserving and Creating Freedom in the New American Republic,* ed. David Thomas Konig (Stan-ford: Stanford University Press, 1995); in *Ohio Frontier* Hurt treats the re-moval of the Wyandots as the point at which the "frontier" phase of Ohio history ended (1–4). On the marginality of Native Americans who re-mained in white-settled regions, see Donna Keith Baron, J. Edward Hood, and Holly V. Izard, "They Were Here All Along: The Native American Pres-ence in Lower-Central New England in the Eighteenth and Nineteenth Centuries," *William and Mary Quarterly* 53 (1996): 561–86.

7. Hinderaker, *Elusive Empires,* 244.

8. On the background to settlers' aspirations, see Allan Kulikoff, *From British Peasants to Colonial American Farmers* (Chapel Hill: University of North Carolina Press, 2000); on speculators, see Daniel M. Friedenberg, *Life, Lib-erty, and the Pursuit of Land: The Plunder of Early America* (Buffalo, NY: Prometheus Books, 1992); Andro Linklater, *Measuring America: How an Un-tamed Wilderness Shaped the United States and Fulfilled the Promise of Democracy* (New York: Walker, 2002).

9. Quoted in Andrew R. L. Cayton, *The Frontier Republic: Ideology and Poli-tics in the Ohio Country, 1780–1825* (Kent, OH: Kent State University Press, 1986), 4.

10. Lee Soltow, "Inequality amidst Abundance: Land Ownership in Early Nineteenth Century Ohio," *Ohio History* 88 (1979): 133–51.

11. Donald J. Ratcliffe, *Party Spirit in a Frontier Republic: Democratic Politics in Ohio, 1793–1821* (Columbus: Ohio State University Press, 1998), 46, 103–4, 271; see also Hurt, *Frontier Ohio,* 175.

12. On relationships between speculators, land developers, and settlers in New York State, see Alan Taylor, *William Cooper's Town: Power and Persuasion on the Frontier of the Early American Republic* (New York: Knopf, 1995); Charles E. Brooks, *Frontier Settlement and Market Revolution: The Holland Land Purchase* (Ithaca: Cornell University Press, 1996); William Wyckoff, *The Developer's Frontier: The Making of the Western New York Landscape* (New Haven: Yale University Press, 1988).

13. Jonathan J. Bean, in "Marketing the 'Great American Commodity': Nathaniel Massie and Land Speculation on the Ohio Frontier, 1783–1813," *Ohio History* 103 (1994): 152–69, concluded that "early Ohio land legislation favored the small farmer" (167). See also Cayton, *Frontier Republic;* Donald J. Ratcliffe, *Party Spirit.*

14. Alfred Tischendorf and E. Taylor Parks, eds., *The Diary and Journal of Richard Clough Anderson, Jr., 1814–1826* (Durham: Duke University Press, 1964), 68.

15. James A. Henretta, "Families and Farms: *Mentalité* in Pre-industrial America," *William and Mary Quarterly* 35 (1978): 3–32. See also Richard L. Bushman, "Family Security in the Transition from Farm to City, 1750–1850," *Journal of Family History* 6 (1981): 238–56.

16. Emily Foster, ed., *American Grit: A Woman's Letters from the Ohio Frontier* (Lexington: University Press of Kentucky, 2002), 14, 37 (emphasis in original).

17. On the long New England tradition of migration from older farming settlements, see David Jaffee, *People of the Wachusett: Greater New England in History and Memory, 1630–1860* (Ithaca: Cornell University Press, 1999).

18. Toby L. Ditz, *Property and Kinship: Inheritance in Early Connecticut, 1750–1820* (Princeton: Princeton University Press, 1986).

19. Jeremiah Root's story is told in Gerald W. McFarland, *A Scattered People: An American Family Moves West* (New York: Pantheon, 1985). The *Northampton* (Mass.) *Hampshire Gazette* (January 31, 1816) published a warning against speculators who were purchasing Massachusetts farms in exchange for fraudulent titles to land in the Connecticut Western Reserve.

20. Jeremy Atack, Fred Bateman, and William N. Parker, "Northern Agriculture and the Westward Movement," in *The Cambridge Economic History of the United States,* vol. 2: *The Long Nineteenth Century,* ed. Stanley L. Engerman and Robert E. Gallman (Cambridge, UK: Cambridge University Press, 2000), 322.

21. William H. Newell, "Inheritance on the Maturing Frontier: Butler County, Ohio, 1803–1865," in *Long-Term Factors in American Economic Growth,* ed. Stanley L. Engerman and Robert E. Gallman, Studies in Income

and Wealth, vol. 51 (Chicago: University of Chicago Press, 1986), 261–306.

22. William Cooper Howells, *Recollections of Life in Ohio from 1813 to 1840* (1895; Gainesville, FL: Scholars' Facsimiles and Reprints, 1963), 110.

23. Quoted in Lee Soltow and Margaret Soltow, "A Settlement that Failed: The French in Early Gallipolis, an Enlightening Letter, and an Explanation," *Ohio History* 94 (1985): 63. On slavery in Ohio, see Ellen Eslinger, "The Evolution of Racial Politics in Early Ohio," in this volume.

24. I discussed household-based farming and exchange practices in New England in my book *The Roots of Rural Capitalism: Western Massachusetts, 1780–1860* (Ithaca: Cornell University Press, 1990).

25. Susan E. Gray, *The Yankee West: Community Life on the Michigan Frontier* (Chapel Hill: University of North Carolina Press, 1996); Francis Wayland Sheperdson, "The Old Granville and the New," *New England Magazine* (March 1899); McFarland, *A Scattered People.*

26. Foster, *American Grit,* 60.

27. Robert A. Wheeler, "Land and Community in Rural Nineteenth Century America: Claridon Township, 1810–1870," *Ohio History* 97 (1988): 101–21. Tamara G. Miller, "'My whole enjoyment and almost my existence depends upon my friends': Family and Kinship in Early Ohio," in this volume.

28. Clark, *Roots of Rural Capitalism,* especially 105–11; Winifred B. Rothenberg, *From Market-Places to a Market-Economy: The Transformation of Rural Massachusetts, 1750–1850* (Chicago: University of Chicago Press, 1992).

29. Foster, *American Grit,* 41.

30. Howells, *Recollections,* 146.

31. In *Recollections* Howells comments on the uses to which cash was put (137–38).

32. Charles Post, "Rural Class Structure and Economic Development: The Transformation of the Northern U.S. Countryside before the Civil War," unpublished paper prepared for a symposium at the Center for Social Theory and Comparative History, University of California, Los Angeles, 1995.

33. Foster, *American Grit,* 59, 87–89.

34. Kenneth Wheeler, "How Colleges Shaped a Public Culture of Usefulness," in this volume. Wheeler notes the high ages of college students in early Ohio; this also replicated patterns discernible in New England up to at least the 1840s: see David F. Allmendinger Jr., *Paupers and Scholars: The Transformation of Student Life in Nineteenth-Century New England* (New York: St. Martins, 1975), especially 136.

35. McFarland, *Scattered People.*

36. Jon Gjerde, *The Minds of the West: Ethnocultural Evolution in the Rural Middle West, 1830–1917* (Chapel Hill: University of North Carolina Press, 1997), 105.

37. Howells, *Recollections,* 50.

38. Foster, *American Grit*, 224, 259.

39. Ohio in 1840 achieved a similar proportion of manufacturing occupations that New York State had exhibited in 1820. The 1820 and 1840 census data on occupations is sketchy and unreliable in many details; above all, it is impossible to determine the bases for assignment to categories, and the division into categories in any case overlooked the widespread practice of "by-employment" in rural areas. However, the data are of some use for comparative purposes.

40. David R. Meyer, "Midwestern Industrialization and the American Manufacturing Belt in the Nineteenth Century," *Journal of Economic History* 49 (1989): 921–37. Rohrbough, in *Trans-Appalachian Frontier*, compared the greater diversification of areas north of the Ohio River that had "no dominant agricultural commodity" with the less-diversified staple-crop regions that emerged to the south (93–114).

41. Mathew Carey, *Essays on Political Economy* (1822; New York: A. M. Kelley, 1968), 72, 97–98; Henry C. Carey, *The Past, the Present, and the Future* (Philadelphia: Carey and Hart, 1848).

42. Soltow and Soltow, "A Settlement that Failed," 63; Alexis de Tocqueville, *Democracy in America*, trans. Henry Reeve, 3rd edition, 2 vols. (Cambridge, MA: Sever and Francis, 1863), 1:464–67.

43. Tischendorf and Taylor, eds., *Diary of Richard Clough Anderson*, 31–32. For a recent discussion of the contrasts between slave and free labor regions in the East, see John D. Majewski, *A House Dividing: Economic Development in Pennsylvania and Virginia before the Civil War* (Cambridge, uk: Cambridge University Press, 2000).

44. On merchants' kinship with farmers, see Miller, "'My whole enjoyment and almost my existence depends upon my friends,'" in this volume; on merchants' business practices, see Naomi R. Lamoreaux, "Rethinking the Transition to Capitalism in the Early American Northeast," *Journal of American History* 90 (September 2003): 437–61.

45. Richard C. Wade, *The Urban Frontier: The Rise of Western Cities, 1790–1830* (Cambridge: Harvard University Press, 1959), focused principally on the settlements that emerged as larger cities; in *River of Enterprise: The Commercial Origins of Regional Identity in the Ohio Valley, 1790–1850* (Bloomington: Indiana University Press, 2002), Kim M. Gruenwald stresses the importance also of "second tier" commercial hubs such as Marietta, the principal focus of her study.

46. Tischendorf and Taylor, eds., *Diary of Richard Clough Anderson*, 31. See Clark, *Roots of Rural Capitalism*, 163–91, and compare Lamoreaux, "Rethinking the Transition to Capitalism."

47. McFarland, *A Scattered People*.

48. On urban commercial hegemony, see William Cronon, *Nature's Metropolis: Chicago and the Great West* (New York: Norton, 1991); on middle-class creation, see Stuart M. Blumin, *The Emergence of the Middle Class: Social Experience in the American City, 1760–1900* (Cambridge, UK: Cambridge Univer-

sity Press, 1989), and Edward J. Balleisen, *Navigating Failure: Bankruptcy and Commercial Society in Antebellum America* (Chapel Hill: University of North Carolina Press, 2001).

49. Rutherford B. Hayes to William McKinley, Cincinnati, November 6, 1866, http://www.ohiohistory.org/onlinedoc/hayes/appendixa.html (consulted June 22, 2003).

50. Quoted in Gjerde, *Minds of the West,* 79.

51. Kim M. Gruenwald, "Marietta's Example of a Settlement Pattern in the Ohio Country: A Reinterpretation," *Ohio History* 105 (1996): 125–44.

52. Gruenwald's *River of Enterprise* discusses the antebellum reorientation of Ohio toward the Northeast and away from the region below the Ohio River. My argument has stressed instead the latency of this orientation throughout Ohio's settlement and development.

AFTERWORD

New Directions in the History of Ohio in the Early American Republic

STUART D. HOBBS

This volume originated in a desire to mark the bicentennial of Ohio statehood by demonstrating its significance in the early history of the United States. While recent historians have paid a good deal of attention to the Ohio Country, their work as a whole has not been effectively integrated into larger national and international narratives.[1] The purpose of *The Center of a Great Empire* is to frame fresh conversations about the complex relationship between Ohio and the American republic.

The early republic was an era of building—building institutions, infrastructure, culture, and society. In many long-settled areas, new construction had to be fit into and alongside older structures. Ohio, however, emerged concurrently with the new nation. The people who came to Ohio brought ideas and institutions that formed the foundation on which they built many of the new institutions that defined the nineteenth-century United States, including political parties, voluntary associations (such as new religious sects), schools and colleges, roads, and canals. Ohio and other states of the Old Northwest provide a unique vantage point on these radical and ubiquitous developments. As John Wigger points out, the dearth of entrenched older denominations in the Ohio Country facilitated the growth of Methodism. The lack of (or removal of) an entrenched past enabled the growth of many other things as well. The late eighteenth and early nineteenth centuries were times of dramatic changes in the Atlantic World, and Ohioans participated creatively in those transformations.

There is more work to be done, and this essay is intended to survey the field and present some topics and questions that bear further investigation. I am aware that one could use the essays in this volume to chart more than one path of future research. The perhaps idiosyncratic path that I map out here is intended not as a final word but as a way to provoke questions and discussion. My own immersion in the multifaceted career of Thomas Worthington and the questions raised by studying him, his family, and his milieu have certainly influenced what I say here, though not in the direction of calling for more studies of him.[2]

Before the Ohio Country was a part of an Atlantic empire, it was Indian country and a contested ground among Native Americans. By the time of the early republic, the Ohio Country was the scene of mounting violence between Native Americans and American settlers. It is here that our exploration of new directions in the history of Ohio appropriately begins. Patrick Griffin shows that what appeared to be just one more skirmish between Indians and settlers (the Big Bottom "Massacre") was in fact a turning point from the white perspective. What were similar turning points from the Indian perspective? It is an admittedly difficult proposition, but more work needs to be done to tell the story of the Ohio Country from the vantage point of Indian country.[3] Furthermore, is it possible to go beyond the political, diplomatic, and military history of Native Americans? Ohio was home to two racially defined communities scorned by most whites: African and Native. One managed to get a foothold in the state and grow despite widespread hostility. The other was forced out. Were there efforts to make common cause? What might come from pursuing such comparisons?

The development of the market economy has occupied historians of the early republic for several years. The market makes a relatively fleeting appearance here, however, mostly in the context of Christopher Clark's discussion of the diversification of the Ohio economy. Clark tells his story primarily from the point of view of Ohio farmers. He alludes to the merchants, however, and the merchants of the Old Northwest are both a group integrally important to economic developments at the time and a body of people about which we could stand to know much more. With annual or semi-annual trips to Baltimore or Philadelphia, merchants in early Ohio brought to their customers a variety of goods, from imported china to wines to textiles. Ohio was integrated into the world market in consumer goods from the beginning. What role did merchants play in developing Ohio manufacturing? In Chillicothe, storekeepers Waddle and Davisson eventually partnered with Thomas Worthington to develop a major pork-packing business. Was this pattern of merchant industrialists typical?

Worthington himself is an interesting case. A large landowner, he brought millwrights with him to Ohio in 1798. Recognizing from the beginning that it was not enough to grow crops, he knew the money was in the processing. Worthington soon ground almost all of the grain grown in Ross County. He acquired Merino sheep and during the decade after 1810 acquired all the machinery necessary to process wool into cloth. His was surely one of the earliest vertically integrated factories west of the Appalachians. He was not very successful at it, but his operation was ambitious. Did other large landowners make similar investments? In other words, who led the development of manufacturing—the agricultural elite (a traditional elite) or the merchants (the rising new middle class)? Moreover, how independent of the East were they? Worthington, after all, died heavily in debt to John Jacob Astor.

Worthington was also indebted to the Chillicothe branch of the Bank of the United States (of which Worthington was a trustee; a cozy relationship indeed). One of the themes of the New Western History is that federal money made possible the economic development of the West, especially of California and the Sunbelt (regions that, ironically, then produced antigovernment politicians). Thomas Worthington was a creature of the central government. During most of his thirty years in Ohio, he held elective or appointive public office at the local, state, or national level. The salaries from these offices were a key source of cash, vital in a cash-poor economy. Worthington's successful pork-packing business was founded on selling his product to U.S. army posts in Louisiana and Arkansas (Worthington discovered the benefits of being a government contractor during the War of 1812—a war he had opposed as a U.S. senator). He tried to interest the army in purchasing shirts from his cloth mill, but did not get a nibble.[4]

Patrick Griffin shows that following the Big Bottom affair the central government would take the lead in settlement, coming in first to clear out the natives and generally set things up for receiving a stream of migrants. This is consistent with the work of other scholars who have shown through studies of the army, the post office, and the land office that the federal government was a powerful and important player in the lives of citizens of the early republic, especially in newly settled areas. The direct and indirect ways in which the federal government promoted economic growth in the Ohio Valley is an important area for further inquiry.[5]

Of course, the state government was most important in the preeminent public works project of the era, the Ohio canals. In this collection, the theme of infrastructure development is given a twist; Kenneth Wheeler examines not the obvious projects but the chartering of colleges and universities and the impact certain key institutions had on Ohio. The "private" denominational universities Wheeler studies had public charters. The distinction between public and private that is so important to us today was not so clear to our early republican forebears. For-profit corporations and what we call not-for-profit corporations both had public responsibilities to a greater or lesser degree. Wheeler shows that Ohio legislators viewed higher education as a public good. Chartering these institutions permitted the state government to promote that public good without spending money. This Wheeler interprets as a positive, if pragmatic, action.

Wheeler asks us to examine institutions as infrastructure. Beyond colleges and universities, there remain other educational institutions, museums, libraries, and historical societies (many of which were founded in the states of the Old Northwest within a few years of statehood, and even in some cases before). How did these institutions fit into the vision of public good held by legislators and the public? How did that vision change over time? Were there differences between states and regions on this issue? Some of the oldest state historical societies are on the eastern seaboard, where they tend to be private nonprofit organizations. States from the Old Northwest, such as Ohio, are known for state historical societies that are both private and public entities. In other states historical functions are completely lodged in state government. Why the difference, and why the hybrid forms in Ohio, Wisconsin, Minnesota, and other places in the Old Northwest? In these times of revived interest in federalism, and at a time when public institutions have taken a beating in political rhetoric and state budgets, the meaning of public institutions and the relationship between public and private organizations could stand deeper thought and inspection.

The political history of Ohio is the most fully studied aspect of the state's history. The strength of Donald Ratcliffe's work has always been the close attention he has paid to the working of politics at the local level. Here he shows that the intensity of partisan conflict produced a more democratic politics than most politicians wanted. States carved from the Northwest Territory after Ohio were less democratic politically because the "more democratic" Jeffersonian Republicans elsewhere did not face a strong challenge from Federalists. While Ratcliffe styles himself a critic of the cultural interpretation of politics, in practice he pays attention to the ideological and social issues that are at the root of the cultural approach. Moreover, he notes the inconsistencies and contradictions that are exposed by a close look at actual political behavior.

Several other essays in this volume suggest that the politics of Ohio, the Ohio Valley, and the Northwest should be considered in close conjunction with national developments. The divisions that Ellen Eslinger finds between those favoring and opposing black equality and slavery indicate that racial issues provide a window into an ideologically fractured society. Women and reform movements provide another point of reference. Politics in a republican/democratic society is ultimately about the question Who are the people? By paying close attention to the rhetoric and the reality of that question, while noting differences across geography as well as time, we will illuminate the workings of our republic in the past while gaining insight that helps us understand its workings in the present.

Politics and economics combine with social and cultural history in the persons of artisans. Sean Wilentz's *Chants Democratic: New York City and the Rise of the American Working Class, 1788–1850* is perhaps the most well known work that explores how artisans responded politically to the changing economy of the early republic.[6] But what about the artisan community and the culture of the Old Northwest? Steven Ross devoted the first, and shortest, part of his book on Cincinnati workers to artisans, however, as Richard Stott has observed, most artisans did not live in urban areas. About the mechanics (as they were called at the time) who lived in villages and the countryside we know very little.[7] Almost from the beginning Chillicothe was home to furniture makers, watchmakers, silversmiths, and a variety of other craftspeople. The rapid settlement of places like Ohio must have been a great opportunity for artisans. Rather than setting up shop in Baltimore or Philadelphia and competing with the master who trained him, an artisan could move west and be the first and only cooper in a community. That monopoly might not last long, but the opportunities would seem to have been great. Were they? How did that success (or lack of it) influence politics? Did artisans in the Old Northwest contribute to the widening of political participation? Christopher Clark in this volume characterizes merchants and lawyers as the political elites of Ohio cities and towns, which would seem to be accurate. Did artisans and workers form a self-conscious opposition group or did they identify with the goals of economic growth and development advocated by the elites? Ratcliffe has described Cincinnati artisans who organized with gentlemen to oppose Federalists in early Ohio.[8] How long did this sort of alliance continue?

What did Ohio artisans contribute to the debate about canals? Did artisans resist internal improvements that made it easier to bring manufactured goods to the interior, thus undermining their businesses (Wilentz's artisans certainly tended to be opposed to the developing industrial basis for the market economy)? Of course the canals were built, and Ohio was integrated more tightly into the growing market economy. How did artisans in Ohio respond to the growth of the market? Were they opposed to it, or were they part of a broad alliance with commercial farmers in support of the market? What role did artisans, especially in small towns, play in the growth of manufacturing in Ohio? Stott notes that most interpretations of artisans follow a declension model: the good old days of handicraft and economic independence were destroyed by the rise of the market economy. This has been the standard interpretation for antimodernists and Marxists. It is time for political, economic, and social historians, however, to make a fresh start by turning their attention to the experience of mechanics in towns and villages across Ohio and the Old Northwest.

While boosters painted a picture of economic progress in nineteenth-century Ohio, Lee Soltow has documented the great inequalities of wealth that persisted throughout this period. Some flesh is put on Soltow's statistics by the Worthington family. Not only did Thomas experience the booms and busts of the nineteenth-century business cycle but it proved impossible for him to pass on his social and economic status to most of his children. Eleanor and Thomas Worthington had ten children, all of whom lived to adulthood; however, as Mary Alice Mairose commented, "Alco-holism, debt, and disgrace played a major role in the lives of . . . [their] offspring." For the five daughters, for example, marriage was not just a matter of love but an economic decision as well. Many of them made matches that appeared to promise social and economic advancement but in fact brought hardship. The Worthington family was unusual in wealth and prestige, but their example challenges easy clichés about economic progress and social mobility. What might the economic history of families across generations tell us about living in the developing market economy?[9]

The cultural history of Ohio is a topic that has long cried for fur-ther exploration. A recent encyclopedia of Ohio artists provides a wealth of data for examining painting and sculpture in Ohio that we can only hope scholars will use as a jumping-off point.[10] More work is needed as well on music, architecture, and literary culture and the institutions that nourished all of these. The fields of art, music, and literary history are often insular. Because Ohio lacks towering fig-ures such as a Nathaniel Hawthorne or Herman Melville, historians of Ohio culture can further the development of a cultural history rooted in social history. At the center of the cultural history of Ohio and the nation is the small-town bourgeoisie. The nineteenth cen-tury was the great century for America's middle class.

Andrew Cayton, in *Ohio: The History of a People,* and Wheeler, in this volume, provide a framework for looking at Ohio's middle class. Cayton emphasizes the goals of self-improvement and gentility among the bourgeoisie.[11] Wheeler addresses the desire to be useful, to make the world a better place. (While Wheeler sees an antibour-geois tendency in the manual labor programs, I see a very bourgeois antibourgeois program.) Cayton describes a more inner directed, Wheeler a more outer directed, middle class, but these descriptions are parallel, rather than mutually exclusive. Using both points of view, historians can interpret the multitude of cultural institutions the Ohio bourgeoisie created as it grew and prospered. Wigger notes that economic mobility was associated with a falling off in reli-gious enthusiasm. While religion and economic progress were both important to the middle class, they also existed in tension. By taking ideas and cultural production seriously in and of themselves and si-multaneously rooting them in their social milieu (taking those val-ues and conditions seriously), historians can come to a much deeper understanding of Americans and American culture.[12]

By the late twentieth century the American middle class seemed to have changed, becoming more insular, more materialistic, and interested more in consumption than in production. What were the factors that nourished the midwestern middle class in its cultural and economic heyday? How did it shape the national culture? These, too, are questions whose answers a study of cultural institutions and the people who founded, funded, and administered them can reveal.

The ideas and methods of material culture study are only beginning to be integrated into cultural and social history. One way to approach the material culture of the early republic is to think of it as the study of the world of goods that were the objects of the market revolution. Farmers and mechanics sold goods in order to make purchases. What did they purchase? How did the quantity and quality of goods available to ordinary people expand over time? Ohio should be a revealing place to study such questions as the transportation infrastructure evolved and the state increasingly became a place for manufacture as well as consumption. Material artifacts were often an expression of regional identity, especially in the case of architecture. Are there additional ways that material culture connected with southern, New England, or other regions, as well as European-immigrant communities, and how did that change? Finally, because consumption displays status, material culture can provide a window into the ways Americans navigated between egalitarian ideology and social hierarchies.

The social history of Ohio in the early republic remains seriously underdeveloped. Tamara Miller illustrates the quality of source material that exists for the history of women, the family, and sexuality. Studies of childhood, education, ethnic communities, and servant life are just some of the topics that remain to be explored in an Ohio context. Servants, for example, were an important part of middle-class households in the nineteenth century. The servants, however, were from different backgrounds than their masters. The Worthingtons initially drew their household help from the freed slaves they brought with them from Virginia. Young girls, especially from surrounding farms, also worked in households at Adena and elsewhere. By the 1830s and 1840s Irish and German immigrants made up an increasingly large part of the servant population. In 1848 the elderly Eleanor Worthington wrote to her daughter, "I am now living with strange dutches that I never heard of till they came to me, yet we get along somehow."[13] The study of household service provides an opportunity for comparing middle- and working-class people, native born and immigrant, all in the context of expanding notions of civic equality. The story of servants and masters enables a view into domestic life, politics, society, gender relations, ethnic relations, economics, mobility, the history of childhood, and a host of other topics. With its strongly republican ideology, Ohio makes an excellent venue in which to study domestic service in the context of the contradictions and paradoxes of social equality, deference, citizenship, and the ideology of economic mobility.

Ohio's free black community provides a fertile field for investigation that combines economics, religion, politics and political ideology, class, race, and gender. Ellen Eslinger describes how the growth of the free black community in Ohio coincided with increased efforts to keep Ohio free of slavery and free of African Americans. The growing controversy resulted in divisions among the white proponents of the Black Laws and colonization and those opposed to slavery and discrimination. Eslinger highlights the need now for concentrated work to recover the voices and experiences of the free blacks themselves.[14] How did Ohio African Americans respond to the passing of ever more stringent Black Laws that subsequently were not uniformly enforced? Did they feel welcome in their local situation and insecure elsewhere? Who migrated out of Ohio and why? This migration included moving to Canada and, for some, moving to Liberia. In what ways were the motivations similar and different, and how did those who stayed behind view those who migrated?

Eslinger notes that many antislavery whites, especially southern Quakers, moved to Ohio in groups. She alludes to groups of manumitted slaves also moving to Ohio communally. In the 1840s, a group of thirty-six slaves freed by their master moved together from Virginia and settled in Gallia County in southern Ohio. Originally, they held land communally. Descendents of the settlers were still found in the area in the late twentieth century. These so-called Lambert Lands settlers organized their community differently from most whites.[15] Was that typical? In what other ways did African American communities differ from white, and why? What happened to them over time? Of course Ohio was the site of a number of important communal societies that were largely white. Were there parallels in ideology, organization, or other issues between white communalism and black?[16] The history of how black communities paralleled, differed, defied, and clashed with surrounding white communities should illuminate both.

Finally, what about region? What is the connection between region and nation, and what is distinctive about Ohio regionally? Clark, Miller, and Wigger provide evidence that connections at the head of the migration stream remained important to Ohio settlers. Miller explicitly says that links with extended family persisted in Marietta after these connections had become less significant for northeastern families. Here is an instance of cultural lag which might suggest that, contrary to the contentions of this volume's editors and contributors, the history of the eastern seaboard really is the history of the United States; the rest of the country just followed along later.

The larger issue is how these migrant connections integrated Ohio into the nation. How did social connections produce economic, cultural, and political ties? Ratcliffe suggests that migration brought to Ohio partisan divisions developed in the East, quickly integrating the new territory into national politics. Did the diversity of settlement produce over time a distinctly Ohio or midwestern culture? Some have argued that the culture of Ohio in the mid-nineteenth century, though self-consciously celebratory of the state, was not in quality different from those of other regions of the country.

Part of the problem is deciding to what region the state belongs. Is it part of the Midwest, a region that seemingly grew out of a political entity (the Northwest Territory), or is it part of the Ohio Valley, a geographical entity? The geographical approach has an obvious advantage over the political one in that it roots Ohio in something primordial—a river—as opposed to something temporal, partisan, and constructed by humans—politics. Andrew Cayton has quoted Jack Temple Kirby's remark that "drainage is destiny," a strong vote for the validity of the Ohio Valley construct. Cayton, who has explored Ohio as a region from both perspectives, has made an eloquent plea for historians to "exploit the contradictions and ambiguities of place constructed around a river that was at once a commercial artery drawing its life from north and south and a political boundary dividing a northern world from a southern one. It is a puzzle we have only begun to contemplate." I hope historians will take up Cayton's cause, especially through the development of comparative local histories.[17]

A discussion of regional identity may seem a strange place to bring up local or microhistory, but I think that more such studies, especially of Ohio towns and cities from this period, are just what is needed to help us understand the regional identity of Ohio.[18] The best microhistory takes local developments and uses them to illuminate the larger trends of the time. The bibliography shows a great deal of attention to Cincinnati, while Chillicothe, Columbus, Dayton, Lancaster, and Marietta, among others, have been examined mostly in unpublished dissertations. Because of the rich literature on Kentucky and Illinois, the opportunity exists to develop a local history that explicitly compares a town such as Portsmouth with other river towns, or a farming community with similar communities, both free and slave. The results of such studies should tell us more about the nature of region as well as the similarities and differences existing north and south of the river. My sense is that the Ohio Valley model will not work as a coherent social, cultural, and economic entity. The river functioned more as a border than a center, and increasingly so as the nineteenth century went on.

The essays in this volume rarely deal explicitly with the theme of the Ohio Valley, yet I believe several of the essays call Kirby's statement seriously into question. The sources of migration streams left Ohio with a strong mid-Atlantic and northeastern tone. At the same time, at least in the early days, drainage *was* destiny as far as commerce was concerned. The cheapest and most efficient way to get goods to wider markets was to send them down the Ohio and Mississippi rivers. Drainage took a population that came largely from the East and forced it to look south and west. But with the development of the Ohio and Erie Canal (completed 1832), followed by railroads, economic ties to the East became predominant. Technology allowed commerce to flow back toward the origins of the migration stream, rather than away. For Ohioans, at least, drainage was not always destiny.

At stake are fundamental issues of causation. What has the most influence on a developing society—geography, culture, or economics? These are big questions, and the history of neither the Ohio Valley nor the Old Northwest will settle them. Nor must they. What should be clear, however, is that the story of Ohio is not just about our past—it has much to tell us about how we think about that past as well.

This volume is one of several that have appeared as a part of the commemoration of the Ohio bicentennial.[19] That the state is rich in historical material and fascinating stories should no longer need to be demonstrated. That those stories are not just relevant to Ohio but are part of the national story and can illuminate our understanding of the past should also be beyond debate. If scholars of the early republic turn their gaze to the interior of North America, they will find that the territory north of the Ohio River was indeed the "centre of a great empire" and our understanding of early American history will be greatly enriched. Bicentennials, based as they are on the arbitrary construct of the calendar, are at one level what Daniel Boorstin called "pseudo-events."[20] Nevertheless, if the Ohio celebration inspires fresh debates and new ways of thinking about our collective past, then the event will have more than justified itself.

Notes

1. Andrew R. L. Cayton, "The State of Ohio's Early History: A Review Essay," *Ohio History* 106 (1997): 192–99.

2. In her review of the reissue of the only book-length biography of Worthington, Mary Alice Mairose does correctly call attention to the need for a modern biography of Worthington. Mary Alice Mairose, "A Facet of a Complex Man," review of Alfred Byron Sears, *Thomas Worthington: Father of Ohio Statehood* (1958; Columbus: Ohio State University Press, 1998). H-Ohio, June 1999, for H-Net. http://www.h-net.org/reviews/showrev.cgi?path= 698928775412 (consulted March 9, 2004).

3. Here I am thinking of something on the model of Daniel K. Richter, *Facing East from Indian Country: A Native History of Early America* (Cambridge: Harvard University Press, 2001).

4. Thomas Worthington to C. Irvine, July 29, 1820, Thomas Worthington Papers, Early Ohio Political Leaders, MIC 96, Roll 12, Box 9, Folder 6, Ohio Historical Society (hereafter OHS).

5. Andrew R. L. Cayton, "'Separate Interests' and the Nation-State: The Washington Administration and the Origins of Regionalism in the Trans-Appalachian West," *Journal of American History* 79 (1992): 39–67; Richard R. John, *Spreading the News: The American Postal System from Franklin to Morse* (Cambridge: Harvard University Press, 1995); Malcolm J. Rohrbough, *The Land Office Business: The Settlement and Administration of American Public Lands, 1789–1837* (New York: Oxford University Press, 1968).

6. Sean Wilentz, *Chants Democratic: New York City and the Rise of the American Working Class, 1788–1850* (New York: Oxford University Press, 1984).

7. Steven Ross, *Workers on the Edge: Work, Leisure, and Politics in Industrializing Cincinnati, 1788–1890* (New York: Columbia University Press, 1985), 3–63; Richard Stott, "Artisans and Capitalist Development," *Journal of the Early Republic* 16 (1996): 257–71.

8. Donald J. Ratcliffe, *Party Spirit in a Frontier Republic: Democratic Politics in Ohio, 1793–1821* (Columbus: Ohio State University Press, 1998), 55–57.

9. Soltow's essays are cited in the bibliography; Mairose, "Facet of a Complex Man."

10. Mary Sayre Haverstock, Jeannette Mahoney Vance, and Brian L. Meggitt, *Artists in Ohio, 1787–1900: A Biographical Dictionary* (Kent, OH: Kent State University Press, 2000).

11. Cayton, *Ohio: The History of a People* (Columbus: Ohio State University Press, 2002), esp. 78–81, 86–88.

12. Wendy Jean Katz, *Regionalism and Reform: Art and Class Formation in Antebellum Cincinnati* (Columbus: Ohio State University Press, 2002), is an example of the sort of cultural history I am talking about.

13. Eleanor Worthington to Elizabeth W. Pomeroy, November 5, 1848, Worthington Family Papers, MSS 54, OHS.

14. Barbara A. Terzian, "'Effusions of Folly and Fanaticism': Race, Gender, and Constitution Making in Ohio, 1802–1923" (PhD diss., Ohio State University, 1999), is another example of recent scholarship which is excellent for its kind but in which blacks are largely a group that is acted upon rather than being actors themselves. Nikki M. Taylor's forthcoming work on the Cincinnati African American community (Ohio University Press) promises to be corrective in this regard.

15. Http://www.zoomnet.net/~histsoc/Lambert.html (consulted January 20, 2004.)

16. See Catherine M. Rokicky, *Creating A Perfect World: Religious and Secular Utopias in Nineteenth-Century Ohio* (Athens: Ohio University Press, 2002).

17. Andrew R. L. Cayton, "Artery and Border: The Ambiguous Development of the Ohio Valley in the Early Republic," *Ohio Valley History* 1 (2001): 19, 25.

18. Richard D. Brown, "Microhistory and the Post-Modern Challenge," *Journal of the Early Republic* 23 (2003): 1–20.

19. These include, choosing just offerings from Ohio University Press, specialized volumes such as Michael Les Benedict and John F. Winkler, eds., *The History of Ohio Law,* 2 vols. (Athens: Ohio University Press, 2004), and the more popularly focused Bicentennial Series, including the volume on utopias cited above as well as works on women, transportation, Native Americans, religion, and migration.

20. Daniel J. Boorstin, *The Image: A Guide to Pseudo-Events in America* (New York: Harper & Row, 1964).

BIBLIOGRAPHY

Ohio in the Early Republic

Like all bibliographies, this one is selective. The principles of selection were as follows:

- The bibliography lists works covering Ohio from the years 1789 to 1850. The bibliography is intended to provide a point of entry for the study of Ohio during the first years of the American nation, so the editors defined that period after the leading professional organization in the field, The Society for Historians of the Early American Republic.

- The bibliography includes works published since 1940. The editors accepted the works of Downes, Utter, and Weisenburger, cited below and published between 1935 and 1942, as being the summation of the first hundred-odd years of historical research on Ohio for this period and thus decided to include only works published after those classics were researched and written.

- The bibliography lists secondary works, not published primary documents.

- The bibliography includes books, articles, and dissertations, but not master's theses.

That said, the editors are not small-minded, and exceptions have been made to many of these rules. The bibliography does include works that begin or end in the period defined but spill out at either end. Most often the difference is just a matter of a few years or perhaps a decade or two. On a few occasions the spillage is larger. For example, James O'Donnell's *Ohio's First Peoples* treats, for most of its length, times well before our stated beginning point, but it is such an important introduction to its subject that all researchers should consult it and its sources. At the other end of the chronological spectrum, David R. Contosta's *Lancaster, Ohio, 1800–2000: Frontier*

Town to Edge City is an important study of a town in a state where studies of communities that are not Cincinnati are rare and thus merited inclusion despite extending well beyond our cutoff point. Some recently published collections of primary sources have been included because of their historiographical significance. A small number of master's theses on topics that are otherwise understudied are also listed.

Note that this bibliography includes published items cited in the chapter notes—if the sources cited were published after 1940. But the essays also cite primary sources and works published before 1940, and these are not included here. In addition, the notes to the essays reference more general works that relate to the larger context of the topics explored. For any topic covered here, the notes to the essays, together with the appropriate section of the bibliography, will give the reader a good overview of relevant works.

General Works

Banta, R. E. *The Ohio*. 1949; Lexington: University Press of Kentucky, 1998.

Barnhart, John D. *Valley of Democracy: The Frontier versus the Plantation in the Ohio Valley, 1775–1818*. Bloomington: Indiana University Press, 1953.

Bond, Beverley W. *The Civilization of the Old Northwest: A Study of Political, Social, and Economic Development, 1788–1812*. New York: Macmillan, 1934.

———. *The Foundations of Ohio*. Vol. 1 of *The History of the State of Ohio*, ed. Carl Frederick Wittke. Columbus: Ohio State Archaeological and Historical Society, 1941.

Booth, Stephane Elise. *Buckeye Women: The History of Ohio's Daughters*. Athens: Ohio University Press, 2001.

Cayton, Andrew R. L. "The State of Ohio's Early History: A Review Essay." *Ohio History* 106 (1997): 192–99.

———. "Artery and Border: The Ambiguous Development of the Ohio Valley in the Early Republic." *Ohio Valley History* 1 (2001): 19–26.

———. *Ohio: The History of a People*. Columbus: Ohio State University Press, 2002.

Cayton, Andrew R. L., and Susan E. Grey, eds. *The American Midwest: Essays on Regional History*. Bloomington: Indiana University Press, 2001.

Cayton, Andrew R. L., and Peter S. Onuf. *The Midwest and the Nation: Rethinking the History of an American Region*. Bloomington: Indiana University Press, 1990.

Downes, Randolph C. *Frontier Ohio, 1788–1803*. Columbus: Ohio State Archaeological and Historical Society, 1935.

Durham, Walter T. "The Southwest and Northwest Territories: A Comparison, 1787–1796." *Tennessee Historical Quarterly* 49 (1990): 188–96.

Fischer, David Hackett, and James C. Kelly. *Bound Away: Virginia and the Westward Movement*. Charlottesville: University Press of Virginia, 2000.

Foster, Emily, ed. *The Ohio Frontier: An Anthology of Early Writings*. Lexington: University Press of Kentucky, 1996.

Grant, H. Roger. *Ohio on the Move: Transportation in the Buckeye State*. Athens: Ohio University Press, 2000.

Gruenwald, Kim M. *River of Enterprise: The Commercial Origins of Regional Identity in the Ohio Valley, 1790–1850*. Bloomington: Indiana University Press, 2002.

Hatcher, Harlan. *The Western Reserve: The Story of New Connecticut in Ohio*. 1966; Kent, OH: Kent State University Press, 1991.

Havighurst, Walter. *Land of Promise: The Story of the Northwest Territory*. New York: Macmillan, 1946.

Heiser, Alta Harvey. *West to Ohio*. Yellow Springs, OH: Antioch Press, 1954.

Hinderaker, Eric. *Elusive Empires: Constructing Colonialism in the Ohio Valley, 1673–1800*. New York: Cambridge University Press, 1997.

Hurt, R. Douglas. *The Ohio Frontier: Crucible of the Old Northwest, 1720–1830*. Bloomington: Indiana University Press, 1996.

Jakle, John A. *Images of the Ohio Valley: A Historical Geography of Travel, 1740 to 1860*. New York: Oxford University Press, 1977.

Knepper, George W. *Ohio and Its People*. 3rd ed. Kent, OH: Kent State University Press, 2003.

Kramer, Frank R. *Voices in the Valley: Mythmaking and Folk Belief in the Shaping of the Middle West*. Madison: University of Wisconsin Press, 1964.

Madison, James H., ed. *Heartland: Comparative Histories of the Midwestern States*. Bloomington: Indiana University Press, 1990.

Miller, James M. *The Genesis of Western Culture: The Upper Ohio Valley, 1800–1825*. Columbus: Ohio State Archaeological and Historical Society, 1938.

Onuf, Peter S. *Statehood and Union: A History of the Northwest Ordinance*. Bloomington: Indiana University Press, 1987.

Parker, Geoffrey, Richard Sisson, and William Russell Coil, eds. *Ohio and the World, 1753–2053: Essays toward a New History of Ohio*. Columbus: Ohio State University Press, 2005.

Peacefull, Leonard, ed. *A Geography of Ohio*. Kent, OH: Kent State University Press, 1996.

Philbrick, Francis Samuel. *The Rise of the West, 1754–1830*. New York: Harper & Row, 1965.

Reid, Robert L., ed. *Always a River: The Ohio River and the American Experience*. Bloomington: Indiana University Press, 1991.

Rohrbough, Malcolm J. *The Trans-Appalachian Frontier: People, Societies, and Institutions, 1775–1850.* New York: Oxford University Press, 1978.

Scheiber, Harry N., ed. *The Old Northwest: Studies in Regional History, 1787–1910.* Lincoln: University Nebraska Press, 1969.

Shriver, Phillip R., and Clarence E. Wunderlin Jr., eds. *The Documentary Heritage of Ohio.* Athens: Ohio University Press, 2000.

Smith, Thomas H. *The Mapping of Ohio: The Delineation of the State of Ohio through the Use of Manuscript Maps, Printed Maps, and Plats, Sketches and Plans from Original Map Makers with a Narrative which Describes Each Map from Contemporary Sources.* Kent, OH: Kent State University Press, 1977.

Utter, William Thomas. *The Frontier State, 1803–1825.* Vol. 2 of *The History of the State of Ohio,* ed. Carl Frederick Wittke. Columbus: Ohio State Archaeological and Historical Society, 1942.

Van Tine, Warren, and Michael Pierce, eds. *Builders of Ohio: A Biographical History.* Columbus: Ohio State University Press, 2003.

Weisenburger, Francis P. *The Passing of the Frontier, 1825–1850.* Vol. 3 of *The History of the State of Ohio,* ed. Carl Frederick Wittke. Columbus: Ohio State Archaeological and Historical Society, 1941.

Native Americans: Culture, Politics, Diplomacy, and War

Calloway, Colin G. "Beyond the Vortex of Violence: Indian-White Relations in the Ohio Country, 1783–1815." *Northwest Ohio Quarterly* 64 (1992): 16–20.

Carter, Harvey Lewis. *The Life and Times of Little Turtle: First Sagamore of the Wabash.* Urbana: University of Illinois Press, 1987.

Cayton, Andrew R. L. "'Noble Actors' upon the 'Theatre of Honor': Power and Civility in the Treaty of Greenville." In *Contact Points: American Frontiers from the Mohawk Valley to the Mississippi,* ed. Andrew R. L. Cayton and Fredrika J. Teute, 235–69. Chapel Hill: University of North Carolina Press for the Omohundro Institute of Early American History and Culture, 1998.

Collins, William Frederick. "John Tipton and the Indians of the Old Northwest." PhD diss., Purdue University, 1997.

Dowd, Gregory Evans. *A Spirited Resistance: The North American Indian Struggle for Unity, 1745–1815.* Baltimore: Johns Hopkins University Press, 1992.

Downes, Randolph C. *Council Fires on the Upper Ohio: A Narrative of Indian Affairs in the Upper Ohio Valley until 1795.* Pittsburgh: University of Pittsburgh Press, 1940.

Edmunds, R. David. *The Shawnee Prophet.* Lincoln: University of Nebraska Press, 1983.

———. *Tecumseh and the Quest for Indian Leadership.* Boston: Little, Brown, 1984.

————. "Main Poc: Potawatomi Wabeno." *American Indian Quarterly* 9 (1985): 259–72.

Farrell, Richard T. "Promoting Agriculture among the Indian Tribes of the Old Northwest, 1789–1820." *Journal of NAL Associates* 3 (1978): 13–18.

Hornbeck, Helen, ed. *Atlas of Great Lakes Indian History.* Norman: Published for the Newberry Library by the University of Oklahoma Press, 1987.

Howard, James Henri. *Shawnee!: The Ceremonialism of a Native Indian Tribe and Its Cultural Background.* Athens: Ohio University Press, 1981.

Jacobs, Wilbur R. "Was the Pontiac Uprising a Conspiracy?" *Ohio State Archaeological and Historical Quarterly* 59 (1950): 26–37.

James, Peter D. "The British Indian Department in the Ohio Country, 1784–1795." *Northwest Ohio Quarterly* 64 (1992): 78–95.

Klopfenstein, Carl Grover. *The Removal of the Indians from Ohio, 1820–1843.* Cleveland: Western Reserve University, 1955.

McConnell, Michael Norman. "The Search for Security: Indian-English Relations in the Trans-Appalachian Region, 1758–1763." PhD diss., College of William and Mary, 1983.

Miriani, Ronald G. "Against the Wind: The Shawnee at Wapakoneta." *Queen City Heritage* 48 (1990): 33–47.

Nelson, Larry L. "Cultural Mediation, Cultural Exchange, and the Invention of the Ohio Frontier." *Ohio History* 105 (1996): 72–91.

————. *A Man of Distinction among Them: Alexander McKee and the Ohio Country Frontier, 1754–1799.* Kent, OH: Kent State University Press, 1999.

Newcomb, William W., Jr. *The Culture and Acculturation of the Delaware Indians.* University of Michigan Museum of Anthropology, Anthropological Papers 10. Ann Arbor, 1956.

O'Donnell, James H. *Ohio's First Peoples.* Athens: Ohio University Press, 2004.

Okerson, Barbara Buhr. "Weyapicrsenweh: Blue Jacket, War Chief of the Shawnees, and the Contest for Possession of the Ohio River Valley." PhD diss., University of Memphis, 1996.

Olmstead, Earl P. "A Day of Shame: The Gnadenhutten Story." *Timeline* 8 (August/September 1991): 20–33.

Richards, James K. "A Clash of Cultures: Simon Girty and the Struggle for the Frontier." *Timeline* 2 (June/July 1985): 2–17.

Satz, Ronald N. "Indian Policy in the Jacksonian Era: The Old Northwest as a Test Case." *Michigan History* 60 (1976): 71–93.

Schutt, Amy C. "'What Will Become of Our Young People?': Goals for Indian Children in Moravian Missions." *History of Education Quarterly* 38 (1998): 268–86.

Shriver, Phillip R. "Know Them No More Forever: The Miami Removal of 1846." *Timeline* 10 (November/December 1993): 30–41.

Smith, Dwight L. "Wayne's Peace with the Indians of the Old Northwest, 1795." *Ohio State Archaeological and Historical Quarterly* 59 (1950): 239–55.

———. "The Problem of the Historic Indian in the Ohio Valley: The Historian's View." *Ohio State Archaeological and Historical Quarterly* 63 (1954): 172–80.

Smith, Robert E. "The Clash of Leadership at the Grand Reserve: The Wyandot Subagency and the Methodist Mission, 1820–1824." *Ohio History* 89 (1980): 181–205.

Sugden, John. *Tecumseh: A Life.* New York: Henry Holt, 1998.

———. *Blue Jacket: Warrior of the Shawnees.* Lincoln: University of Nebraska Press, 2000.

Tanner, Helen Hornbeck. "Cherokees in the Ohio Country." *Journal of Cherokee Studies* 3 (1978): 94–102.

———. "The Glaize in 1792: A Composite Indian Community." *Ethnohistory* 25 (1978): 15–39.

Taylor, Alan. "Captain Hendrick Aupaumut: The Dilemmas of an Intercultural Broker." *Ethnohistory* 43 (1996): 431–57.

Trennert, Robert A., Jr. "William Medill's War with the Indian Traders, 1847." *Ohio History* 82 (1973): 46–62.

Weslager, C. A. *The Delaware Indians: A History.* New Brunswick, NJ: Rutgers University Press, 1972.

———. *The Delaware Indian Westward Migration: With the Texts of Two Manuscripts, 1821–22, Responding to General Lewis Cass's Inquiries about Lenape Culture and Language.* Wallingford, PA: Middle Atlantic Press, 1978.

Politics

Alexander, Roberta Sue. *A Place of Recourse: A History of the U.S. District Court for the Southern District of Ohio, 1803–2003.* Athens: Ohio University Press, 2005.

Allen, Michael. "The Federalists and the West, 1783–1803." *Western Pennsylvania Historical Magazine* 61 (1978): 315–32.

Barlow, William R. "Ohio's Congressmen and the War of 1812." *Ohio History* 72 (1963): 175–94.

Benedict, Michael Les, and John F. Winkler, eds. *The History of Ohio Law.* 2 vols. Athens: Ohio University Press, 2004.

Berquist, Goodwin F., and Paul C. Bowers Jr. *The New Eden: James Kilbourne and the Development of Ohio.* Lanham, MD: University Press of America, 1983.

Bloom, Jo Tice. "The Congressional Delegates from the Northwest Territory." *The Old Northwest* 3 (1977): 3–21.

Blue, Frederick J. "The Ohio Free Soilers and Problems of Factionalism." *Ohio History* 76 (1967): 17–32.

Bochin, Hal W. "Tom Corwin's Speech against the Mexican War: Courageous but Misunderstood." *Ohio History* 90 (1981): 33–53.

Booraem, Hendrik. "William Henry Harrison Comes to Cincinnati." *Queen City Heritage* 45 (1987): 2–22.

Borer, Alan. "William Henry Harrison and the Rhetoric of History." *Northwest Ohio Quarterly* 68 (1996): 116–32.

Bradford, Henry David. "The Background and Formation of the Republican Party in Ohio, 1844–1861." PhD diss., University of Chicago, 1947.

Brisbin, Richard A., Jr. "Before Bureaucracy: State Courts and the Administration of Public Services in the Northwest, 1787–1830." *The Old Northwest* 10 (1984): 141–74.

Brown, David Scott. "The Political Culture of the Whig Party in Ohio." PhD diss., University of Toledo, 1995.

Brown, Jeffrey P. "Frontier Politics: The Evolution of a Political Society in Ohio, 1788–1814." PhD diss., University of Illinois, Urbana-Champaign, 1979.

———. "Samuel Huntington: A Connecticut Aristocrat on the Ohio Frontier." *Ohio History* 89 (1980): 420–38.

———. "The Ohio Federalists, 1803–1815." *Journal of the Early Republic* 2 (1982): 261–82.

———. "William McMillan and the Conservative Cincinnati Jeffersonians." *The Old Northwest* 12 (1986): 117–35.

———. "Arthur St. Clair and the Northwest Territory." *Northwest Ohio Quarterly* 59 (1987): 75–90.

Brown, Jeffrey P., and Andrew R. L. Cayton, eds. *The Pursuit of Public Power: Political Culture in Ohio, 1787–1861.* Kent, OH: Kent State University Press, 1994.

Buchstein, Frederick D. "Josiah Warren: The Peaceful Revolutionist." *Cincinnati Historical Society Bulletin* 32 (1974): 61–71.

Cayton, Andrew R. L. *The Frontier Republic: Ideology and Politics in the Ohio Country, 1780–1825.* Kent, OH: Kent State University Press, 1986.

———. "The Contours of Power in a Frontier Town: Marietta, Ohio, 1788–1803." *Journal of the Early Republic* 6 (1986): 103–26.

———. "Land, Power, and Reputation: The Cultural Dimension of Politics in the Ohio Country." *William and Mary Quarterly* 47 (1990): 266–86.

———. "'Separate Interests' and the Nation-State: The Washington Administration and the Origins of Regionalism in the Trans-Appalachian West." *Journal of American History* 79 (1992): 39–67.

———. "Radicals in the Western World: The Federalist Conquest of Trans-Appalachian North America." In *Federalists Reconsidered,* ed. Barbara Oberg and Doron Ben-Atar, 77–96. Charlottesville: University Press of Virginia, 1998.

Davis, David Brion. "The Significance of Excluding Slavery from the Old Northwest in 1787." *Indiana Magazine of History* 84 (1988): 75–89.

Dubin, Barbara Hinda. "A Critical Review of the Social and Educational Theories of Josiah Warren and His Individualist School of Anarchism." PhD diss., University of Illinois, Urbana-Champaign, 1973.

Dudley, Charlotte W. "Jared Mansfield: United States Surveyor General." *Ohio History* 85 (1976): 231–46.

Elkins, Stanley M., and Eric L. McKitrick. "A Meaning for Turner's Frontier: Democracy in the Old Northwest." *Political Science Quarterly* 69 (1954): 321–53.

Erickson, Leonard. "Politics and the Repeal of Ohio's Black Laws, 1837–1849." *Ohio History* 82 (1973): 154–75.

Etcheson, Nicole. *The Emerging Midwest: Upland Southerners and the Political Culture of the Old Northwest, 1787–1861.* Bloomington: Indiana University Press, 1996.

Finkelman, Paul R. "Slavery and the Northwest Ordinance: A Study in Ambiguity." *Journal of the Early Republic* 6 (1986): 343–70.

Flack, Irwin F. "Who Governed Cincinnati?: A Comparative Analysis of Government and Social Structure in a Nineteenth Century River City, 1819–1860." PhD diss., University of Pittsburgh, 1978.

Fox, Stephen C. "Politicians, Issues, and Voter Preference in Jacksonian Ohio: A Critique of an Interpretation." *Ohio History* 86 (1977): 155–70.

———. "The Bank Wars, the Idea of 'Party,' and the Division of the Electorate in Jacksonian Ohio." *Ohio History* 88 (1979): 253–76.

———. *The Group Bases of Ohio Political Behavior, 1803–1848.* New York: Garland Publishing, 1989.

Franz, Patricia L. "Ohio v. the Bank: An Historical Examination of Osborn v. The Bank of the United States." *Journal of Supreme Court History* 23 (1999): 112–37.

Gilbert, Abby L. "Thomas Ewing, Sr.: Ohio's Advocate for a National Bank." *Ohio History* 82 (1973): 4–24.

Grupenhoff, John T. "Politics and the Rise of Political Parties in the Northwest Territory and Early Ohio to 1812 with Emphasis on Cincinnati and Hamilton County." PhD diss., University of Texas, 1962.

Gunderson, Robert G. "John W. Bear, 'The Buckeye Blacksmith.'" *Ohio State Archaeological and Historical Quarterly* 61 (1952): 262–71.

Hall, Bowman N. "The Economic Ideas of Josiah Warren, First American Anarchist." *History of Political Economy* 6 (1974): 95–108.

Harrold, Stanley C., Jr. "Forging an Antislavery Instrument: Gamaliel Bailey and the Foundation of the Ohio Liberty Party." *The Old Northwest* 2 (1976): 371–87.

———. "The Southern Strategy of the Liberty Party." *Ohio History* 87 (1978): 21–36.

Kindig, Everett William. "Western Opposition to Jackson's Democracy: The Ohio Valley as a Case Study, 1827–1836." PhD diss., Stanford University, 1974.

Maizlish, Stephen E. *The Triumph of Sectionalism: The Transformation of Ohio Politics, 1844–1856.* Kent, OH: Kent State University Press, 1983.

Mangin, Michael. "Freemen in Theory: Race, Society, and Politics in Ross County, Ohio, 1796–1850." PhD diss., University of California, San Diego, 2002.

Marcus, Alan I. "National History through Local: Social Evils and the Origin of Municipal Services in Cincinnati." *American Studies* 22 (1981): 23–39.

Matijasic, Thomas D. "Whig Support for African Colonization: Ohio as a Test Case." *Mid-America* 66 (1984): 79–91.

Melhorn, Donald F., Jr. *"Lest We Be Marshall'd": Judicial Powers and Politics in Ohio, 1806–1812.* Akron: University of Akron Press, 2003.

Minor, Richard Clyde. "James Preston Poindexter, Elder Statesman of Columbus." *Ohio State Archaeological and Historical Quarterly* 56 (1947): 266–86.

Miriani, Ronald G. "Lewis Cass and Indian Administration in the Old Northwest, 1815–1836." PhD diss., University of Michigan, 1974.

Onuf, Peter S. "From Constitution to Higher Law: The Reinterpretation of the Northwest Ordinance." *Ohio History* 94 (1985): 5–33.

———. "The Toledo War and American Federalism." *Northwest Ohio Quarterly* 59 (1987): 135–52.

Overman, William D. "Early Ohio Postal Routes." *Ohio State Archaeological and Historical Quarterly* 55 (1946): 21–29, 401–6.

Palmer, Beverly Wilson. "Towards a National Antislavery Party: The Giddings-Sumner Alliance." *Ohio History* 99 (1990): 51–71.

Parker, Wyman W. "Edwin M. Stanton at Kenyon." *Ohio State Archaeological and Historical Quarterly* 60 (1951): 233–56.

Pershing, Benjamin H. "The Admission of Ohio to the Union." *Ohio State Archaeological and Historical Quarterly* 63 (1954): 240–53.

Pitcavage, Mark. "'Burthened in Defence of Our Rights': Opposition to Military Service in Ohio During the War of 1812." *Ohio History* 104 (1995): 142–62.

Pocock, Emil. "Popular Roots of Jacksonian Democracy: The Case of Dayton, Ohio, 1815–30." *Journal of the Early Republic* 9 (1989): 489–515.

Porter, Eugene O. "Boundary and Jurisdictional Problems of the Kentucky-Ohio Border." *Ohio State Archaeological and Historical Quarterly* 55 (1946): 155–64.

Potts, Louis W. "Manasseh Cutler, Lobbyist." *Ohio History* 96 (1987): 101–23.

Preston, Emmett D. "The Fugitive Slave Acts in Ohio." *The Journal of Negro History* 28 (1943): 422–77.

Ratcliffe, Donald J. "The Experience of Revolution and the Beginnings of Party Politics in Ohio, 1776–1816." *Ohio History* 85 (1976): 186–230.

———. "Politics in Jacksonian Ohio: Reflections on the Ethnocultural Interpretation." *Ohio History* 88 (1979): 5–36.

———. "Voter Turnout in Early Ohio." *Journal of the Early Republic* 7 (1987): 223–51.

———. *Party Spirit in a Frontier Republic: Democratic Politics in Ohio, 1793–1821.* Columbus: Ohio State University Press, 1998.

———. *The Politics of Long Division: The Birth of the Second Party System in Ohio, 1818–1828.* Columbus: Ohio State University Press, 2000.

Rayback, Joseph G. "The Liberty Party Leaders of Ohio: Exponents of Anti-Slavery Coalition." *Ohio State Archaeological and Historical Quarterly* 57 (1948): 165–78.

Reilley, Edward C. "Politico-Economic Considerations in the Western Reserve's Early Slavery Controversy." *Ohio State Archaeological and Historical Quarterly* 52 (1943): 141–57.

Rubenstein, Asa Lee. "Richard Clough Anderson, Nathaniel Massie, and the Impact of Government on Western Land Speculation and Settlement, 1774–1830." PhD diss., University of Illinois, Urbana-Champaign, 1986.

Rutenbeck, Jeff. "Partisan Press Coverage of Anti-Abolitionist Violence: A Study of Early Nineteenth-Century 'Viewsflow.'" *Journal of Communication Inquiry* 19 (1995): 126–41.

Salisbury, Robert S. "William Windom: The Formative Years." *The Old Northwest* 2 (1986): 439–56.

Sears, Alfred B. "The Political Philosophy of Arthur St. Clair." *Ohio State Historical and Archaeological Quarterly* 49 (1940): 41–57.

———. *Thomas Worthington: Father of Ohio Statehood.* 1958; Columbus: Ohio State University Press, 1998.

Shade, William G. *Banks or No Banks: The Money Issue in Western Politics, 1832–1865.* Detroit: Wayne State University Press, 1972.

Sharp, James Roger. *The Jacksonians versus the Bank: Politics in the States after the Panic of 1837.* New York: Columbia University Press, 1970.

Shetrone, Henry C. "Caleb Atwater: Versatile Pioneer." *Ohio State Archaeological and Historical Quarterly* 54 (1945): 79–88.

Spraul-Schmidt, Judith. "The Origins of Modern City Government: From Corporate Regulation to Municipal Corporation in New York, New Orleans, and Cincinnati, 1785–1870." PhD diss., University of Cincinnati, 1990.

Stegemoeller, James E. "That Contemptible Bauble: The Birth of the Cincinnati Whig Party, 1834–1836." *Cincinnati Historical Society Bulletin* 39 (1981): 201–23.

Stevens, Harry R. *The Early Jackson Party in Ohio.* Durham, NC: Duke University Press, 1957.

Stewart, James Brewer. *Joshua R. Giddings and the Tactics of Radical Politics.* Cleveland: Press of Case Western Reserve University, 1970.

Still, John S. "The Life of Ethan Allen Brown, Governor of Ohio." PhD diss., Ohio State University, 1951.

Stuckey, James Herbert. "The Formation of Leadership Groups in a Frontier Town: Canton, Ohio, 1805–1855." PhD diss., Case Western Reserve University, 1976.

Terzian, Barbara A. "'Effusions of Folly and Fanaticism': Race, Gender, and Constitution Making in Ohio, 1802–1923." PhD diss., Ohio State University, 1999.

Thurston, Helen M. "The 1802 Ohio Constitutional Convention and the Status of the Negro." *Ohio History* 81 (1972): 15–37.

Trester, Delmer J. "David Tod and the Gubernatorial Campaign of 1844." *Ohio State Archaeological and Historical Quarterly* 62 (1953): 162–78.

Volpe, Vernon L. "The Ohio Election of 1838: A Study in the Historical Method." *Ohio History* 95 (1986): 85–100.

———. "Benjamin Wade's Strange Defeat." *Ohio History* 97 (1988): 122–32.

———. *Forlorn Hope of Freedom: The Liberty Party in the Old Northwest, 1838–1848.* Kent, OH: Kent State University Press, 1990.

Wilhelmy, Robert W. "Senator John Smith and the Aaron Burr Conspiracy." *Cincinnati Historical Society Bulletin* 28 (1970): 38–60.

Wilson, Gordon L. "Arthur St. Clair and the Administration of the Old Northwest, 1788–1802." PhD diss., University of Southern California, 1957.

Winkle, Kenneth J. *The Politics of Community: Migration and Politics in Antebellum Ohio.* Cambridge, UK: Cambridge University Press, 1988.

Winship, Marion Nelson. "Enterprise in Motion in the Early American Republic: The Federal Government and the Making of Thomas Worthington." *Business and Economic History* 23 (1994): 81–91.

Wittke, Carl. "Ohioans and the Canadian-American Crisis of 1837–1838." *Ohio State Archaeological and Historical Quarterly* 58 (1949): 21–34.

Zsoldos, Silvia Tammisto. "The Political Career of Thomas Ewing, Sr." PhD diss., University of Delaware, 1977.

Military

Bird, Harrison. *War for the West, 1790–1813.* New York: Oxford University Press, 1971.

Bowlus, Bruce. "A 'Signal Victory': The Battle for Fort Stephenson, August 1–2, 1813." *Northwest Ohio Quarterly* 63 (1991): 43–57.

Brod, Raymond Michael. "Maps as Weapons in the Conquest of Old American Northwest, 1608 to 1829." PhD diss., University of Illinois, Chicago, 2000.

Brown, Alan S. "The Role of the Army in Western Settlement: Josiah Harmar's Command, 1785–1790." *Pennsylvania Magazine of History and Biography* 93 (1969): 161–78.

Carroll, George. "Lewis Wetzel: Warfare Tactics on the Frontier." *West Virginia History* 50 (1991): 79–90.

Case, Thomas R. "The Battle of Fallen Timbers." *Northwest Ohio Quarterly* 35 (1963): 54–68.

Coles, Harry Lewis. *The War of 1812.* Chicago: University of Chicago Press, 1966.

Crisman, Kevin J. "Cleared for Action: Inland Navies in the War of 1812." *Timeline* 6 (April/May 1989): 2–19.

DeRegnaucourt, Tony, and Tom Parker. *General Anthony Wayne and the Ohio Indian Wars: A Collection of Unpublished Letters and Artifacts.* Arcanum, OH: Upper Miami Valley Archaeological Research Museum, 1995.

Edel, Wilbur. *Kekionga!: The Worst Defeat in the History of the U.S. Army.* Westport, CT: Praeger, 1997.

Gifford, Jack Jule. "The Northwest Indian War, 1784–1795." PhD diss., University of California, Los Angeles, 1964.

Gunderson, Robert G. "William Henry Harrison: Apprentice in Arms." *Northwest Ohio Quarterly* 65 (1993): 3–29.

Horsman, Reginald. "The British Indian Department and the Resistance to General Anthony Wayne, 1793–1795." *Mississippi Valley Historical Review* 49 (1962): 269–90.

Huber, John Parker. "General Josiah Harmar's Command: Military Policy in the Old Northwest, 1784–1791." PhD diss., University of Michigan, 1968.

Knopf, Richard C. "Fort Miamis: The International Background." *Ohio State Archaeological and Historical Quarterly* 61 (1952): 146–66.

Mahon, John K. *The War of 1812.* Gainesville: University of Florida Press, 1972.

Melhorn, Donald F., Jr. "'A Splendid Man': Richardson, Ft. Meigs and the Story of Metoss." *Northwest Ohio Quarterly* 69 (1997): 133–60.

Michael, Steven B. "Ohio and the Mexican War: Public Response to the 1846–1848 Crisis." PhD diss., Ohio State University, 1985.

———. "A Year's Campaign: Dewitt C. Loudon's Mexican War." *Timeline* 9 (April/May 1992): 18–33.

Millett, Allan R. "Caesar and the Conquest of the Northwest Territory: The Wayne Campaign, 1792–1795." *Timeline* 14 (May/June 1997): 2–21.

———. "Caesar and the Conquest of the Northwest Territory: The Harrison Campaign, 1811." *Timeline* 14 (July/August 1997): 2–19.

———. "Caesar and the Conquest of the Northwest Territory: The Second Harrison Campaign, 1813." *Timeline* 14 (September/October 1997): 2–21.

Millett, Stephen M. "Bellicose Nationalism in Ohio: An Origin of the War of 1812." *Canadian Review of Studies in Nationalism* 1 (1974): 221–40.

Nelson, Larry L. *Men of Patriotism, Courage and Enterprise: Fort Meigs in the War of 1812.* Canton, OH: Daring Books, 1985.

Nelson, Paul David. "Anthony Wayne's Indian War in the Old Northwest, 1792–1795." *Northwest Ohio Quarterly* 56 (1984): 115–40.

Odom, William O. "Destined for Defeat: An Analysis of the St. Clair Expedition of 1791." *Northwest Ohio Quarterly* 65 (1993): 68–93.

Peckham, Howard H. "Josiah Harmar and His Indian Expedition." *Ohio State Archaeological and Historical Quarterly* 55 (1946): 227–41.

Scamyhorn, Richard, and John Steinle. *Stockades in the Wilderness: The Frontier Defenses and Settlements of Southwestern Ohio, 1788–1795.* Dayton: Landfall Press, 1986.

Simmons, David A. "The Military and Administrative Abilities of James Wilkinson in the Old Northwest, 1792–1793." *The Old Northwest* 3 (1977): 237–50.

Slosson, Preston. "The Significance of the Treaty of Greene Ville." *Ohio State Archaeological and Historical Quarterly* 55 (1946): 1–11.

Smith, Dwight L. "Wayne and the Treaty of Greene Ville." *Ohio State Archaeological and Historical Quarterly* 63 (1954): 1–7.

Steinle, John. "Unlucky Soldier: Josiah Harmar's Frontier Struggle." *Timeline* 8 (April/May 1991): 2–17.

Sword, Wiley. *President Washington's Indian War: The Struggle for the Old Northwest, 1790–1795.* Norman: University of Oklahoma Press, 1985.

Walsh, William Patrick. "The Defeat of Major General Arthur St. Clair, November 4, 1791: A Study of the Nation's Response, 1791–1793." PhD diss., Loyola University of Chicago, 1977.

Williams, Gary S. *The Forts of Ohio: A Guide to Military Stockades.* Caldwell, OH: Buckeye Books, 2003.

Reform

Alilunas, Leo. "Fugitive Slave Cases in Ohio prior to 1850." *Ohio History* 49 (1940): 160–84.

Baily, Marilyn. "From Cincinnati, Ohio, to Wilberforce, Canada: A Note on Antebellum Colonization." *Journal of Negro History* 58 (1973): 427–40.

Dannenbaum, Jed. "Drink and Disorder: Temperance Reform in Cincinnati, 1841–1874." PhD diss., University of California, Davis, 1978.

———. "Immigrants and Temperance: Ethnocultural Conflict in Cincinnati, 1845–1860." *Ohio History* 87 (1978): 125–39.

DeBlasio, Donna Marie. "Her Own Society: The Life and Times of Betsy Mix Cowles, 1810–1876." PhD diss., Kent State University, 1980.

Gamble, Douglas A. "Joshua Giddings and the Ohio Abolitionists: A Study in Radical Politics." *Ohio History* 88 (1979): 37–56.

Gara, Larry. "The Underground Railroad: Legend and Reality. *Timeline* 5 (August/September 1988): 18–31.

Geary, Linda L. *Balanced in the Wind: A Biography of Betsey Mix Cowles.* Lewisburg: Bucknell University Press; and London and Cranbury, NJ: Associated University Presses, 1989.

Harris, Marc. "The Process of Voluntary Association: Organizing the Ravenna Temperance Society, 1830." *Ohio History* 94 (1985): 158–70.

Hollins, Dennis Charles. "A Black Voice of Antebellum Ohio: A Rhetorical Analysis of *The Palladium of Liberty,* 1843–1844." PhD diss., Ohio State University, 1978.

Marcus, Alan I. "The Failure of Empowerment: The Mid-Nineteenth Century Benevolent Campaign in Cincinnati." *Queen City Heritage* 50 (1992): 37–48.

Matijasic, Thomas D. "Conservative Reform in the West: The African Colonization Movement in Ohio, 1826–1839." PhD diss., Miami University, 1982.

――――. "Abolition vs. Colonization: The Battle for Ohio." *Queen City Heritage* 45 (1987): 27–40.

Middleton, Stephen. "The Fugitive Slave Issue in Southwest Ohio: Unreported Cases." *The Old Northwest* 14 (1988): 285–310.

――――. *Ohio and the Antislavery Activities of Attorney Salmon Portland Chase, 1830–1849.* New York: Garland, 1990.

――――. "Cincinnati and the Fight for the Law of Freedom in Ohio, 1830–1856." *Locus* 4 (1991): 59–73.

――――. "Law and Ideology in Ohio and Kentucky: The Kidnapping of Jerry Phinney." *Filson Club History Quarterly* 67 (1993): 347–72.

Miller, Randall M. "The Union Humane Society: A Quaker-Gradualist Anti-Slavery Society in Early Ohio." *Quaker History* 61 (1972): 91–106.

Nye, Russel B. "Marius Robinson: A Forgotten Abolitionist Leader." *Ohio State Archaeological and Historical Quarterly* 55 (1946): 138–54.

Oates, Stephen B. "Years of Trial: John Brown in Ohio." *Timeline* 2 (February/March 1985): 2–13.

O'Dell, Richard F. "The Early Antislavery Movement in Ohio." PhD diss., University of Michigan, 1948.

Post, Albert. "The Anti-Gallows Movement in Ohio." *Ohio State Archaeological and Historical Quarterly* 54 (1945): 104–12.

Ratcliffe, Donald J. "Captain James Riley and Antislavery Sentiment in Ohio, 1819–1824." *Ohio History* 81 (1972): 76–94.

Rokicky, Catherine M. *Creating a Perfect World: Religious and Secular Utopias in Nineteenth-Century Ohio.* Athens: Ohio University Press, 2002.

Rosenbloom, Nancy Jean. "Cincinnati's Common Schools: The Politics of Reform, 1829–1853." PhD diss., University of Rochester, 1982.

Sheeler, J. Reuben. "The Struggle of the Negro in Ohio for Freedom." *The Journal of Negro History* 31 (1946): 208–26.

Siebert, Wilbur H. "Beginnings of the Underground Railroad in Ohio." *Ohio State Archaeological and Historical Quarterly* 56 (1947): 70–93.

Volpe, Vernon L. "Theodore Dwight Weld's Antislavery Mission in Ohio." *Ohio History* 100 (1991): 5–18.

Watson, Robert Meredith, Jr. "The Anatomy of a Crusade: A Western Reserve Township and the War against Slaveholders, 1831–1865." PhD diss., Memphis State University, 1978.

Weaver, Randall. "Confronting the Soul-Destroyers: James Bradley and the Abolitionist Movement's Origins." *Journal of Unconventional History* 11 (2000): 11–27.

Social

Anderson, M. Christine, and Nancy E. Bertaux. "Poor Men but Hard-Working Fathers: The Cincinnati Orphan Asylum and Parental Roles in the Nineteenth-Century Working Class." *Ohio History* (2002): 145–82.

Beller, Edward. "From Community toward State in the Northwest Territory (1787–1803)." PhD diss., City University of New York, 1983.

Bentley, Anna Briggs. *American Grit: A Woman's Letters from the Ohio Frontier.* Ed. Emily Foster. Lexington: University Press of Kentucky, 2002.

Berwanger, Eugene H. *The Frontier against Slavery: Western Anti-Negro Prejudice and the Slavery Extension Controversy.* Urbana: University of Illinois Press, 1967.

Bobersky, Alexander T., and David T. Stephens. "Cultural Faultline? An Examination of Early Settlement Patterns along the Boundary of the Western Reserve." *Pioneer America Society Transactions* 11 (1988): 87–95.

Bray, Robert, and Paul Bushnell. "From New England to the Old Northwest: The American Odyssey of the Jeremiah Greenman Family." *Journal of the Illinois State Historical Society* 69 (1976): 201–12.

Brown, Jeffrey P. "Chillicothe's Elite: Leadership in a Frontier Community." *Ohio History* 96 (1987): 140–56.

Brown, Marion A. "Mid-Nineteenth Century Mechanics and Scientists: A Reluctant Alliance." *Queen City Heritage* 50 (1992): 25–35.

Buley, R. Carlyle. *The Old Northwest: Pioneer Period, 1815–1840.* 2 vols. Bloomington: Indiana University Press, 1950.

Carter, Ruth C. "Cincinnatians and Cholera: Attitudes toward the Epidemics of 1832 and 1849." *Queen City Heritage* 50 (1992): 32–48.

Cashin, Joan E. "Black Families in the Old Northwest." *Journal of the Early Republic* 15 (1995): 449–75.

Cayton, Andrew R. L. "'A Quiet Independence': The Western Vision of the Ohio Company." *Ohio History* 90 (1981): 5–32.

———. "The Failure of Michael Baldwin: A Case Study in the Origins of Middle-Class Culture on the Trans-Appalachian Frontier." *Ohio History* 95 (1986): 34–48.

———. "Marietta and the Ohio Company." In *Appalachian Frontiers: Settlement, Society and Development in the Preindustrial Era,* ed. Robert D. Mitchell, 187–200. Lexington: University Press of Kentucky, 1991.

Chaddock, Robert Emmet. *Ohio before 1850: A Study of the Early Influence of Pennsylvania and Southern Populations in Ohio.* New York: AMS Press, 1967.

Davis, James E. "'New Aspects of Men and New Forms of Society': The Old Northwest, 1790–1820." *Journal of the Illinois State Historical Society* 69 (1976): 164–72.

Davis, Lenwood G. "Nineteenth Century Blacks in Ohio: An Historical View." In *Blacks in Ohio History: A Conference to Commemorate the Bicentennial of the American Revolution,* ed. Rubin F. Weston, 4–10. Columbus: Published for the Ohio American Revolution Bicentennial Advisory Commission by the Ohio Historical Society, 1976.

Dwarko, Daniel Agyei. "The Settler in the Maumee Valley: Henry, Lucas and Wood Counties, Ohio, 1830–1860." PhD diss., Bowling Green State University, 1981.

Ellingson, Stephen. "Understanding the Dialectic of Discourse and Collective Action: Public Debate and Rioting in Antebellum Cincinnati." *American Journal of Sociology* 101 (1995): 100–44.

Erickson, Charlotte. "British Immigrants in the Old Northwest, 1815–1860." In *The Frontier in American Development: Essays in Honor of Paul Wallace Gates,* ed. David M. Ellis, 323–56. Ithaca: Cornell University Press, 1969.

Fabe, Joan Howison. "The Trial and Error Period of Euro-American Settlement in Hamilton County, Ohio, 1773–1795." PhD diss., University of Cincinnati, 1988.

Faries, Elizabeth. "The Miami Country, 1750–1815, as Described in Journals and Letters." *Ohio State Archaeological and Historical Quarterly* 57 (1948): 48–67.

Fisk, William L., Jr. "The Scotch-Irish in Central Ohio." *Ohio State Archaeological and Historical Quarterly* 57 (1948): 111–25.

Folk, Patrick Allen. "'The Queen City of Mobs': Riots and Community Reactions in Cincinnati, 1788–1848." PhD diss., University of Toledo, 1978.

Ford, Bridget. "American Heartland: The Sentimentalization of Religion and Race Relations in Cincinnati and Louisville, 1820–1860." PhD diss., University of California, Davis, 2002.

French, David. "Puritan Conservatism and the Frontier: The Elizur Wright Family on the Connecticut Western Reserve." *The Old Northwest* 1 (1975): 85–95.

Fry, Mildred Covey. "Women on the Ohio Frontier: The Marietta Area." *Ohio History* 90 (1981): 54–73.

Glaab, Charles N. "Jesup W. Scott and a West of Cities." *Ohio History* 73 (1964): 3–12.

Glazer, Walter S. "Participation and Power: Voluntary Associations and the Functional Organization of Cincinnati in 1840." *Historical Methods Newsletter* 5 (1972): 151–68.

Griffler, Keith P. *Front Line of Freedom: African Americans and the Forging of the Underground Railroad in the Ohio Valley.* Lexington: University Press of Kentucky, 2004.

Gruenwald, Kim M. "Settling the Old Northwest: Changing Family and Commercial Strategies in the Early Republic." PhD diss., University of Colorado, Boulder, 1994.

———. "Marietta's Example of a Settlement Pattern in the Ohio Country: A Reinterpretation." *Ohio History* 105 (1996): 125–44.

Hall, Virginius C. "Ohio in Knee Pants." *Ohio State Archaeological and Historical Quarterly* 56 (1947): 1–15.

Hawley, Steven Anthony. "Black Swamp Babies: An Historical Analysis of Family and Fertility in Northwest Ohio, 1830–1860." PhD diss., Bowling Green State University, 1989.

Harris, Marc. "Social Entrepreneurs: Economic Enterprisers and Social Reformers on Ohio's Western Reserve, 1795–1845." PhD diss., Johns Hopkins University, 1984.

Hildreth, William H. "Mrs. Trollope in Porkopolis." *Ohio State Archaeological and Historical Quarterly* 58 (1949): 35–51.

Hoag, Andrew Breton. "Probate Relationships and the Establishment of Wood County, Ohio, 1820–1840." PhD diss., University of Michigan, 1991.

Hodgson, Traci A. "Egalitarian Transformations: Gender, Religious Culture, and Family Government on the Western Reserve of Ohio, 1800–1830." PhD diss., Boston University, 1997.

Horsman, Reginald. "Hunger in a Land of Plenty: Marietta's Lean Years." *Timeline* 19 (January/February 2002): 20–31.

Hudson, John C. "North American Origins of Middlewestern Frontier Populations." *Annals of the Association of American Geographers* 78 (1988): 395–413.

Hutslar, Donald A. "'God's Scourge': The Cholera Years in Ohio." *Ohio History* 105 (1996): 174–91.

Jordan, Wayne. "The People of Ohio's First County." *Ohio State Archaeological and Historical Quarterly* 49 (1940): 1–40.

Kaatz, Martin Richard. *The Black Swamp: A Study in Historical Geography.* Washington, DC: Association of American Geographers, 1955.

Kenney, Alice. "A Dutch Pioneer: Zachariah Price De Witt Moves West." *Halve Maen* 57 (1983): 3–5, 23, 25.

Kessler, John S., and Donald B. Ball. *North From the Mountains: A Folk History of the Carmel Melungeon Settlement, Highland County, Ohio.* Macon, GA: Mercer University Press, 2001.

Knowles, Anne Kelly. *Calvinists Incorporated: Welsh Immigrants On Ohio's Industrial Frontier.* Chicago: University of Chicago Press, 1997.

Kramer, Howard D. "An Ohio Doctor in the Early Navy." *Ohio State Archaeological and Historical Quarterly* 60 (1951): 155–74.

Lawson, Ellen N., and Marlene Merrill. "The Antebellum 'Talented Thousandth': Black College Students at Oberlin Before the Civil War." *Journal of Negro Education* 52 (1983): 142–55.

Leet, Don R. *Population Pressure and Human Fertility Response: Ohio, 1810–1860.* New York: Arno Press, 1978.

Lottich, Kenneth V. "Culture Transplantation in the Connecticut Reserve." *Bulletin of the Historical and Philosophical Society of Ohio* 8 (1959): 155–66.

———. *New England Transplanted: A Study of the Development of Educational and Other Cultural Agencies in the Connecticut Western Reserve in Their National and Philosophical Setting.* Dallas: Royal Pub. Co., 1964.

Luckett, Judith Ann Blodgett. "Protest, Advancement and Identity: Organizational Strategies of Northern Free Blacks, 1830 to 1860." PhD diss., Johns Hopkins University, 1993.

McFarland, Gerald W. *A Scattered People: An American Family Moves West.* New York: Pantheon Books, 1985.

McManis, Michael Allen. "The New England Presence on the Midwestern Landscape." *The Old Northwest* 9 (1983): 125–33.

McTighe, Michael J. "'True Philanthropy' and the Limits of the Female Sphere: Poor Relief and Labor Organizations in Ante-Bellum Cleveland." *Labor History* 27 (1986): 227–56.

Miller, Tamra G. "'Seeking to Strengthen the Ties of Friendship': Women and Community in Southeastern Ohio, 1788–1850." PhD diss., Brandeis University, 1995.

———. "'Those with Whom I Feel Most Nearly Connected': Kinship and Gender in Early Ohio." In *Midwestern Women: Work, Community, and Leadership at the Crossroads*, ed. Lucy Eldersveld Murphy and Wendy Hamand Venet, 121–40. Bloomington: Indiana University Press, 1997.

Morris, James M. "Communes and Cooperatives: Cincinnati's Early Experiments in Social Reform." *Cincinnati Historical Society Bulletin* 33 (1975): 57–80.

Morrison, Grant. "Interregional Entrepreneurship in the 1830's: The Role of New Yorkers in the Founding of an Ohio Corporation." *The Old Northwest* 7 (1981): 23–40.

Mussey, Barrows. "Yankee Chills, Ohio Fever." *The New England Quarterly* 22 (1949): 435–51.

Pallante, Martha. "The Trek West: Early Travel Narratives and Perceptions of the Frontier." *Michigan Historical Review* 21 (1995): 83–99.

Pankratz, John R. "New Englanders, the Written Word and the Errand into Ohio, 1788–1830." PhD diss., Cornell University, 1988.

Pih, Richard W. "Negro Self-Improvement Efforts in Ante-Bellum Cincinnati, 1836–1850." *Ohio History* 78 (1969): 179–87.

Porter, Lorle. *Sara's Table: "Keeping House" in Ohio, 1800–1950.* Zanesville, OH: New Concord Press, 2001.

Power, Richard Lyle. *Planting Corn Belt Culture: The Impress of the Upland Southerner and Yankee in the Old Northwest.* Indianapolis: Indiana Historical Society, 1953.

Rodabaugh, James H. "The Negro in Ohio." *Journal of Negro History* 31 (1946): 9–29.

Rogers, George Truett. "A Biography of David Jones, 1736–1820: His Religious, Military, and Community Life." PhD diss., University of Colorado, 1976.

Ruggles, Alice McGuffey. "A Buckeye Boarding-School in 1821." *Ohio State Archaeological and Historical Quarterly* 53 (1944): 251–68.

Scharf, Lois. "'I Would Go Wherever Fortune Would Direct': Hannah Huntington and the Frontier of the Western Reserve." *Ohio History* 97 (1988): 5–28.

Soltow, Lee, and Margaret Soltow. "The Settlement that Failed: The French in Early Gallipolis: An Enlightening Letter, and an Explanation." *Ohio History* 94 (1985): 46–67.

Swierenga, Robert P. "The Settlement of the Old Northwest: Ethnic Pluralism in a Featureless Plain." *Journal of the Early Republic* 9 (1989): 73–105.

Taylor, Clare. "Paddy's Run: A Welsh Settlement in Ohio." *Welsh History Review* 11 (1983): 302–16.

Taylor, Henry Louis. "The Northwest Ordinance and the Place of Ohio in African-American History." *The Old Northwest* 14 (1988): 131–44.

———, ed. *Race and the City: Work, Community, and Protest in Cincinnati, 1820–1970.* Urbana: University of Illinois Press, 1993.

Taylor, Nikki M. *Frontiers of Freedom: Cincinnati's Black Community 1802–1868.* Athens: Ohio University Press, 2005.

Tolzmann, Don Heinrich. "The German Image of Cincinnati Before 1830." *Queen City Heritage* 42 (1984): 31–38.

———, ed. *Das Ohiotal—The Ohio Valley: The German Dimension.* New York: P. Lang, 1993.

Tucker, David A., Jr. "Notes on Cholera in Southwestern Ohio." *Ohio State Historical and Archaeological Quarterly* 49 (1940): 378–85.

Trotter, Joe William. *River Jordan: African American Urban Life in the Ohio Valley.* Lexington: University Press of Kentucky, 1998.

Wade, Richard C. "The Negro in Cincinnati, 1800–1830." *Journal of Negro History* 39 (1954): 43–57.

Warnes, Kathy. "Elizabeth Turner McCormick, Woman Voyageur." *Inland Seas* 55 (1999): 187–91.

Wendler, Marilyn Van Voorhis. "Doctors and Diseases on the Ohio Frontier." *Ohio History* 89 (1980): 222–42.

Wesley, Charles H. *Negro Americans in Ohio: A Sesquicentennial View.* Wilberforce: Central State College, 1953.

Western Reserve Studies Symposium (3rd: 1988: Painesville, Ohio). *Transplanting and Innovating: New Patterns on the Reserve, 1830–1880.* Painesville, OH: Lake Erie College Press, 1988.

Weston, Rubin F., ed. *Blacks in Ohio History: A Conference to Commemorate the Bicentennial of the American Revolution.* Columbus: Published for the Ohio American Revolution Bicentennial Advisory Commission by the Ohio Historical Society, 1976.

Wheeler, Robert A. "Land and Community in Rural Nineteenth-Century America: Claridon Township, 1810–1870." *Ohio History* 97 (1983): 101–21.

White, John R. "Preliminary Excavations at the Austin Cabin Complex, 1976." *Chesopiean* 18 (1980): 40–59.

Wilhelm, Hubert G. H. *The Origin and Distribution of Settlement Groups: Ohio: 1850.* Athens, OH: H. G. H. Wilhelm, 1982.

———. "A Pennsylvania Homestead in the Virginia Settlement Region of Ohio." *Pioneer America Society Transactions* 15 (1992): 33–40.

Wittke, Carl. "The Germans of Cincinnati." *Bulletin of the Historical and Philosophical Society of Ohio* 20 (1962): 3–14.

Wolcott, Merlin D. "Frontier Adventure: The Life of Alexander Clemons." *Northwest Ohio Quarterly* 49 (1976): 19–33.

Cultural and Intellectual

Baluk, Ulana Lydia. "Proprietary Museums in Antebellum Cincinnati: 'Something to Please You and Something to Learn.'" PhD diss., University of Toronto, 2000.

Barnhart, Terry A. "An American Menagerie: The Cabinet of Squier and Davis." *Timeline* (December 1985/January 1986): 2–17.

———. "James McBride: Historian and Archaeologist of the Miami Valley." *Ohio History* 103 (1994): 23–40.

Bigelow, Ann Clymer. "Columbus's Pioneer Doctor John M. Edmiston: The Fabric of His Life and Death." *Ohio History* 110 (2001): 5–25.

Blue, Frederick J. "Salmon P. Chase, First Historian of the Old Northwest." *Ohio History* 98 (1989): 52–69.

Brammer, Mauck. "Winthrop B. Smith: Creator of the Eclectic Educational Series." *Ohio History* 80 (1971): 45–59.

Brown, David Scott. "Jesup Scott's Great West: Promotion and Persuasion on the Ohio Frontier." *Northwest Ohio Quarterly* 71 (1999): 81–102.

Buerki, Robert A. "Interpreting Nineteenth-Century Pharmacy Practice: The Ohio Experience." *Journal of American Culture* 12 (1989): 93–102.

Carter, Denny. "Cincinnati as an Art Center, 1830–1865." In *The Golden Age: Cincinnati Painters of the Nineteenth Century Represented in the Cincinnati Art Museum,* 13–21. Cincinnati: Cincinnati Art Museum, 1979.

Cazden, Robert E. "The German Book Trade in Ohio Before 1848." *Ohio History* 84 (1975): 57–77.

Chamberlain, Georgia Edwina. "The Art Heritage of Summit County, 1800–1900." MA thesis, Western Reserve University, 1948.

Clark, George Peirce. "An Early Report on Oberlin College." *Ohio State Archaeological and Historical Quarterly* 63 (1954): 279–82.

Clark, Thomas D. "Building Libraries in the Early Ohio Valley." *Journal of Library History* 6 (1971): 101–19.

Clifton, Lucile. "Beginnings of Literary Culture in Columbus, Ohio, 1812–1840." PhD diss., Ohio State University, 1948.

———. "The Early Theater in Columbus, Ohio, 1820–1840." *Ohio State Archaeological and Historical Quarterly* 62 (1953): 234–46.

Daniels, Elizabeth. "The Specter of the Deadly Woodlands." *Timeline* 5 (October/November 1988): 44–54.

Devine, Michael J. "The Historical Paintings of William Henry Powell." *Ohio History* 89 (1980): 65–77.

Dillon, Kathleen M. "Painters and Patrons: The Fine Arts in Cincinnati, 1820–1860." *Ohio History* 96 (1987): 7–32.

Dittrick, Howard. "An Ancestor of Ohio Medicine: Fairfield Medical School (1812–1840)." *Ohio State Archaeological and Historical Quarterly* 61 (1952): 365–70.

Dorn, Michael L. "Climate, Alcohol, and the American Body Politic: The Medical and Moral Geographies of Daniel Drake (1775–1852)." PhD diss., University of Kentucky, 2003.

Dunlop, M. H. "Curiosities Too Numerous to Mention: Early Regionalism and Cincinnati's Western Museum." *American Quarterly* 36 (1984): 524–48.

Durrell, Jane. "Upstairs at Mrs. Amelung's." *Cincinnati Historical Society Bulletin* 35 (1977): 33–42.

Edwards, Linden F. "Body Snatching in Ohio During the Nineteenth Century." *Ohio State Archaeological and Historical Quarterly* 59 (1950): 329–51.

Emch, Lucille B. "Ohio in Short Stories, 1824–1839." *Ohio State Archaeological and Historical Quarterly* 53 (1944): 209–50.

Endres, Fredric F. "Frontier Obituaries as Cultural Reflectors: Toward 'Operationalizing' Carey's Thesis." *Journalism History* 11 (1984): 54–60.

Farrell, Richard T. "Daniel Drake: The Ohio Valley's Benjamin Franklin." *Cincinnati Historical Society Bulletin* 23 (1965): 243–56.

Fees, Paul Rodger. "New England's Image of the Old Northwest and Its Incorporation of Western Cultural Symbols, 1783–1820." PhD diss., Brown University, 1982.

Fisk, William L., Jr. "The Early Years of Muskingum College." *The Old Northwest* 5 (1979): 19–44.

Fletcher, Juanita D. "Against the Consensus: Oberlin College and the Education of American Negroes, 1835–1865." PhD diss., American University, 1974.

Fletcher, Robert Samuel. "Bread and Doctrine at Oberlin." *Ohio State Archaeological and Historical Quarterly* 49 (1940): 58–67.

Forman, Jonathan. "The Medical Journals of the Period, 1835–1858." *Ohio State Archaeological and Historical Quarterly* 49 (1940): 361–66.

———. "The Worthington Medical College." *Ohio State Archaeological and Historical Quarterly* 50 (1941): 373–79.

———. "Dr. Alva Curtis in Columbus: The *Thomasonian Recorder* and Columbus' First Medical School." *Ohio State Archaeological and Historical Quarterly* 51 (1942): 332–40.

———. " Ohio Medical History." *Ohio State Archaeological and Historical Quarterly* 53 (1944): 303–12.

Franklin, Cathy Rogers. "James Gillespie Birney, the Revival Spirit, and *The Philanthropist*." *American Journalism* 17 (2000): 31–51.

Goldfarb, Stephen. "Science and Democracy: A History of the Cincinnati Observatory, 1842–1872." *Ohio History* 78 (1969): 172–78.

Goodheart, Lawrence B. "Abolitionists vs. Academics: The Controversy at Western Reserve College, 1832–1833." *History of Education Quarterly* 22 (1982): 421–33.

Goodman, Paul. "The Manual Labor Movement and the Origins of Abolitionism." *Journal of the Early Republic* 13 (1993): 355–88.

Green, Judith Abigail. "Religion, Life, and Literature in *The Western Messenger*." PhD diss., University of Wisconsin, Madison, 1981.

Greenberg, Gerald S. "Beman Gates and *The Marietta Intelligencer*, 1839–56." *Publishing History* 38 (1995): 55–75.

———. "Caleb Emerson, Nineteenth-Century Newspaper Publisher of Marietta, Ohio." *Publishing History* 43 (1998): 33–52.

Habich, Robert David. "The History and Achievement of *The Western Messenger*, 1835–1841." PhD diss., Pennsylvania State University, 1982.

Haverstock, Mary Sayre, Jeannette Mahoney Vance, and Brian L. Meggitt. *Artists in Ohio, 1787–1900: A Biographical Dictionary*. Kent, OH: Kent State University Press, 2000.

Hertzog, Lucy Stone. "The Rise of Homeopathy." *Ohio State Archaeological and Historical Quarterly* 49 (1940): 332–46.

Hibbard, Francis C. "Origin of Some Early Belmont County Newspapers." *Ohio State Archaeological and Historical Quarterly* 55 (1946): 78–182.

Hilgert, Earle. "Calvin Ellis Stowe: Pioneer Librarian of the Old West." *Library Quarterly* 50 (1980): 324–51.

Hitchcock, Walter Theodore. "Timothy Walker: Antebellum Lawyer." PhD diss., University of Mississippi, 1980.

Hobbs, Stuart D. "National Historic Landmark Nomination: Adena, the Thomas Worthington House." Columbus: Ohio Historic Preservation Office, 2003.

Holsinger, M. Paul. "Timothy Walker: Blackstone For the New Republic." *Ohio History* 84 (1975): 145–57.

Hoover, Thomas N. "The Beginnings of Higher Education in the Northwest Territory." *Ohio State Archaeological and Historical Quarterly* 50 (1941): 244–60.

Horine, Emmet Field. *Daniel Drake, 1785–1852: Pioneer Physician of the Midwest*. Philadelphia: University of Pennsylvania Press, 1961.

Irrmann, Robert H. "The Library of an Early Ohio Farmer." *Ohio State Archaeological and Historical Quarterly* 57 (1948): 185–93.

Irvine, Russell W., and Donna Zani Dunkerton. "The Noyes Academy, 1834–35: The Road to the Oberlin Collegiate Institute and the Higher Education of African-Americans in the Nineteenth Century." *Western Journal of Black Studies* 22 (1998): 260–73.

Jordan, Philip D. "Samuel Robinson: Champion of the Thomasonian System." *Ohio State Archaeological and Historical Quarterly* 51 (1942): 263–70.

Kaestle, Carl F. "Public Education in the Old Northwest: 'Necessary to Good Government and the Happiness of Mankind.'" *Indiana Magazine of History* 84 (1988): 60–74.

Katz, Wendy Jean. *Regionalism and Reform: Art and Class Formation in Antebellum Cincinnati*. Columbus: Ohio State University Press, 2002.

Kime, Wayne R. "Pierre M. Irving and the *Toledo Blade*." *Northwest Ohio Quarterly* 47 (1975): 131–50.

King, Arthur D. "Cincinnati Doctors Before Daniel Drake, 1788–1807." *Cincinnati Historical Society Bulletin* 23 (1965): 119–27.

Lottich, Kenneth V. "Educational Leadership in Early Ohio." *History of Education Quarterly* 2 (1962): 52–61.

Loveland, Anne C. "The Nation's Guest: Lafayette's Visit." *Timeline* 11 (July/August 1994): 2–17.

Luker, Richard Michael. "The Western Reserve and a Legacy for Higher Education: Faculty Self-Governance at Oberlin College under the Finney Compact, 1834–1846." PhD diss., University of Akron, 1985.

Lupold, Harry Forrest. "'Oh, the Pain of It All,' the Birth and Death of an Ohio Medical College." *The Old Northwest* 12 (1986): 319–31.

MacKenzie, Donald R. "The Itinerant Artist in Early Ohio." *Ohio History* 73 (1964): 41–46.

———. "Early Ohio Painters: Cincinnati, 1830–1850." *Ohio History* 73 (1964): 111–18.

———. "Early Ohio Painters: The Prewar Years." *Ohio History* 73 (1964): 254–62.

Matthews, Samuel. "John Isom Gaines: The Architect of Black Public Education." *Queen City Heritage* 45 (1987): 41–48.

McDermott, John Francis. "J. C. Wild, Western Painter and Lithographer." *Ohio State Archaeological and Historical Quarterly* 60 (1951): 111–25.

McMullen, Haynes. "The Use of Books in the Ohio Valley Before 1850." *Journal of Library History* 1 (1966): 43–56, 73.

Merrill, Marlene D. "Daughters of America Rejoice: The Oberlin Experiment." *Timeline* 4 (October/November 1987): 12–21.

Mills, Edward C. "Dentistry and Dental Education." *Ohio State Archaeological and Historical Quarterly* 49 (1940): 386–97.

———. "Dental Education in Ohio, 1838–1858." *Ohio State Archaeological and Historical Quarterly* 51 (1942): 294–312.

Muehl, Siegmar. "Eduard Muhl: Cincinnati's Radical German-American Newspaper Man, 1840–1843." *Queen City Heritage* 56 (1998): 2–12.

Mulligan, Robert W. "Xavier: 1831–1861." *Cincinnati Historical Society Bulletin* 37 (1979): 7–22.

Nerone, John Charles. "The Press and Popular Culture in the Early Republic: Cincinnati, 1793–1848." PhD diss., University of Notre Dame, 1982.

Oliver, John William, Jr., James A. Hodges, and James H. O'Donnell, eds. *Cradles of Conscience: Ohio's Independent Colleges and Universities.* Kent, OH: Kent State University Press, 2003.

Osborne, William N. *Music in Ohio: A Celebration of the Rich and Varied Musical History of Ohio.* Kent, OH: Kent State University Press, 2003.

Paterson, Robert G. "The Role of the 'District' as a Unit in Organized Medicine in Ohio." *Ohio State Archaeological and Historical Quarterly* 49 (1940): 367–77.

———. "Local Boards of Health in Ohio during the Period, 1835–1858." *Ohio State Archaeological and Historical Quarterly* 50 (1941): 380–83.

Peckham, Howard H. "Books and Reading on the Ohio Valley Frontier." *The Mississippi Valley Historical Review* 44 (1958): 649–63.

Perko, F. Michael. "To Enlighten the Rising Generation: School Formation in Cincinnati, 1821–1836." *Queen City Heritage* 43 (1985): 33–48.

Pinta, Emil R. "Samuel M. Smith, 'Dr. Cure-Awl's' Assistant at the Ohio Lunatic Asylum: His 1841 Case-Reports on Insanity." *Ohio History* 107 (1998): 58–75.

Roark, Elisabeth L. "John Frankenstein's Portrait of Godfrey Frankenstein and the Aesthetics of Friedrich Schiller." *American Art* 15 (2001): 74–83.

Schwartz, Abby S. "Nicholas Longworth: Art Patron of Cincinnati." *Queen City Heritage* 46 (1988): 17–32.

Shira, Donald D. "Contributions of Ohio Physicians to the Inventions of the Period, 1835–1858." *Ohio State Archaeological and Historical Quarterly* 49 (1940): 315–21.

———. "The Organization of the Ohio State Medical Society and Its Relation to the Ohio Medical Convention." *Ohio State Archaeological and Historical Quarterly* 50 (1941): 366–72.

Shoemaker, F. L. "Samuel Galloway: An Educational Statesman of First Rank." *History of Education Journal* 5 (1954): 105–17.

Stevens, Edward, Jr. "Books and Wealth on the Frontier: Athens County and Washington County, Ohio, 1790–1859." *Social Science History* 5 (1981): 417–44.

———. "Literacy and the Worth of Liberty." *Historical Social Research* 4 (1985): 65–81.

Stevens, Harry R. "The Haydn Society in Cincinnati, 1819–24." *Ohio State Archaeological and Historical Quarterly* 52 (1943): 95–119.

———. "Folk Music on the Midwestern Frontier 1788–1825." *Ohio State Archaeological and Historical Quarterly* 57 (1948): 126–46.

Stewart, Robert G. "Auguste Hervieu, A Portrait Painter in Cincinnati." *Queen City Heritage* 47 (1989): 23–31.

Stuckey, Ronald L. *Frontier Botanist: William Starling Sullivant's Flowering-Plant Botany of Ohio (1830–1850).* Columbus: Department of Botany, College of Biological Sciences, Ohio State University, 1991.

Studebaker, Sue. *Ohio Is My Dwelling Place: Schoolgirl Embroideries, 1803–1850.* Athens: Ohio University Press, 2002.

Sutton, Walter. "Cincinnati as a Publishing and Book Trade Center, 1796–1830." *Ohio State Archaeological and Historical Quarterly* 56 (1947): 117–43.

Swift, Mary Grace. "Terpsichore in the Western Athens: Ante-Bellum Ballet in the Queen City." *Cincinnati Historical Society Bulletin* 35 (1977): 79–97.

Szaraz, Stephen Charles. "History, Character, and Prospects: Daniel Drake and the Life of the Mind in the Ohio Valley, 1785–1852." PhD diss., Harvard University, 1993.

Szubiski , Chester Stanley. "Ohio Medical History." *Ohio State Archaeological and Historical Quarterly* 53 (1944): 371–89.

Tryon, W. S. "Ticknor and Fields' Publications in the Old Northwest, 1840–1860." *Mississippi Valley Historical Review* 34 (1948): 589–610.

Tucker, Louis L. "The Semicolon Club of Cincinnati." *Ohio History* 73 (1964): 13–26.

———. "Cincinnati: Athens of the West, 1830–1861." *Ohio History* 75 (1966): 10–25.

———. "Clio Comes to the Old Northwest." *Cincinnati Historical Society Bulletin* 38 (1980): 221–32.

Ulrich, Dennis Nicholas. "Samuel P. Hildreth: Physician and Scientist on the American Frontier, 1783–1863." PhD diss., Miami University, 1983.

Vitz, Robert C. *The Queen and the Arts: Cultural Life in Nineteenth-Century Cincinnati*. Kent, OH: Kent State University Press, 1989.

———. "The Troubled Life of James Handasyd Perkins." *Queen City Heritage* 53 (1995): 40–48.

Waite, Frederick D. "Thomasonianism in Ohio." *Ohio State Archaeological and Historical Quarterly* 49 (1940): 322–31.

Waller, Adolph E. "Dr. John Milton Bigelow, 1804–1878: An Early Ohio Physician-Botanist." *Ohio State Archaeological and Historical Quarterly* 51 (1942): 313–31.

———. "Ohio Medical History." *Ohio State Archaeological and Historical Quarterly* 53 (1944): 313–38.

———. "The Vaulting Imagination of John L. Riddell. *Ohio State Archaeological and Historical Quarterly* 54 (1945): 331–60.

———. "Dr. John Locke: Early Ohio Scientist (1792–1856)." *Ohio State Archaeological and Historical Quarterly* 55 (1946): 346–73.

Wheeler, Kenneth H. "The Antebellum College in the Old Northwest: Higher Education and the Defining of the Midwest." PhD diss., Ohio State University, 1999.

Wheeler, Robert A. "The Literature of the Western Reserve." *Ohio History* 100 (1991): 101–28.

Wilson, John. "Cincinnati Artists and the Lure of Germany in the Nineteenth Century." *Queen City Heritage* 57 (1999): 2–19.

Wyrick, Charles R. "Concert and Criticism in Cincinnati, 1840–1850." Master of Music thesis, University of Cincinnati, 1965.

Religion

Allbeck, Willard Dow. *A Century of Lutherans in Ohio*. Yellow Springs, OH: Antioch Press, 1966.

Andrews, Edward Deming. "The Shaker Mission to the Shawnee Indians." *Winterthur Portfolio* 7 (1971): 113–28.

Backman, Milton Vaughn. *The Heavens Resound: A History of the Latter-Day Saints in Ohio, 1830–1838*. Salt Lake City, Utah: Desert Book Co., 1983.

Bakken, Dawn Elizabeth. "Putting the Shakers 'In Place': Union Village, Ohio, 1805–1815." PhD diss., Indiana University, 1998.

Barnes, Sherman B. "Shaker Education." *Ohio State Archaeological and Historical Quarterly* 62 (1953): 67–76.

Beauregard, Erving E. "A Clergyman Pioneer in Ohio." *Fides Et Historia* 24 (1992): 97–111.

Binsfeld, Edmund L. "Francisca Bauer: The Sister of the Woods." *Ohio Historical Quarterly* 69 (1960): 353–66.

Blodgett, Geoffrey. "Father Finney's Church." *Timeline* 14 (January/February 1997): 20–33.

Boase, Paul H. "Slavery and the Ohio Circuit Rider." *Ohio Historical Quarterly* 64 (1955): 195–205.

———. "Moral Policemen on the Ohio Frontier." *Ohio Historical Quarterly* 68 (1959): 38–53.

———. "The Fortunes of a Circuit Rider." *Ohio History* 72 (1963): 91–115.

Brown, E. Leonard. "Quaker Migration to 'Miami Country,' 1798–1861." PhD diss., Michigan State University, 1974.

Brown, John Haldane. "Presbyterian Social Influences in Early Ohio." *Journal of Presbyterian History* 30 (1952): 209–35.

Brunger, Ronald A. "Methodist Circuit Riders." *Michigan History* 51 (1967): 252–67.

Burke, James L., and Donald E. Bensch. "Mount Pleasant and the Early Quakers of Ohio." *Ohio History* 83 (1974): 220–55.

Butalia, Tarunjit Singh, and Dianne P. Small, eds. *Religion in Ohio: Profiles of Faith Communities*. Athens: Ohio University Press, 2004.

Cole, Charles C., Jr. "Finney's Fight against the Masons." *Ohio State Archaeological and Historical Quarterly* 59 (1950): 270–86.

———. *Lion of the Forest: James B. Finley, Frontier Reformer.* Lexington: University Press of Kentucky, 1994.

Connor, Elizabeth. *Methodist Trail Blazer: Philip Gatch 1751–1834: His Life in Maryland, Virginia and Ohio.* Rutland, VT: Academy Books, 1970.

Conrad, Maia Turner. "'Struck in Their Hearts': David Zeisberger's Moravian Mission to the Delaware Indians in Ohio, 1767–1808." PhD diss., College of William and Mary, 1998.

DeRogatis, Amy. "Moral Geography: The Plan of Union Mission to the Western Reserve, 1787–1833." PhD diss., University of North Carolina, Chapel Hill, 1998.

Des Champs, Margaret Burr. "Early Presbyterianism along the North Bank of the Ohio River." *Journal of Presbyterian History* 28 (1952): 207–20.

Dichtl, John Raymond. "Frontiers of Faith: Transplanting Catholicism to the West in the Early Republic." PhD diss., Indiana University, 2000.

Dillon, Merton L. "Benjamin Lundy: Quaker Radical." *Timeline* 3 (June/July 1986): 28–41.

Durnbaugh, Donald F. "'Strangers and Exiles': Assistance Given by the Religious Society of Friends to the Separatist Society of Zoar in 1817–1818." *Ohio History* 109 (2000): 71–92.

Eller, David Barry. "The Brethren in the Western Ohio Valley, 1790–1850: German Baptist Settlement and Frontier Accommodation." PhD diss., Miami University, 1976.

Fortin, Roger. *Faith and Action: A History of the Catholic Archdiocese of Cincinnati, 1821–1996.* Columbus: Ohio State University Press, 2002.

Friends on the Landscape: A Preliminary Examination of the Society of Friends—Their Settlement and Architecture in Clinton, Highland and Warren Counties, 1795–1860. Cincinnati: Miami Purchase Association, 1981.

Gara, Lenna Mae. "An Expedition Against the Shakers." *Timeline* 10 (May/June 1993): 46–53.

Ginzberg, Lori D. "Women in an Evangelical Community: Oberlin, 1835–1850." *Ohio History* 89 (1980): 78–88.

Goldman, Karla. "The Path to Reform Judaism: An Examination of Religious Leadership in Cincinnati, 1841–1855." *American Jewish History* 90 (2002): 35–50.

Gorrell, Donald K. "Ohio Origins of the United Brethren in Christ and the Evangelical Association." *Methodist History* 15 (1977): 95–106.

Grandstaff, Mark R., and Milton V. Backman Jr. "The Social Origins of Kirtland Mormons." *Brigham Young University Studies* 30 (1990): 47–66.

Hamil, Fred Coyne. "The Establishment of the Second Moravian Mission on the Pettquotting." *Ohio State Archaeological and Historical Quarterly* 58 (1949): 207–12.

Hill, Marvin S., Keith C. Rooker, and Larry T. Wimmer. "The Kirtland Economy Revisited: A Market Critique of Sectarian Economics." *Brigham Young University Studies* 17 (1977): 387–475.

Howard, Victor B. "The Doves of 1847: The Religious Response in Ohio to the Mexican War." *The Old Northwest* 5 (1979): 237–67.

Huber, Donald I. *Educating Lutheran Pastors in Ohio, 1830–1980: A History of Trinity Lutheran Seminary and Its Predecessors.* Lewiston, NY: Edwin Mellen Press, 1989.

———. "White, Red, and Black: The Wyandot Mission at Upper Sandusky." *Timeline* 13 (May/June 1996): 2–17.

Hurdus, Adam, and Ophia D. Smith. "The Swedenborgians in Early Cincinnati." *Ohio State Archaeological and Historical Quarterly* 53 (1944): 106–34.

Johnson, Charles A. "Early Ohio Camp Meetings, 1801–1816." *Ohio State Archaeological and Historical Quarterly* 61 (1952): 32–50.

Johnson, Frank E. "Constructing the Church Triumphant: Methodism and the Emergence of the Midwest, 1800–1856." PhD diss., Michigan State University, 1996.

———. "'Inspired By Grace': Methodist Itinerants in the Early Midwest." *Methodist History* 35 (1997): 81–94.

Johnson, James E. "Charles G. Finney and Oberlin Perfectionism." *Journal of Presbyterian History* 46 (1968): 42–57, 128–38.

Klein, Lisa M. *Be It Remembered: The Story of Trinity Episcopal Church on Capitol Square.* Wilmington, OH: Orange Frazer Press, 2003

Lesick, Lawrence Thomas. *The Lane Rebels: Evangelicalism and Antislavery in Antebellum America.* Metuchen, NJ: Scarecrow Press, 1980.

Lindley, Harlow. "Friends and the Shawnee Indians at Wapakoneta." *Ohio State Archaeological and Historical Quarterly* 54 (1945): 33–39.

Luce, W. Ray. "Building the Kingdom of God: Mormon Architecture Before 1847." *Brigham Young University Studies* 30 (1990): 33–45.

Marcus, Alan I. "Am I My Brother's Keeper: Reform Judaism in the American West, Cincinnati, 1840–1870." *Queen City Heritage* 44 (1986): 3–19.

Marquardt, H. Michael. "Martin Harris: The Kirtland Years, 1831–1870." *Dialogue* 35 (2002): 1–40.

Marsik, Stanley J. "The Moravian Brethren Unitas Fratrum and American Indians in the Northwest Territory." *Czechoslovak and Central European Journal* 9 (1990): 47–74.

Matijasic, Thomas D. "The African Colonization Movement and Ohio's Protestant Community." *Phylon* 46 (1985): 16–24.

McCormick, Virginia E., and Robert W. McCormick. "Episcopal Versus Methodist: Religious Competition in Frontier Worthington." *Ohio History* 107 (1998): 5–21.

McTighe, Michael J. *A Measure of Success: Protestants and Public Culture in Antebellum Cleveland.* Albany: State University of New York Press, 1994.

Mostov, Stephen G. "A 'Jerusalem' on the Ohio: The Social and Economic History of Cincinnati's Jewish Community, 1840–1875." PhD diss., Brandeis University, 1981.

Murray, John E., and Metin M. Cosgel. "Market, Religion, and Culture in Shaker Swine Production, 1788–1880." *Agricultural History* 72 (1998): 552–73.

Newell, Linda King, and Valeen Tippitts Avery. "Sweet Counsel and Seas of Tribulation: The Religious Life of the Women in Kirtland." *Brigham Young University Studies* 20 (1980): 151–62.

Noricks, Ronald H. "'Jealousies and Contentions': The Plan of Union and the Western Reserve, 1801–37." *Journal of Presbyterian History* 60 (1982): 130–43.

Norton, Walter A. "Comparative Images: Mormonism and Contemporary Religions as Seen by Village Newspapermen in Western New York and Northeastern Ohio, 1820–1833." PhD diss., Brigham Young University, 1991.

Olmstead, Earl P. *Blackcoats among the Delaware: David Zeisberger on the Ohio Frontier.* Kent, OH: Kent State University Press, 1991.

Pankratz, John R. "Reading the Revival: The Connecticut Evangelical Magazine and the Communications Circuit on the Early Western Reserve." *Journal of Presbyterian History* 77 (1999): 237–46.

Parker, Russell D. "The Philosophy of Charles G. Finney: Higher Law and Revivalism." *Ohio History* 82 (1973): 142–53.

Perko, F. Michael. "A Time to Favor Zion: A Case Study of Religion as a Force in American Educational Development, 1830–1870." PhD diss., Stanford University, 1981.

———. "Two Bishops, the Bible, and the Schools: An Exercise in Differential Biography." *Vitae Scholasticae* 3 (1984): 61–93.

Piercy, Harry D. "Shaker Medicines." *Ohio State Archaeological and Historical Quarterly* 63 (1954): 336–48.

Pritchard, Linda K. "Religious Change in a Developing Region: The Social Contexts of Evangelicalism in Western New York and the Upper Ohio Valley During the Mid-Nineteenth Century." PhD diss., University of Pittsburgh, 1980.

Raphael, Marc Lee. *Jews and Judaism in a Midwestern Community, Columbus, Ohio, 1840–1975.* Columbus: Ohio Historical Society, 1979.

Robison, Elwin C. "Heavenly Aspirations and Earthly Realities: Four Northeast Ohio Religious Utopias." *Timeline* 17 (November/December 2000): 2–25.

Rokicky, Catherine M. "Lydia Finney and Evangelical Womanhood." *Ohio History* 103 (1994): 170–89.

Rubinstein, Judah, and Jane Avner. *Merging Traditions: Jewish Life in Cleveland.* Kent, OH: Kent State University Press, 2004.

Sarna, Jonathan D., and Nancy H. Klein. *The Jews of Cincinnati.* Cincinnati: Center for Study of the American Jewish Experience, Hebrew Union College-Jewish Institute of Religion, 1989.

Shevitz, Amy Hill. "Streams: Small Jewish Communities on the Banks of the Ohio." PhD diss., University of Oklahoma, 2002.

Smith, Ophia D. "The Beginnings of the New Jerusalem Church in Ohio." *Ohio State Archaeological and Historical Quarterly* 61 (1952): 235–61.

———. "The Rise of the New Jerusalem Church in Ohio." *Ohio State Archaeological and Historical Quarterly* 61 (1952): 380–409.

Smith, Timothy L. "The Ohio Valley: Testing Ground For America's Experiment in Religious Pluralism." *Church History* 60 (1991): 461–79.

Snyder, K. Alan. "Charles Finney: Should Christianity Mix With Politics?" *Continuity* 23 (1999): 65–82.

Specht, Neva Jean. "Mixed Blessing: Trans-Appalachian Settlement and the Society of Friends, 1780–1813." PhD diss., University of Delaware, 1997.

Stein, Stephen J. "'A Candid Statement of Our Principles': Early Shaker Theology in the West." *Proceedings of the American Philosophical Society* 133 (1989): 503–19.

Thomas, N. Gordon. "The Millerite Movement in Ohio." *Ohio History* 81 (1972): 95–107.

Thornburg, Opal. "Cultural Resources of Quaker Pioneers in Ohio: A Glimpse of the Home Community of Marcus Mote, Artist." *Bulletin of the Friends Historical Association* 44 (1955): 94–99.

Thornton, Willis. "Gentile and Saint at Kirtland." *Ohio State Archaeological and Historical Quarterly* 63 (1954): 8–33.

Townsend, Charles. "Peter Cartwright's Circuit Riding Days in Ohio." *Ohio History* 74 (1965): 90–98.

Vitz, Robert C. "A Calvinist of the Old School: Joshua Lacy Wilson in Cincinnati, 1808–1846." *Queen City Heritage* 50 (1992): 3–16.

Welsh, Edward Burgett. "Origins of Ohio Presbyterianism." *Journal of Presbyterian History* 43 (1965): 16–27.

Western Reserve Studies Symposium. Ninth symposium: *Parameters of Faith: Religion in the Western Reserve*, October 7–8, 1994, Cleveland, Ohio. Cleveland: Case Western Reserve University, 1994.

Wigger, John H. *Taking Heaven by Storm: Methodism and the Rise of Popular Christianity in America.* New York: Oxford University Press, 1998.

Willey, Larry G. "The Reverend John Rankin: Early Ohio Antislavery Leader." PhD diss., University of Iowa, 1976.

———. "John Rankin, Antislavery Prophet, and the Free Presbyterian Church." *American Presbyterians* 72 (1994): 157–71.

Williams, David Newell. "The Theology of the Great Revival in the West as Seen through the Life and Thought of Barton Warren Stone." PhD diss., Vanderbilt University, 1979.

Williams, Peter W. "Ohio's Religious Landscape." *Timeline* 17 (May/June 2000): 2–15.

Zoar: An Ohio Experiment in Communalism. Columbus: Ohio Historical Society, 1952.

Material Culture

Brcak, Nancy J. "Country Carpenters, Federal Buildings: An Early Architectural Tradition in Ohio's Western Reserve." *Ohio History* 98 (1989): 131–46.

Clark, Ricky. "A Bride's Quilt from New Connecticut: Rebellion or Reflection?" *Hayes Historical Journal* 6 (1987): 29–39.

Clark, Ricky, George W. Knepper, and Ellice Ronsheim. *Quilts in Community: Ohio's Traditions.* Nashville: Rutledge Hill Press, 1991.

Clark, Roger W. "Cincinnati Coppersmiths." *Cincinnati Historical Society Bulletin* 23 (1965): 256–72.

Connell, E. Jane, and Charles R. Muller. "Ohio Furniture, 1788–1888." *Magazine Antiques* 125 (1984): 462–68.

Contosta, David R. "Origins of Early Domestic Architecture in Lancaster, Ohio." *The Old Northwest* 7 (1981): 201–16.

Cunningham, Patricia A. "The Woven Record: Nineteenth-Century Coverlets and Textile Industries in Northwest Ohio." *Northwest Ohio Quarterly* 56 (1984): 43–76.

Dittrick, Howard. "Urinalysis, Instruments of Precision, the Stethoscope, et cetera, of the Period, 1835–1858." *Ohio State Archaeological and Historical Quarterly* 49 (1940): 347–60.

Hageman, Jane Sikes. *The Furniture Makers of Cincinnati, 1790–1849.* Cincinnati: Lithographed by Merten Company, 1976.

———. *Ohio Furniture Makers.* 2 vols. Cincinnati: J. S. Hageman, 1984.

Hudson, Harriet E. "The Temple Form Houses of Wellington, Ohio." *The Old Northwest* 13 (1987): 237–54.

Hutslar, Donald A. *The Architecture of Migration: Log Construction in the Ohio Country, 1750–1850.* Athens: Ohio University Press, 1986.

———. "Lock, Stock, and Barrel: Ohio Muzzle-Loading Rifles." *Timeline* 9 (June/July 1992): 2–17.

Johannesen, Eric. "Simeon Porter: Ohio Architect." *Ohio History* 74 (1965): 169–90.

———. "Charles W. Heard, Victorian Architect." *Ohio History* 77 (1968): 130–42.

———. *Ohio College Architecture before 1870.* Columbus: Ohio Historical Society, 1969.

Jones, Joann Crecelius. "The Development of the Firelands Furniture Industry, 1815–1850." MA thesis, Ohio State University, 1971.

Lucas, Patrick Lee. "Realized Ideals: Grecian-Style Buildings as Metaphors for Democracy on the Trans-Appalachian Frontier." PhD diss., Michigan State University, 2002.

Miller, George L., and Silas D. Hurry. "Ceramic Supply in an Economically Isolated Frontier Community: Portage County of the Ohio Western Reserve, 1800–1825." *Historical Archaeology* 17 (1983): 80–92.

Noble, Vergil E. "The Archaeology of American Canals." *Michigan Archaeologist* 37 (1991): 35–44.

Prosser, Daniel. "The Hellenic Ideal: The Ohio Statehouse." *Timeline* 10 (July/August 1993): 46–54.

Rusk, Sarah H. "Hezekiah Eldredge, Architect-Builder of St. John's Church, Cleveland, Ohio." *Journal of the Society of Architectural Historians* 25 (1966): 50–58.

Saint-Pierre, Adrienne E. "Luther Edgerton's 'Cloathing Books': A Record of Men's Ready-to-Wear from the Early Nineteenth Century." *Dublin Seminar for New England Folklife, Annual Proceedings* 22 (1997): 212–32.

Shine, Carolyn R. "Hunting Shirts and Silk Stockings: Clothing Early Cincinnati." *Queen City Heritage* 45 (1987): 23–48.

Snyder, Tricia, Gil Snyder, and Paul A. Goudy. *Zoar Furniture, 1817–1898: A Preliminary Study.* New Philadelphia, OH: Tuscarawas County Historical Society, 1978.

Steiner, Catherine McQuaid, and Schuyler Eaton Cone. *Ornate & Simple Forms: Pomeroy Furniture & Fashion, 1840–1880.* Athens, OH: C. M. Steiner, S. E. Cone, 1990.

Steiner, Catherine McQuaid, and Bruce E. Steiner. *High Style and Vernacular: Ohio Furniture, Decorative Arts, and Craftsmen, 1800–1850: Chillicothe, Ironton, Lancaster, St. Clairsville, Zanesville.* Published for the exhibition "High Style and Vernacular: Ohio Furniture, Decorative Arts, and Craftsmen, 1800–1850," The Dairy Barn Southeastern Ohio Cultural Arts Center, April 1–24, 1988. Athens, OH: C. M. Steiner, B. E. Steiner, 1988.

Streifthau, Donna Largent. "Cincinnati Cabinet- and Chair-Makers, 1819–1830." PhD diss., Ohio State University, 1970.

Economic

Abbott, Carl John. "The Divergent Development of Cincinnati, Indianapolis, Chicago and Galena, 1840–1860: Economic Thought and Economic Growth." PhD diss., University of Chicago, 1971.

Adams, Dale W. "Chartering the Kirtland Bank." *Brigham Young University Studies* 23 (1983): 467–82.

Allen, Michael. "Alligator Horses: Ohio and Mississippi River Flatboatmen, Keelboatmen, and Raftsmen, 1763–1860." PhD diss., University of Washington, 1985.

Arms, Richard G. "From Disassembly to Assembly—Cincinnati: The Birthplace of Mass-Production." *Bulletin of the Historical and Philosophical Society of Ohio* 17 (1959): 195–203.

Ashendel, Anita. "'She Is the Man of the Concern': Entrepreneurial Women in the Ohio Valley, 1790–1860." PhD diss., Purdue University, 1997.

Atherton, Lewis Eldon. *Main Street on the Middle Border.* Bloomington: Indiana University Press, 1954.

———. *The Frontier Merchant in Mid-America.* Columbia: University of Missouri Press, 1971.

Barringer, Sallie H., and Bradford W. Scharlott. "The Cincinnati Mercantile Library as a Business-Communications Center, 1835–1846." *Libraries & Culture* 26 (1991): 388–401.

Bean, Jonathan J. "Marketing 'the Great American Commodity': Nathaniel Massie and Land Speculation on the Ohio Frontier, 1783–1813." *Ohio History* 103 (1994) 152–69.

Becker, Carl M. "Mill, Shop, and Factory: The Industrial Life of Dayton, Ohio, 1830–1900." PhD diss., University of Cincinnati, 1971.

Becker, Carl M., and Leland R. Johnson. "History at the Bar: Navigability of the Great Miami River." *Journal of Transport History* 12 (1991): 148–68.

Berry, Thomas Senior. *Western Prices Before 1861: A Study of the Cincinnati Market.* Cambridge, MA: Harvard University Press, 1943.

Brown, Marion A. *The Second Bank of the United States and Ohio, (1803–1860): A Collision of Interests.* Lewiston, NY: Edwin Mellen Press, 1998.

Cayton, Andrew R. L. "The Rise and Fall of a Frontier Entrepreneur: Commerce and Nationalism in the Career of Senator John Smith." In *The Human Tradition in Antebellum America,* ed. Michael A. Morrison, 67–82. Wilmington, DE: Scholarly Resources, 2000.

Cole, Susanne M. DeBerry. "Going to the Market: Women's Work and the Market Economies of Antebellum Cincinnati, 1789–1860." PhD diss., Miami University, 1997.

Conlin, Mary Lou. *Simon Perkins of the Western Reserve.* Cleveland: Western Reserve Historical Society, 1968.

Crawford, Stanton C. "A Springboard on Saw Mill Run." *Western Pennsylvania Historical Magazine* 49 (1966): 97–110.

Danhof, Clarence H. *Change in Agriculture: The Northern United States, 1820–1870.* Cambridge, MA: Harvard University Press, 1969.

Denney, Ellen Wilson. "Surveyor Speculation in the Virginia Military Tract: The Territorial Period." *Cincinnati Historical Society Bulletin* 34 (1976): 175–88.

Dittrick, Howard. "Cleveland Doctors and Their Fees (about 1840)." *Ohio State Archaeological and Historical Quarterly* 54 (1945): 361–70.

———. "A Cleveland Drug Store of 1835." *Ohio State Archaeological and Historical Quarterly* 55 (1946): 338–45.

Dodds, Gilbert F. *Early Agriculture in Franklin County.* Columbus, OH: The Franklin County Historical Society, 1954.

Duckett, Kenneth W. "Ohio Land Patents." *Ohio History* 72 (1963): 51–60.

Ende, Eleanor Von, and Thomas Weiss. "Consumption of Farm Output and Economic Growth in the Old Northwest, 1800–1860." *Journal of Economic History* 53 (1993): 308–18.

Farrell, Richard T. "Internal Improvement Projects in Southwestern Ohio, 1815–1834." *Ohio History* 80 (1971): 4–23.

Finn, Chester E. "The Ohio Canals: Public Enterprise on the Frontier." *Ohio State Archaeological and Historical Quarterly* 51 (1942): 1–40.

Fisk, William L., Jr. "Merino Mania." *Timeline* 14 (January/February 1997): 42–51.

Ford, Ashley L. "Life on the Ohio: A Captain's View." *Queen City Heritage* 57 (1999): 19–26.

Frohman, Charles E. "The Milan Canal." *Ohio State Archaeological and Historical Quarterly* 57 (1948): 237–46.

Greer, Thomas H. "Economic and Social Effects of the Depression of 1819 in the Old Northwest." *Indiana Magazine of History* 44 (1948): 227–43.

Haeger, John Denis. "Eastern Financiers and Institutional Change: The Origins of the New York Life Insurance and Trust Company and the Ohio Life Insurance and Trust Company." *Journal of Economic History* 39 (1979): 259–73.

Harte, Brian. "Land in the Old Northwest: A Study of Speculation, Sales, and Settlement on the Connecticut Western Reserve." *Ohio History* 101 (1992): 114–39.

Havighurst, Walter. *Wilderness for Sale: The Story of the First Western Land Rush.* New York: Hastings House, 1956.

Henlein, Paul C. "Shifting Range-Feeder Patterns in the Ohio Valley before 1860." *Agricultural History* 31 (1957): 1–12.

————. *Cattle Kingdom in the Ohio Valley, 1783–1860.* Lexington: University Press of Kentucky, 1959.

Horton, John J. *The Jonathan Hale Farm: A Chronicle of the Cuyahoga Valley.* Cleveland: Western Reserve Historical Society, 1990.

Hurt, R. Douglas. "Bettering the Beef: Felix Renick and the Ohio Company for Importing English Cattle." *Timeline* 10 (March/April 1993): 24–29.

Hutchinson, William Thomas. *The Bounty Lands of the American Revolution in Ohio.* New York: Arno Press, 1979.

Hutslar, Donald A. "Ohio Water Powered Sawmills." *Ohio History* 84 (1975): 5–56.

Jakle, John A. "Salt on the Ohio Valley Frontier, 1770–1820." *Annals of the Association of American Geographers* 59 (1969): 687–709.

James, Peter D. *The National Road.* Indianapolis: Bobbs-Merrill, 1948.

Jones, Robert Leslie. "A History of Local Agricultural Societies in Ohio to 1865." *Ohio State Archaeological and Historical Quarterly* 52 (1943): 120–40.

————. "The Horse and Mule Industry in Ohio to 1865." *Mississippi Valley Historical Review* 33 (1946): 61–88.

————. "The Dairy Industry in Ohio prior to the Civil War." *Ohio State Archaeological and Historical Quarterly* 56 (1947): 46–69.

————. "The Beef Cattle Industry in Ohio prior to the Civil War." *Ohio Historical Quarterly* 64 (1955): 168–94, 287–319.

————. *History of Agriculture in Ohio to 1880.* Kent, OH: Kent State University Press, 1983.

Kingsley, Ronald F. "Chestnut Grove: An Early 19th-Century Lime Burning Industry in the Connecticut Western Reserve." *North American Archaeologist* 14 (1993): 71–85.

————. "The Gillett Brothers and the Mid-Nineteenth Century Black Powder Mill, Portage County, Ohio: An Entrepreneurship Presaging the Industrial Era." *North American Archaeologist* 22 (2001): 259–82.

Klingaman, David C., and Richard K. Vedder, eds. *Essays in Nineteenth Century Economic History: The Old Northwest.* Athens: Ohio University Press, 1975.

————. *Essays on the Economy of the Old Northwest.* Athens: Ohio University Press, 1987.

Knodell, Jane. "Interregional Financial Integration and the Banknote Market: The Old Northwest, 1815–1845." *Journal of Economic History* 48 (1988): 287–98.

————. "The Demise of Central Banking and the Domestic Exchanges: Evidence from Antebellum Ohio." *Journal of Economic History* 58 (1998): 714–30.

Larew, Marilyn Melton. "The Cincinnati Branch of the Second Bank of the United States and Its Effect on the Local Economy, 1817–1836." PhD diss., University of Maryland, 1978.

Mabry, William Alexander. "Industrial Beginnings in Ohio." *Ohio State Archaeological and Historical Quarterly* 55 (1946): 242–53.

Mak, James. "Production, Consumption, and the Distribution of Agricultural Surpluses and Deficits in Ohio, 1840–1860." PhD diss., Purdue University, 1970.

———. "Intraregional Trade in the Antebellum West: Ohio, a Case Study." *Agricultural History* 46 (1972): 489–97.

Marvin, Walter Rumsey. "Columbus and the Railroads of Central Ohio before the Civil War." PhD diss., Ohio State University, 1953.

———. "Ohio's Unsung Penitentiary Railroad." *Ohio State Archaeological and Historical Quarterly* 63 (1954): 254–69.

Melvin, Patricia Mooney. "Steamboats West: The Legacy of a Transportation Revolution." *The Old Northwest* 7 (1982): 339–57.

Mennel, Robert M. "'The Family System of Common Farmers': The Origins of Ohio's Reform Farm." *Ohio History* 89 (1980): 125–56, 279–322.

Newell, William H. "Inheritance on the Maturing Frontier: Butler County, Ohio, 1803–1865." In *Long-Term Factors in American Economic Growth,* ed. Stanley L. Engerman and Robert E. Gallman, *Studies in Income and Wealth,* vol. 51, 261–306. Chicago: University of Chicago Press, 1986.

Parker, Wyman W. "Printing in Gambier, Ohio, 1829–1884." *Ohio State Archaeological and Historical Quarterly* 62 (1953): 55–66.

Pattison, William David. *Beginnings of the American Rectangular Land Survey System, 1784–1800.* 1957; Columbus: Ohio Historical Society, 1970.

———. "The Survey of the Seven Ranges." *Ohio Historical Quarterly* 68 (1959): 115–40.

Porter, Eugene O. "Financing Ohio's Pre–Civil War Railroads." *Ohio State Archaeological and Historical Quarterly* 57 (1948): 215–26.

Potts, Louis W. "Visions of America, 1787–1788: The Ohio of Reverend Manasseh Cutler." *Ohio History* 111 (2002): 101–20.

Preston, Daniel. "Thomas Kelsey, Hardluck Entrepreneur." *Ohio History* 104 (1995): 127–41.

———. "Reapers, Harvesters, and Steam Threshers: The Interdependence of Agriculture and Manufacturing in the Miami Valley." *Queen City Heritage* 54 (1996): 2–18.

Previts, Gary John, and William D. Samson. "Exploring the Contents of the Baltimore and Ohio Railroad Annual Reports: 1827–1856." *Accounting Historians Journal* 27 (2000): 1–42.

Rastatter, Edward Herbert. "The Economic Impact of the Speculator on the Distribution of Public Lands in the United States: Ohio, 1820 to 1840." PhD diss., University of Virginia, 1965.

Ray, John Bernard. "Zane's Trace, 1796–1812: A Study in Historical Geography." PhD diss., Indiana University, 1968.

Rich, David. "The Toledo Mechanics' Association: The City's First Labor Union." *Northwest Ohio Quarterly* 46 (1973–74): 12–19.

Rohrbough, Malcolm J. *The Land Office Business: The Settlement and Administration of American Public Lands, 1789–1837.* New York: Oxford University Press, 1968.

Ross, Steven Joseph. *Workers on the Edge: Work, Leisure, and Politics in Industri-alizing Cincinnati, 1788–1890.* New York: Columbia University Press, 1985.

Samson, William D., and Gary John Previts. "Reporting for Success: The Baltimore and Ohio Railroad and Management Information, 1827–1856." *Business and Economic History* 28 (1999): 235–54.

Scharf, Jon, and Rick Stager. "It All Started with Steamboats: The Niles Works and the Origins of Cincinnati's Machine Tool Industry." *Queen City Heritage* 54 (1996): 34–48.

Scharlott, Bradford W. "The Telegraph and the Integration of the U.S. Economy: The Impact of Electrical Communications on Interregional Prices and the Commercial Life of Cincinnati." PhD diss., University of Wisconsin, Madison, 1986.

Scheiber, Harry N. "Urban Rivalry and Internal Improvements in the Old Northwest, 1820–1860." *Ohio History* 71 (1962): 227–39.

———. "Entrepreneurship and Western Development: The Case of Micajah T. Williams." *Business History Review* 37 (1963): 345–68.

———. "State Policy and the Public Domain: The Ohio Canal Lands." *Journal of Economic History* 25 (1965): 86–113.

———. "The Commercial Bank of Lake Erie, 1831–1843." *Business History Review* 40 (1966): 47–65.

———. *Ohio Canal Era: A Case Study of Government and the Economy, 1820–1861.* Athens: Ohio University Press, 1968.

———. "Alfred Kelley and the Ohio Business Elite, 1822–1859." *Ohio History* 87 (1978): 365–92.

———. "The Pennsylvania and Ohio Canal: Transport Innovation, Mixed Enterprise, and Urban Commercial Rivalry, 1825–1861." *The Old Northwest* 6 (1980): 105–35.

Schob, David E. *Hired Hands and Plowboys: Farm Labor in the Midwest, 1815–1860.* Urbana: University of Illinois Press, 1975.

Schroder, Alan Max. "A Quantitative Study of the Effect of the Credit System of Public Land Sales on the Economic Growth of Ohio, 1801–1832." PhD diss., Kent State University, 1980.

Shannon, Timothy J. "The Ohio Company and the Meaning of Opportunity in the American West, 1786–1795." *New England Quarterly* 64 (1991): 393–413.

Soltow, Lee. "Inequality amidst Abundance: Land Ownership in Early Nineteenth Century Ohio." *Ohio History* 88 (1979): 133–51.

———. "Land Fragmentation as an Index of History in the Virginia Military District of Ohio." *Explorations in Economic History* 20 (1983): 263–73.

Stephens, David T., and Alexander T. Bobersky. "Analysis of Land Sales, Steubenville Land Office, 1800–1820." *Pioneer America Society Transactions* 13 (1989): 1–9.

———. "The Origins of Land Buyers, Steubenville Land Office, 1800–1820." *Material Culture* 22 (1990): 37–45.

Stevens, Harry R. "Bank Enterprisers in a Western Town, 1815–1822." *Business History Review* 29 (1955): 139–56.

———. "Samuel Watts Davies and the Industrial Revolution in Cincinnati." *Ohio Historical Quarterly* 70 (1961): 95–127.

Stover, Stephen L. "Early Sheep Husbandry in Ohio." *Agricultural History* 36 (1962): 101–7.

Streifthau, Donna L. "Fancy Chairs and Finials: Cincinnati Furniture Industry, 1819–1830." *Cincinnati Historical Society Bulletin* 29 (1971): 171–200.

Teaford, Jon C. "The State and Industrial Development: Public Power Development in the Old Northwest." *The Old Northwest* 1 (1975): 11–34.

Van Fossan, W. H. "Sandy and Beaver Canal." *Ohio State Archaeological and Historical Quarterly* 55 (1946): 165–77.

vonEnde, Eleanor Theresa. "Conjectural Estimates of Economic Growth for the Old Northwest, 1800 to 1860." PhD diss., University of Kansas, 1990.

Wheeler, David L. "The Beef Cattle Industry in the Old Northwest, 1803–1860." *Panhandle-Plains Historical Review* 47 (1974): 28–45.

White, C. Albert. *A History of the Rectangular Survey System*. Washington, DC: U.S. Department of the Interior, Bureau of Land Management, 1983.

———. *Initial Points of the Rectangular Survey System*. Westminster, CO: Produced for Professional Land Surveyors of Colorado, Inc., by the Publishing House, 1996.

White, John R. "The Rebirth and Demise of Ohio's Earliest Blast Furnace: An Archaeological Postmortem." *Midcontinental Journal of Archaeology* 21 (1996): 217–45.

Whiteman, Maxwell. "Notions, Dry Goods, and Clothing: An Introduction to the Study of the Cincinnati Peddler." *Jewish Quarterly Review* 53 (1963): 306–21.

Wilson, Ellen Susan. "Speculators and Land Development in the Virginia Military Tract: The Territorial Period." PhD diss., Miami University, 1982.

———. "Gaining Title to the Land: The Case of the Virginia Military Tract." *The Old Northwest* 12 (1986): 65–82.

Cities and Towns

Aaron, Daniel. *Cincinnati, Queen City of the West, 1819–1838*. Columbus: Ohio State University Press, 1992.

Anderson, Celestine Estelle. "The Invention of the 'Professional' Municipal Police: The Case of Cincinnati, 1788 to 1900." PhD diss., University of Cincinnati, 1979.

Blum, Carol Jean. "'A Devotion to the West': The Settlement of Cincinnati, 1788–1810." *Queen City Heritage* 48 (1990): 3–19.

Bowers, Paul C., Jr., and Goodwin F. Berquist Jr. "Worthington, Ohio: James Kilbourn's Episcopal Haven on the Western Frontier." *Ohio History* 85 (1976): 247–62.

Cayton, Andrew R. L., and Paula Riggs. *City into Town: The City of Marietta, Ohio, 1788–1988.* Marietta, OH: Marietta College, Dawes Memorial Library, 1991.

Cole, Charles C., Jr. *A Fragile Capital: Identity and the Early Years of Columbus, Ohio.* Columbus: Ohio State University Press, 2001.

Contosta, David R. *Lancaster, Ohio, 1800–2000: Frontier Town to Edge City.* Columbus: Ohio State University Press, 1999.

Daniel, Robert L. *Athens, Ohio: The Village Years.* Athens: Ohio University Press, 1997.

Dwyer, Doris Dawn. "A Century of City-Building: Three Generations of the Kilgour Family in Cincinnati, 1798–1914." PhD diss., Miami University, 1979.

Farrell, Richard T. "Cincinnati in the Early Jackson Era, 1816–1834: An Economic and Political Study." PhD diss., Indiana University, 1967.

———. "Cincinnati, 1800–1830: Economic Development through Trade and Industry." *Ohio History* 77 (1968): 111–29.

Glazer, Walter S. *Cincinnati in 1840: The Social and Functional Organization of an Urban Community during the Pre–Civil War Period.* Columbus: Ohio State University Press, 1999.

Grimm, Harold J. "The Founding of Franklinton: Its Significance Today." *Ohio State Archeological and Historical Quarterly* 56 (1947): 323–30.

Heald, Edward Thornton. *Bezaleel Wells: Founder of Canton and Steubenville, Ohio.* Canton: Stark County Historical Society, 1942.

Matthews, James Swinton. "Expressions of Urbanism in the Sequent Occupance of Northeastern Ohio." PhD diss., University of Chicago, 1949.

McCormick, Virginia E., and Robert W. McCormick. *New Englanders on the Ohio Frontier: The Migration and Settlement of Worthington, Ohio.* Kent, OH: Kent State University Press, 1998.

McManis, Michael Allen. "Range Ten, Town Four: A Social History of Hudson, Ohio, 1799–1840." PhD diss., Case Western Reserve University, 1976.

Miller, Carol Poh, and Robert A. Wheeler. *Cleveland: A Concise History, 1796–1996.* Bloomington: Indiana University Press, 1997.

Miller, Glenn Richard. "Transportation and Urban Growth in Cincinnati, Ohio, and Vicinity: 1788–1980." PhD diss., University of Cincinnati, 1983.

Phillips, Josephine E. "The Naming of Marietta." *Ohio State Archaeological and Historical Quarterly* 55 (1946): 106–37.

Pocock, Emil. "Evangelical Frontier: Dayton, Ohio, 1796–1830." PhD diss., Indiana University, 1984.

Preston, Daniel F. "Market and Mill Town: Hamilton, Ohio, 1795–1860." PhD diss., University of Maryland, College Park, 1987.

Roomann, Raja R. *Urban Growth and the Development of an Urban Sewer System: City of Cincinnati, 1800–1915*. Cincinnati: RONNHU Publishers, 2001.

Rose, William Ganson. *Cleveland: The Making of a City*. Kent, OH: Kent State University Press, 1990.

Schneider, Norris F. *Y-Bridge City: The Story of Zanesville*. Cleveland: World, 1950.

Seat, William R., Jr. "A Rebuttal to Mrs. Trollope: Harriet Martineau in Cincinnati." *Ohio Historical Quarterly* 68 (1959): 276–89.

Stevens, Harry R. "David Everett Wade (1763–1842): Patriot, Tanner, Deacon, Alderman." *Bulletin of the Historical and Philosophical Society of Ohio* 13 (1955): 181–90.

Stewart, Leola M. "Sandusky: Pioneer Link between Sail and Rail." *Ohio State Archaeological and Historical Quarterly* 57 (1948): 227–36.

Still, Bayrd. "Patterns of Mid-Nineteenth Century Urbanization in the Middle West." *Mississippi Valley Historical Review* 28 (1941): 187–206.

Utter, William Thomas. *Granville: The Story of an Ohio Village*. Granville, OH: Denison University, 1956.

Wade, Richard C. *The Urban Frontier: The Rise of Western Cities, 1790–1830*. Cambridge, MA: Harvard University Press, 1959.

Walton, John. "The Men of Losantiville." *Filson Club History Quarterly* 47 (1973): 309–22.

West, Earl Irvin. "Early Cincinnati's 'Unprecedented Spectacle.'" *Ohio History* 79 (1970): 5–17.

Wolfe, Phillip J., and Warren J. Wolfe. "Prospects for the Gallipolis Settlement: French Diplomatic Dispatches." *Ohio History* 103 (1994): 41–56.

Wunder, John, ed. *Toward an Urban Ohio: A Conference to Commemorate the Bicentennial of the American Revolution*. Columbus: Published for the Ohio American Revolution Bicentennial Advisory Commission by the Ohio Historical Society, 1977.

CONTRIBUTORS

Andrew R. L. Cayton is distinguished professor of history at Miami University in Oxford, Ohio. He has written extensively on the history of Ohio, including *Ohio: The History of a People*. His most recent book is *The Dominion of War: Liberty and Empire in North America, 1500–2000*, co-authored by Fred Anderson.

Christopher Clark is professor of North American history at the University of Warwick in the United Kingdom. His book *The Roots of Rural Capitalism: Western Massachusetts, 1780–1860* won the Frederick Jackson Turner Award of the Organization of American Historians. Most recently he co-edited *Letters from an American Utopia: The Stetson Family and the Northampton Association, 1843–1847*.

Ellen Eslinger is professor of history at DePaul University and the author of *Citizens of Zion: The Social Origins of Camp Meeting Revivalism* and editor of *Running Mad for Kentucky: Frontier Travel Accounts*.

Patrick Griffin is associate professor of history at Ohio University and the author of *The People with No Name: Ireland's Ulster Scots, America's Scots Irish, and the Creation of a British Atlantic World, 1689–1764*.

Stuart D. Hobbs is the director of the Ohio State University history department's History in the Heartland, a continuing education program for middle and high school history teachers. His publications include *The End of the American Avant Garde*.

Tamara Gaskell Miller is the editor of the *Pennsylvania Magazine of History and Biography* and *Pennsylvania Legacies*, both published by The Historical Society of Pennsylvania, and a contributor to the edited volume *Midwestern Women: Work, Community, and Leadership at the Crossroads*.

Donald J. Ratcliffe is Lecturer in American History at the University of Oxford in the United Kingdom. He has also taught at the University of Durham and the Ohio State University. Ratcliffe has written extensively on Ohio political history, most recently in *Party Spirit in a Frontier Republic: Democratic Politics in Ohio, 1793–1821* and *The Politics of Long Division: The Birth of the Second Party System in Ohio, 1818–1828.*

Kenneth H. Wheeler is assistant professor of history at Reinhardt College in Waleska, Georgia, and a contributor to the volume *Builders of Ohio.*

John Wigger is associate professor of history at the University of Missouri–Columbia. He is the author of *Taking Heaven by Storm: Methodism and the Rise of Popular Christianity in America,* and co-editor, with Nathan Hatch, of *Methodism and the Shaping of American Culture.*

INDEX

Michigan, 152; higher education in, 106
Middlebury College (Vermont), 112, 115
middle-class culture, 4, 6–7, 116,
    172–73; and family, 123–24
Midwest, the, 146–47, 175–76
Mifflin, Thomas, 27, 28
Miles, Billy and Rachel, 89
Miller, Tamara Gaskell, 153, 173, 175
Milner, Beverly, 90
Montgomery County, 90
Moravian Indians. *See* Delawares
Morrow, Jeremiah, 92
Mount Vernon, Ohio, 136, 138, 139

naming patterns, 125, 128–30, 133–35,
    142n17
National Cash Register Company, 105
New England, 107, 151, 152, 153, 154,
    157, 158, 173; education in, con-
    trasted with Old Northwest, 110–14;
    family life, 122–39, 141n17; politics,
    contrasted with Ohio, 44, 56; con-
    trasted with South, 17
Nixon family, 127, 129, 131
Northwest Ordinance of 1787, 2, 14–15;
    government under, 39–40, slavery
    and, 81, 83–84; suffrage and, 49; vot-
    ing practices under, 39
Northwest Territory, 39, 82–83, 130
Nye, Minerva, 21

Oberlin College (Ohio), 109, 110, 111,
    115, 116; and coeducation, 113, 114
Ogelthorpe College (Georgia), 110
Ohio Company of Associates, 1, 15, 25,
    44, 84
Ohio River: as River Jordan, 5
Ohio University, 106
Ohio Valley: as region, 175–76
Oneida Institute, 110
Onuf, Peter S., 105–6
Ottawas, 14, 21
Otterbein College (Ohio), 111

Patterson, John, 105, 116
Patterson, Robert, 90
Pelham, Peter, 66–67
Petit family, 130–31
Philanthropist, The, 84
politics, 4, 170; bibliography, 184–89;
    Ohio contrasted with Canadian,
    47–48; local party conventions,
    53–54; party competition and democ-
    racy, 52, 53, 54–55; racial, 86–90,

91–92; religion and, 46–47, 67–71;
    Ohio contrasted with other states',
    43, 44, 48, 51, 56; in territories, 51, 55
population, 3, 4, 150; and family struc-
    ture in Washington County, 124–28,
    133–36; inequalities in Ohio, 171;
    migration out of Ohio, 152, 155; mi-
    gration to Ohio, 152–53, 157; occu-
    pations, 155–56, 164n39; of Old
    Northwest colleges, 113; persistence
    rates in Old Northwest, 141nn10–11
Portsmouth, Ohio, 176
Post, Charles: "market discipline," 154
Presbyterians, 96, 106; and slavery, 84,
    85, 90
Princeton College (New Jersey), 112
Progressive Era reform, 105, 116
public culture, 4, 105–9, 116
Putnam, Rufus, 17, 20, 21, 25, 26

Quakers, 151, 153; and slavery, 84, 96
Quinn, James, 66, 74

race, 3, 4, 82, 148–49, 167, 170, 173–75,
    178n14
Randolph-Macon College (Virginia), 112
Rankin, John, 85, 95, 96, 99n9
Ratcliffe, Donald, 147, 150, 170
Reckard family, 126, 129–30
reform: history of, bibliography, 191–92
regional dimension of Ohio history,
    175–76; critique of, 146–47; and edu-
    cation, 107–16; and family, 122–39,
    141n17
religion, 1, 4, 5, 7, 166, 172; and educa-
    tion, 109–11, 114–16; and family,
    132; history of, bibliography, 203–8;
    and politics, 46–47, 67–71; and race,
    84–86; and Underground Railroad,
    96–97
Republican Party, 70
Republican Society of Cincinnati, 42
Ripley, Ohio, 85, 96
Rockefeller, John D., 4, 158
Rohrbough, Malcolm J., 146
Romanticism, 6–8
Root, Jeremiah, 151, 152
Ross, Steven, 170
Ross County, 85, 89, 168
Rotundo, E. Anthony: on "usefulness," 109
rural life, 146–60

Sale, John, 5
Scott, James D., 90